UNDERSTANDING
JANE SMILEY

Understanding Contemporary American Literature
Matthew J. Bruccoli, Series Editor

Volumes on

Edward Albee • Nicholson Baker • John Barth • Donald Barthelme
The Beats • The Black Mountain Poets • Robert Bly
Raymond Carver • Chicano Literature
Contemporary American Drama
Contemporary American Horror Fiction
Contemporary American Literary Theory
Contemporary American Science Fiction • James Dickey
E. L. Doctorow • John Gardner • George Garrett • John Hawkes
Joseph Heller • John Irving • Randall Jarrell • William Kennedy
Ursula K. Le Guin • Denise Levertov • Bernard Malamud
Carson McCullers • W. S. Merwin • Arthur Miller
Toni Morrison's Fiction • Vladimir Nabokov • Gloria Naylor
Joyce Carol Oates • Tim O'Brien • Flannery O'Connor
Cynthia Ozick • Walker Percy • Katherine Anne Porter
Reynolds Price • Thomas Pynchon • Theodore Roethke • Philip Roth
Hubert Selby, Jr. • Mary Lee Settle • Isaac Bashevis Singer
Jane Smiley • Gary Snyder • William Stafford • Anne Tyler
Kurt Vonnegut • Tennessee Williams • August Wilson

UNDERSTANDING JANE SMILEY

Neil Nakadate

University of South Carolina Press

Published in Columbia, South Carolina, by the
University of South Carolina Press

Manufactured in the United States of America

03 02 01 00 5 4 3 2

Library of Congress Cataloging-in-Publication Data

Nakadate, Neil.
Understanding Jane Smiley / Neil Nakadate.
p. cm. — (Understanding contemporary American literature)
Includes bibliographical references (p.) and index.

ISBN 1-57003-251-3
1. Smiley, Jane—Criticism and interpretation. 2. Women and literature—United States—History—20th century. I. Title. II. Series.
PS3569.M39 Z79 1999
813'.54—dc21 98-40224

For my brother Jim
For my sisters Jean Keiko and Ann

CONTENTS

EDITOR'S PREFACE

The volumes of *Understanding Contemporary American Literature* have been planned as guides or companions for students as well as good nonacademic readers. The editor and publisher perceive a need for these volumes because much of the influential contemporary literature makes special demands. Uninitiated readers encounter difficulty in approaching works that depart from the traditional forms and techniques of prose and poetry. Literature relies on conventions, but the conventions keep evolving; new writers form their own conventions—which in time may become familiar. Put simply, *UCAL* provides instruction in how to read certain contemporary writers—identifying and explicating their material, themes, use of language, point of view, structures, symbolism, and responses to experience.

The word *understanding* in the titles was deliberately chosen. Many willing readers lack an adequate understanding of how contemporary literature works; that is, what the author is attempting to express and the means by which it is conveyed. Although the criticism and analysis in the series have been aimed at a level of general accessibility, these introductory volumes are meant to be applied in conjunction with the works they cover. They do not provide a substitute for the works and authors they introduce, but rather prepare the reader for more profitable literary experiences.

M. J. B.

ACKNOWLEDGMENTS

Jane Smiley has been particularly helpful on several occasions in providing biographical information and information on the composition and publication of her work. I am particularly appreciative of an extended, two-session interview she granted during August and November 1996.

Several others have provided assistance and support at various stages of my research and during the writing, revising, and editing of this book, including Bobbie Bristol, Molly Brown, Susan Carlson, Brenda Daly, Keith Fynaardt, Sheryl Kamps, Ann Kotas, Sarah McGrath, Michael Mendelson, Dale Ross, and Faye P. Whitaker.

A portion of this book was written during a 1996–1997 Faculty Improvement Leave supported by Iowa State University.

UNDERSTANDING
JANE SMILEY

CHAPTER ONE

Understanding Jane Smiley

Career

The themes and issues of Jane Smiley's fiction—and occasionally its incidental details—owe much to her experience with family life as a dynamic and diverse phenomenon. Her father's absence, her mother's independence and ambition, and her constant interaction with step- and half-siblings and cousins were among the salient facts of Smiley's childhood and youth. Similarly, Smiley's intellectual growth, prodded and sustained by reading on a wide range of topics and across academic disciplines, has had a significant impact on the ideas and arguments of her fiction.

Jane Smiley's mother was born Frances Graves in 1921 in Shoshone, Idaho, grew up in Wood River, Illinois, and in 1943 left home to join the Women's Army Corps (against her father's wishes). Her mother told Smiley that she had "had a great longing to leave the Midwest" and seek sophistication, and that she found it as an army journalist in Paris in the spring of 1944, arriving in Europe on a ship carrying three thousand American soldiers.[1] Smiley's father, James LaVerne Smiley, born in 1915, and originally from Kalamazoo, Michigan, was a December 1941 graduate of the United States Military Academy who saw service in World War II; he met Frances Graves in France in 1945. A brief romance ended in 1946 when Frances left the army and began a career in journalism, writing for the *Memphis Press Scimitar* in Tennessee; James Smiley began a career in aeronautical engineering, eventually working for Hughes Aircraft in Los Angeles. James reestablished contact by letter in 1948 and, after a whirlwind romance, they married on 7 December.

Jane Graves Smiley was born on 26 September 1949 in Los Angeles County Hospital. By the time she was a year old, her father was seeking treatment at veterans hospitals in Wyoming and Michigan for mental problems—quite possibly was what is now referred to as post-traumatic stress disorder. (James LaVerne Smiley died in February 1982.) When Jane was four, her parents divorced, her mother taking her to Saint Louis and beginning work, first for the McDonald-Douglas in-house paper and then for the *Globe Democrat* and the *Post-Dispatch* as women's page editor. Jane spent the days with her maternal grandmother and had frequent contact with her mother's sisters Jane and Ruth and brother David and their families. Smiley grew particularly close to her Aunt Jane's daughter Lucy and Aunt Ruth's son Carl, Jr. (Jody), who were "more like brother and sister to me," but reports being "close to all my cousins," and from the outset enjoyed being part of a large, extended family. A key reason for this enjoyment was that "they all loved story-telling, particularly stories about the family . . . what so and so did and why they did it." Her grandparents (who "believed in corporal punishment" but were also "very affectionate") loved colorful expressions, and "everybody in the family was a raconteur." Smiley's conclusion is that "I was well raised by the combination."[2]

Growing up with myriad family stories, Smiley learned about (on her father's side) grandparents Florence Upjohn and Homer Smiley, and about Homer's father, a photographer in Illinois, and about Homer's father's father, an immigrant to Nova Scotia. She learned that her father was the oldest surviving son among six siblings. Jane also heard stories about (on her mother's side) Ethel Ingeborg Doolittle and David Berger Graves, her maternal grandfather tracing his lineage back from Missouri to Tennessee and Virginia—and seeking a future in Idaho with a brother who was allegedly involved in a fatal barroom fight. Smiley's maternal grandmother was an itinerant schoolteacher in Shoshone, Idaho, when the two brothers took her in as a lodger and David persuaded her to marry him. As a child, Smiley's mother was old enough to witness her father and uncle struggle with their ranch, fight with each other, lose money, and finally relinquish their property, her parents working their way back to the Midwest by way of Laredo, Texas. Frances Graves was herself the oldest of five siblings. These and other family members and their storied and unstoried lives—not to mention the rich implications of "family" as a focus for fiction and of storytelling as a craft—were neither to be forgotten nor later left unmined by Smiley as a writer of fiction, beginning with *Barn Blind* and *At Paradise Gate*. Looking back on the gossip-rich prewriting time of her childhood and youth, Smiley has said that "The first novel I ever knew was our family."[3]

In 1960, when Jane was eleven, her mother married William J. Nuelle, who had custody of two adopted children by a previous marriage, Susan and William; the couple then had two children of their own, David and Frances (Francie). Jane Smiley and her step- and half-siblings grew up in Webster Groves, Missouri, where she attended several public and private schools, including John Burroughs School for grades 7–12. Smiley recalls that her schoolgirl interests included English, history, and horses. Smiley first rode when she was four, and had two horses during her girlhood; she describes riding them as "my great passion" and years later could recall clearly the circumstances of their respective deaths. Her passion for equestrian sports is reflected with some regularity in her writing, both fiction and nonfiction. During her early adolescence Smiley went in two years from a "normal-sized seventh grader" of 5 feet and 75 pounds to 6 feet and 125 pounds. "My junior high years," she recalls, "were mostly taken up with growth." (Smiley eventually grew to 6 feet, 2 inches.)

Smiley's intellectual and creative growth and her growth as a reader have long been interdependent, and continue to be reflected in a steady output of reviews for the *New York Times Book Review* and other publications. Recalling her adolescence she remembers, for example, reading O. E. Rölvaag's *Giants in the Earth* and John H. Storer's *The Web of Life* in the eighth grade—the stark realism of the former and the ecological insights of the latter becoming embedded in her memory. Crucially for Smiley's future thinking and writing, Storer's book "reinforced that sense I had of the variousness and interconnectedness of land, animals, plants, people, town and countryside, prairie and civilization."[4] The "web of life" is clearly a dominant principle in *A Thousand Acres* and *Moo,* for example, and is also fundamental to understanding *The Greenlanders.* Smiley also recalls reading *David Copperfield* in ninth grade and being struck by Dickens's style and "the complexity and liveliness of the novel as a form." From the seventh through twelfth grades she also read Shakespeare, one play per year, beginning with *Twelfth Night* and ending with *King Lear.* But while she liked drama—"the action and liveliness on the stage . . . plenty was happening"—the plays "were not quite dark enough to be right for me and there was too much talk." Impatient with drama, Smiley understood fiction to be markedly different, a form holding the potential for other options. Years later she could articulate this potential, observing that "narrative gives more direct access to the inner life, allows the writer to reveal the disjuncture between what is felt and what appears, and to suggest emotions so powerful that their complete expression must fail, resulting in silence."[5]

The summer after her high school graduation in June 1967, Smiley worked as a horse groom at a camp in Virginia. In the fall she enrolled at Vassar, having chosen it (with her mother's help) from several highly selective women's colleges to which she had been accepted; Smiley would later characterize herself as a test-validated and self-confident female "member of the SAT generation." At Vassar she accepted as normal both the notions of women's education and personal ambition and her own simple but ambitious version of a career plan: "To read as many books as possible and to get as much praise for my own writing as possible." She was sustained by an institutional milieu in which both she and other women took such ambitions seriously. And,

Smiley adds, "If the plan was for us to get married and raise children, it was not communicated directly to us."[6]

As an English major at Vassar, Smiley engaged in an extensive examination of English literature from Old English on, perhaps most memorably under the mentorship of Professor Harriet Hawkins, from whom she got supportive feedback on early creative efforts and through whom she seriously addressed *King Lear* for the first time. "I became aware of how my reaction to the play did not conform to the standard interpretation of it. Harriet's was, simultaneously, a voice of authority, dispensing the conventional wisdom about the play, but also a woman's voice, slightly recasting the whole argument."[7] Hawkins's pedagogical recasting was, of course, an early model for feminist interpretation, one that Smiley was to emulate creatively two decades later in the writing of *A Thousand Acres.* At Vassar Smiley also read extensively the established novelists of the Western tradition, not excluding the Russians, and received her B.A. in 1971. Following graduation, Smiley pursued her interest in history, archaeology, and cultural study by serving as a "digger" in a medieval excavation at Winchester, England—the first of several experiences that eventuated in her writing *The Greenlanders.*

In December 1969 (during her sophomore year) Smiley, who had "never dated anyone," had visited Yale University as part of an exchange, during the course of which she introduced herself to John B. Whiston, a native of Wyoming and member of the basketball team. She began a relationship with Whiston, and the following summer Smiley and Whiston, a radical student activist, lived in a leftist commune in New Haven, where there was much earnest discussion of economic and political philosophy; Smiley worked in electronics factories in East Haven and West Haven but made "a bad factory worker." During this period of both personal and national urgency and ideological self-consciousness, and in part through her extensive discussions with Whiston and fellow commune members, Smiley was made aware of the inevitable gap between ideas and social action, as well as the ironies that emerge when ideology and personal relationships test each other. In addition, Smiley was always conscious of being both a participant and an observer, and her "drab, urban" experience at a time of intense personal and intellectual growth yielded striking insights on the interaction of cultural forces and private lives.[8] Smiley and Whiston married in September 1970.

It is worth noting that, like Smiley herself, many of the adult characters of her fiction between *Duplicate Keys* and *Moo* came of age during the years of the New Frontier and the U.S. space program, the Great Society and the civil rights movement, and the disruptive energies invoked by the Vietnam War. By generation, education, and direct personal experience, and whether by accident or choice, most of them have been shaped by the social, cultural, and intellectual forces of that era. Yet once the more immediate questions concerning "the bomb," "the pill," "the moon," and "the war" have been addressed in some fashion, they find themselves having to build productive lives that are intelligible with reference to their beginnings without becoming cultural artifacts. In a few instances—for example,

Alexandra Day in "Dynamite," Bob Miller in "Good Will," and Chairman X in *Moo*—setting aside the legacies of counterculture does not prove easy.

The decision by Whiston and Smiley to choose Iowa rather than Virginia as the site of his graduate work in medieval history (she herself had not been accepted into the Iowa Writer's Workshop) was the result of relatively little discussion, mostly having to do with proximity to relatives. Smiley was later to wonder more than once at the casualness of the move, given her steadily increasing awareness of environmental degradation at the hands of agriculture and technology, and was particularly to recall it when writing *A Thousand Acres.* Smiley engaged in life as a "graduate student wife," in her case living in a rented farmhouse (at $25 per month) well outside of Iowa City and "making teddy bears in a factory" (at $1.65 per hour).[9] Smiley and Whiston ate a lot ("If I cooked it then it had ingredients that I *knew* were in it"), talked a lot, and "I watched *The Waltons* on T.V. all the time . . . my favorite show": "We had a little domestic life." Smiley recalls wanting very much—given that "that was the era of the back-to-the-land movement"—"to live a pastoral, idyllic life" of gardening, canning, having a windmill, and using solar power. She would eventually revisit, in both positive and negative variations, this early interest in domestic environment shaped by the hand of a human maker—in *Catskill Crafts: Artisans of the Catskill Mountains* (1988) and in the novella "Good Will" (1989). Smiley also recalls reading at this time Barry Commoner's *The Closing Circle: Nature, Man, and Technology* (1971), which concerned, among other things, the unwelcome presence of pesticides and nitrates in well water; Smiley notes that "that stuck with me all the way through *A Thousand Acres.*"[10]

Meanwhile, Smiley had talked Professor John C. McGalliard into letting her audit his course in Old Norse at the University of Iowa, one of several crucial moves that was to contribute immediately to her growth as a student of language and writer of narrative prose, and eventually to her creation of *The Greenlanders.* In December 1972 Smiley was accepted into the doctoral program in English at Iowa, and she began formal study the following month. She completed her master's degree in 1975, also the year in which she and Whiston divorced. Encouraged by Rush Rankin and Stuart Dybek, writing students who had read some of her fiction, Smiley had also worked her way toward at last being accepted into the Writer's Workshop—by studying the fiction of others already enrolled in it and sharpening her own technique. Her participation in the workshop began in the fall of 1974; her contemporaries included Alan Gurganis, Joanne Meschery, Richard Bausch, and Barbara Grossman (now in publishing), and preceding them slightly were T. C. Boyle, Tracy Kidder, and Dybek. In the course of her graduate education, Smiley studied not only Old Norse, fiction writing, and literature ("a lot of novel courses"), but also Gothic, Sanskrit, Old Irish, Old and Middle English (including Beowulf and Chaucer), Shakespeare, linguistics, poetry writing, and contemporary literary theory. Smiley recalls that in terms of a literary "work ideal" her models were Jane Austen, George Eliot, and Virginia Woolf: "I wanted to be the greatest, like them." As for her orientation toward literary study, it was at this time that Smiley began to resist the determinedly philological, exegetical, and theoretical; her recollection is that "the nuts and bolts of language study preserved me from too much literary theory."[11]

During the 1976–1977 academic year Smiley traveled to Iceland on a Fulbright-Hays study grant, living alone and with the intention of working toward a doctoral dissertation on the Icelandic sagas—"marvelous, marvelous works" that "are accessible to the modern mind" by virtue of the individualism and social conflict conveyed through them. Iceland proved windy, damp, desolate, and lonely, and living there she felt "an enormous sense of self-consciousness." (Perhaps in part to escape all this, Smiley took a midyear break, at one point staying for three weeks in New York City with an old Iowa City friend named Jane Temple Howard, whose generosity in letting friends impose on her had resulted in her losing track of how many keys were circulating. *Duplicate Keys* is dedicated to Howard.) It was a time of "no fun, no culture, no companionship [only one friend], no writing, and no big house," during which she read a lot of bulky European fiction—including Tolstoy, Flaubert, Christiana Stead, and Halldór Laxness—and conceived her own first two novels, as well as *The Greenlanders.* She also wrote short fiction, in part out of desperation. "I had a regimen of self-improvement," driven by the feeling that "If I didn't write [fiction] during a day then my life was worthless . . . so I got in the habit of writing every day"—a habit she still keeps.[12]

Once she was back in Iowa City, Smiley persuaded Professor Jack Leggatt to allow her submission of a creative dissertation—a collection of short fiction titled "Harmes and Feares"—rather than a research project on the sagas, a temporary crisis arising when her first typist got only three-fifths through the manuscript, having been stopped by "the sexy parts."[13] In 1978 Smiley also married William Silag, a historian, with whom she has two daughters, Phoebe and Lucy. After several temporary academic appointments, during which *Barn Blind* (1980) was published and *At Paradise Gate* (1981) written, Smiley accepted a position on the faculty in English at Iowa State University in Ames, the site of her teaching and writing career from 1981 to 1997.

At Iowa State Smiley began teaching world literature, literature courses that focused on various modes and genres, and graduate and undergraduate fiction writing; she also began to write and publish stories and novels at an energetic pace. With her New York murder mystery *Duplicate Keys* (1984) in press, she entered a crucial fourteen-month period, ending in July 1985, during which she wrote *The Greenlanders* (1988) and then the title story of *The Age of Grief* (1987). In the summer of 1984, domestic routine and preliminary research in Ames gave way to an extended research trip to England, Denmark, and Greenland. On several occasions Smiley has mentioned the mixture of anarchic creative energy ("I was frantic with inspiration," she recalls in "Shakespeare in Iceland") and marital dissatisfaction that contributed to her eventual divorce from Silag in February 1986—and a *Greenlanders* manuscript of over 1,100 pages. Smiley has also said that "The Age of Grief" in turn fed off the energy generated for the massive *Greenlanders* manuscript and by the thoughts and emotions triggered by the failure of her marriage; this resulted in a contemporary prose as figurative and introspective as the language of *Greenlanders* was plain.[14] In print, the 558-page *Greenlanders* was to earn a modest but devoted readership, and *The Age of Grief* a large and enthusiastic one; with both books Smiley went into relatively wide translation and the international fiction market.

In July 1987 Smiley married Stephen Mortensen, whom she had known in Iowa City almost fifteen years earlier, and with whom she has a son, Axel James. Two years later, Knopf published together in a single volume titled *Ordinary Love and Good Will* (1989) a pair of novellas through which Smiley explored further the themes of marriage and family life, and experimented with narrative form. "Good Will" was traditional in form but challenged the assumptions of an egotistical practitioner of back-to-the-land ideology; "Ordinary Love" was a conscious attempt at nontraditional plotting, in which family conversation and its revelations replaced climax and epiphany as the crucial focus.

As early as the summer of 1987 (if not Harriet Hawkins's class at Vassar) Smiley had thought about recasting *King Lear,* and a series of tentative probings merged on an end-of-winter drive up Interstate 35 during the following March, when she scanned the still-bleak landscape and realized that she could successfully set her *Lear* in Iowa—that is, on fertile and productive, but also environmentally compromised, land. The critical reception of *A Thousand Acres* (1991) was generally positive, but the novel's popular success was assured when it was awarded the Pulitzer Prize for fiction in 1992. Smiley's appropriation of Shakespeare was generally considered successful, as was her integration into the novel of several key social issues and cultural concerns. In the wake of the recognition brought on by her novel of patriarchy, commodification, and abuse in the heartland, Smiley was named a Fellow of the American Academy of Arts and Letters in 1994.[15]

The comic novel *Moo* (1995) was a deliberate departure—and to many readers a surprising one—from Smiley's greatest earlier successes and her recently successful reworking of Shakespearean tragedy. Smiley's intimate understanding of the culture of land-grant higher education resulted in a Dickensian roster of characters from the full spectrum of university life, a great deal of readerly concern for an overweight (because overindulged) porcine research project named Earl Butz, and an opportunity for many to reconsider the ease with which they had categorized Smiley as only a writer of "domestic realism" and family stories. In addition, *Moo* proved puzzling to more than a few reviewers, who found the novel less bitingly satirical than critically sympathetic, written less in the vein of Swift (or even Thackeray) than that of George Eliot. Still not interested in being categorized and understood too quickly, Smiley then undertook yet another project likely to surprise advocates of *The Age of Grief* and *Ordinary Love and Good Will,* a historical "romance" set in Kansas Territory in 1855–56. Given Smiley's earlier variations on the epic, tragic, and comic modes, however, it was perhaps appropriate that *The All-True Travels and Adventures of Lidie Newton* (1998) emerged as a realist challenge to some of the romantic and sentimental premises of the antebellum nineteenth century—that is, an "anti-romance." "The thing that keeps me writing novels," Smiley has said,

> is that when you choose the form itself and also the particular type you're going to write, then you have all these rules and conventions to deal with . . . the form works in a certain way . . . and so the pleasure of writing the novel is recognizing what the form both can do and can't do, and trying to make it work for you while also recognizing that there are some ways it can't work for you. You have to give up something in order to get something . . . and this has been true of every single form that I've tried to write and that's been one of the great pleasures of writing fiction.

Smiley wrote *Lidie Newton* following a cross-country move to Carmel Valley, California, in 1996 that enabled her to concentrate on her writing and to engage more passionately than before with equestrian pursuits. The novel appeared following her resignation from the faculty at Iowa State and shortly after the dissolution of her marriage to Mortensen. Clearly a woman of wide-ranging intellectual interests and a prolific writer inclined to pose creative problems for herself, Smiley would hardly seem a likely candidate for predictions regarding future work.

Overview

As a teacher of fiction writing Jane Smiley works with "a theory of the story" that is at once analytical and rhetorical (in the formal, Aristotelian sense of that word). For Smiley, a story involves "an exchange of expectations, or let's say a negotiation about expectations on the part of both the reader and the writer.

The student writer's responsibility is not to fulfill the reader's expectations but to understand them, and to use that understanding to manipulate them." In her classes, Smiley says, "We talk about things that are very basic [e.g., plotting, character transformation, setting, language, "willing suspension of disbelief"], but we talk about them as an exchange: How do you get your reader to invest in this piece of fiction, and once the reader has made his investment, how do you not jeopardize it, or, if you're going to jeopardize it, how do you regain it?"[16] Smiley sees the production of literature as an ongoing process of discovery, negotiation, and exchange—a serious rhetorical transaction. The reading and writing of fiction constitute a particular, and uniquely demanding, kind of discourse.

Later in the same interview, Smiley glosses her use of "exchange" as a concept, suggesting how the discourse works: "It's an exchange between the student and the teacher, an exchange between the writer and the culture. The culture exists apart from the writer and the writer hopes to bring his or her individuality to bear on the culture, but also to be penetrated by the culture, so that the product is a recognizable cultural product but also unique to that writer. I have to believe simultaneously in the individuality of the writer and the reality of the culture, that they both exist and that there can be an exchange between the two." To this Smiley adds, "And to believe that is basically to have a formalist, or structuralist, theory of literature. That's what I have and that's how to do it."[17] In this context, Smiley's "Reflections on a Lettuce Wedge" essay, which some readers of her novels and stories might otherwise consider odd, extends understanding of her theory and her approach to fiction. In what she herself has referred to as a "diatribe," Smiley comments on the production and consumption of food, in the United States generally and the Midwest specifically, and on unimaginative, unenlightened, heartland cuisine. At one point she says this:

> I do think that people tend to use the earth better if they take delight in its fruits. Eating is one of the sensuous things we do many times a day, day after day, year after year. Eating is our oftenest repeated connection to our agricultural roots. It seems to me that there are two choices: We can continue to process our food, as through a machine, from field to table, and continue to content ourselves with mechanically opening our jaws and processing it through our alimentary canals, or we can sow the seed, harvest the fruits, bring care and interest to the preparation of meals, and take our daily reward in the pleasures of aroma, flavor, and visceral satisfaction. We can decide that what doesn't taste good cannot be good for us. We can resist having our appetites dulled in the name of the countless mouths one single American farmer and all his machinery, petrochemicals, and sacrificed topsoil are alleged to feed. The future begins at dinnertime.[18]

This statement constitutes not only an oblique reference to some of the issues that inspired the writing of *A Thousand Acres* (1991), thus far Smiley's most widely read book, but also a suggestion of the intelligent eye with which she accounts for the details of life and the technique with which she shapes human experience into stories. That intelligent eye is often focused on Smiley's immediate surroundings and acquaintances; more than once she has acknowledged turning the personal into the fictional. "All of the people I'm comfortable with," Smiley once said, "no matter where they live, probably come from the Midwest,"[19] and this consistently includes many of the people that live (or live on) in her fiction. But more expansively and ambitiously, in her novels and stories, as in the lettuce wedge essay, exploratory threads connect the private lives of her characters with society on a larger scale, with American culture broadly viewed, and with the natural world. Smiley's fiction is a discourse on, and across, American culture.

The issues Smiley raises are not, in any responsible analysis, strictly Midwestern issues—though the issues may be most poignantly joined in the heartland, as she argues in her essay "So Shall We Reap,"[20] and though she has demonstrated convincingly that what might be called a Midwestern sensibility can offer an incisive, no-nonsense perspective on a wide range of matters. For example, the implications of habitat destruction and endemic herbicide use extend far beyond Iowa and *A Thousand Acres,* as when produce is shipped or in the Mississippi drainage floods. *The Greenlanders* (1988) is at once a "doomsday" book for a fourteenth-century outpost of Western European progress and an intimation of apocalypse for an age on the verge of environmental, if not nuclear, catastrophe. The academy-cum-corporation assault on a virgin cloud forest in Central America, comically undercut in *Moo* (1995), is finally serious business of global importance. This is not to say that Smiley's writing constitutes a definitive ethical statement on the political, economic, or technological implications of contemporary life. But it should be clear that the larger motives and conditions of human affairs at the end of the twentieth century are, consciously and significantly, the intellectual currency and situational reality of much that is putatively Midwestern and apparently domestic in her fiction. Smiley takes politics, economics, science, and technology seriously—and personally.

Not surprisingly, then, the intelligence and technical skill that Smiley brings to her writing are accompanied by an unapologetic willingness to analyze and evaluate American life, not only through her fiction and her frequent reviews of fiction, but also in numerous occasional pieces such as "Reflections on a Lettuce Wedge," "Family Values," "Can Mothers Think?" and "The Call of the Hunt." Smiley attributes her sense of security in writing and commenting on contemporary American experience to the longtime residency status of the Graves and Smiley family lines—their established position in the United States, in the Midwest, in the propertied middle class. She is, of course, conscious that her own situation stands in marked contrast to that of many other American writers, writers whose history and circumstances dictate radically different personal and professional perspectives and strategies. But for Smiley as a writer, the unchangeable fact is that she has always felt "totally at home" and written "with absolute confidence that I belonged here, hence could observe, criticize, judge."[21]

Yet despite emerging from a sense of establishment, Smiley's is not a fiction focused on movers and shakers. "Certainly the concerns of my short stories and novellas have been fairly mainstream ones," she has written, "the life and the sensibility of the educated middle class somewhere away from the coasts."[22] Her people are fundamentally capable; they are typically observant and often articulate and well read. But they are "ordinary" rather than otherwise. Their ordinariness is often framed by family life as the domain in which character is shaped and stories lived through, beginning with *Barn Blind* (1980) and continuing through *At Paradise Gate* (1981), *Ordinary Love and Good Will* (1989), and *A Thousand Acres.* Even *The Greenlanders* drew attention for the concern Smiley gave to the workaday preoccupations of her doomed settlement, and the historical premise of the book's creation was that the story had to end not in epic triumph, but in squalid apocalypse. Smiley's people are creatures of less talk and more sensibility, cautious (sometimes to a fault) rather than impulsive; they are creatures of introspection, observation, intelligence, and needful conversations in search of an occasion to be played out.

Smiley's characters are also less distracted and self-indulgent than those of Ann Beattie (an exception might be the narrator-protagonist of "Dynamite"), less cheeky and quirky than those of Amy Hempel, less emotionally displaced than those of Richard Ford, less psychically detached than those of Anne Tyler, less manic and grotesque than those of T. C. Boyle. The closest contemporary fictional relations of Smiley's people may be the characters of Sue Miller's and Alice Munro's fiction, Norman Maclean's family in *A River Runs Through It,* and Evan S. Connell's Mr. and Mrs. Bridge. Smiley's characters come to us out of the salvaged artifacts and emotional residue of family history and everyday life; utterance, gesture, and physical detail create texture and a sense of experience, and these in turn engage our attention, curiosity, and understanding. From Greenland to academia, Smiley's people are bound by the unexceptional imperatives of appetite and daily expectation. They are what they eat, and how they produce it, where they buy it, how and when and with whom they prepare and consume it.[23]

Smiley's articulation of the details and issues that inform the lives of her characters—from food and horses to feminism and environmental consciousness—should not be taken lightly. *The Greenlanders,* her own favorite among the novels, is merely Smiley's most starkly ambitious fusion of intellect and imagination. That is, learning and knowing are not only possible (postmodern and poststructuralist claims aside) but, in Smiley's mind, necessary. In taking on the writing of fiction, as in confronting the possibilities of experience, it is (in a phrase used in one of her stories) always worth finding out for yourself. And as Dave Hurst in "The Age of Grief" and Ginny Smith in *A Thousand Acres* make clear, knowledge carries devastating potential, but knowing is always better than not knowing. In fact, whether and how an individual comes to know and understand the fundamental issues is at the heart of Smiley's work, and in several stories and novels a measure of its success. One of Smiley's methods of demonstrating this is to develop narration in terms of passive and active characters, watchers and "doers." Her early novels and some of the stories in *The Age of Grief* are only modestly successful precisely because key characters—including those that dominate point of view—remain largely passive or ineffectually reactive, witnesses who observe much but understand and do little. For Alice Ellis in *Duplicate Keys* (1984), at once curious and tentative with regard to Susan and vexed but indulgent toward the band, this tendency almost proves fatal.

The Age of Grief contains numerous passive-active character pairings, with the center of narrative consciousness more often lying in the reticent observer rather than in the imaginative risk-taker—Florence (as opposed to Frannie) in "The Pleasure of Her Company," Kirby (not Mieko) in "Long Distance," and of course Dave rather than Dana Hurst in the title story. In many of the passive characters in Smiley's earlier work, the gap between vision and action results in stumbling pathos, and the reader may find it difficult to invest for long in a point of view that (like Axel Karlson in *Barn Blind*) sees so much for so long without doing anything about it. In other characters, the gap between vision and action is crossed, and the crossing results in painful but finally wise ironies that they find themselves obliged to appreciate.

In fact, a major shift in Smiley's fiction is manifested in "The Age of Grief," when Dave Hurst passes from watching and feeling into feeling and knowing, subsequently bringing vigilant meditation—that is, an active contemplation—into the service of his threatened domestic world. At virtually the same creative moment, in *The Greenlanders,* Gunnar Asgeirsson brings himself and the reader as close to peace as brutal circumstance and medieval understanding allow by emerging from brooding grief into the wisdom of unapologetic comprehension—that is, recognition of his condition and his fate. Beginning with "The Age of Grief," *The Greenlanders,* and *A Thousand Acres,* Smiley uses point of view to demonstrate intellectual and emotional cognition—articulate feeling. In the words of her November 1996 interview, once having chosen the relatively restrictive point of view of her "smart and meditative" but also somewhat "talky"

Iowa Goneril, Smiley had to "substitute revelation for action." Her interest in the life of the mind is an interest in demonstrating how people live because of the way they think (one of the signs of which is periodic reference to what her characters read). Since Smiley the writer is also more than casually familiar with various traditions of fiction, her affinity to the cerebral-intellectual modernists—James, Joyce, Woolf, and Mansfield, for example, more than the experiential and psychological Conrad, Lawrence, and Faulkner—seems particularly worth mentioning.

Once past the apprentice work (on character, pace, and climax) of her first three novels, and having deposited in her early short fiction some of the more distracting baggage of the 1960s and early 1970s, Smiley could take on radical political imperatives that by the 1980s had been muted and recast as "social issues" linked to the rapidly expanding rhetoric of gender politics, sexual identity, "privatization," "family values," and environmental awareness. For Smiley the writer (rather than factory worker), the ideology, collective occasions, and performative gestures of the 1960s have been dispersed and moderated into the publicly unmarked (but hardly uneventful or unimportant) confrontations of middle-class experience, especially domestic life, in which conflict is more likely to end up in therapy or the courtroom than the newspapers. By the time she wrote *A Thousand Acres,* Smiley was aware that no agenda—including feminism and gender issues, agricultural policy and environmental pollution, higher education and home-schooling, racial identity and social class, research grants and foreign policy—stands alone in a multivalent American culture. Everything is part of the web of life; everything connects.

Smiley engages her readers by attending to the quotidian motions of the mind and heart, exploring them across narrative genres and time, and from the most intimate to the most expansive sites and spaces. In doing so, her orientation to experience and her manner of telling are those of the ironic realist rather than of the romantic myth-maker; she is more Jamesian than Faulknerian. Like Austen's protagonists, Smiley's characters are at once straightforward and reticent, privately and individually memorable but publicly unremarked; a rereading of her work finds them less talkative and more introspective than remembered. More often than not, she catches them when they are too preoccupied to fret, too drained for self-pity, too tired for dramatic gestures, too chastened by the way things have gone to be looking for advice. Smiley's world, as in *The Greenlanders* and *Ordinary Love and Good Will,* can be an unforgiving one; its errors (inevitably less than cosmic but still bound to attract the attention of fate) are irreversible, its regrets deep, and its pain lasting. Smiley's world is one of nearly invisible and often unattended tragedies and catastrophes—betrayal, bewilderment, grief, and even the prospect of individual and collective doom.

But Smiley's fiction is, finally, a moral fiction, a fiction of responsibilities, choices, costs to be paid, and messes to clean up, rather than a cathartic fiction of apocalypse. In John Gardner's definition, "real art creates myths a society can live instead of die by . . . [and] such myths are not mere hopeful fairy tales but the products of careful and disciplined thought."[24] For Smiley as a writer this means consciously trying to give her readers "a rhythm that is mine . . . a stylistic rhythm that stays the same no matter what style I'm using . . . a kind of deliberate rhythm [that] might be analogous to an andante movement in a piece of music." It is "a deliberative pace where you witness something and you contemplate it, you witness it, you contemplate. . . ." Her method works in terms of "a kind of subtle control exerted [on the reader], that the world is asserted to be . . . an understandable world, and there's a subtle kind of reassurance there because the promise is that we'll get to the end and we'll know that it has meaning." In fact, a central tenet of Smiley's is that "daily life is understandable" to us as bystanders and witnesses, that it is finally a matter of cause and effect. And Smiley's conviction is that, in addition to vision and honesty, "it takes courage to accept cause and effect as the only understandable thing." In this belief in the realness, accessibility, and connectedness of causation, meaning, and truth—rather than uncertainty, indeterminacy, and interminable contestation—Smiley is devotedly anti-postmodern and anti-poststructuralist, as at least one critic contends.[25]

To live in the quotidian world of Jane Smiley is to exercise will and to make decisions and choices, and to watch their implications play out over time. In a contemporary culture of hyperbolic claims and expectations, these decisions and choices sometimes push individuals and groups toward pathetic and melodramatic "effects" rather than tragic ones, but the effects, Smiley contends, must still be dealt with in the end.

CHAPTER TWO

Barn Blind

In "Horse Love," a short memoir concerning her early (and ongoing) affection for equestrian sports, Smiley comments on the importance of "the act of dreaming." Recalling her early adolescence, Smiley asserts that

> It is the act of dreaming that is important, the daily process of putting together a future that a girl can move toward with confidence and desire. If she is lucky, as I was, the adoration she feels will fix itself on a transitional object, on someone or something like a horse, that is present but basically indifferent, something that can be left behind when the girl discovers her need for reciprocity. If she is really lucky, she will find in that time long hours of solitude, so that the fantasies can elaborate and develop on their own, owing relatively little to group ideas or adult ideas about what is respectable, worthwhile, or even possible for a girl like her, for in their detail and their idiosyncrasy is their strength, their power to carry her through the ever-increasing demands and prescriptions of high school and young womanhood. The desire to have a particular future, and the energy behind that desire, eventually translate to the sense of accomplishment and self-esteem that permit a woman to make a life that she is happy to live.[1]

In *Barn Blind* (1980), Margaret Karlson is unlucky. She is several years beyond the fourteen of Smiley's memoir, but Margaret's inability to dream a future, despite this age difference, is a frightening commentary on everything that is wrong on the Karlson farm.

By the middle of *Barn Blind* Margaret, having abandoned the kaleidoscope of college life that a highly regimented and repressed girlhood on the Karlson farm has made her incapable of negotiating, has been fully reclaimed by the oppressive regimen. In denial of the real world of urges and choices, the farm is a sheltered place "outside the normal grip of time, an arena of endless summer, endless exertion, endless security. Change was something she no longer quite believed in."[2] Margaret notices "that she had become a good daughter" (116), awakening even before the alarm rings to an obsessively neat room and her responsibility for filling out the family's chore-assignment sheet. She seems well on her way to emulating her mother, becoming another Kate. Margaret's notion that "perfection was just within reach" (117), which could in another young woman be taken ironically as a sign of naivete, is here only a disturbing measure of distorted vision and bewilderment of spirit. Particularly in light of Smiley's comments in "Horse Love," the disheartening implications of a late-adolescent woman who no longer believes in change are difficult to overlook.

Given Kate's ability to dictate the terms and oppressive conditions of Karlson life, it will be impossible for Margaret ever to approach her mother's significance to the family, let alone take her place. For one thing, Kate has so come to dominate the life of farm and family (the two become all but indistinguishable) that she has, for all her children, become the only and ultimate reference point for discipline and order. She gives Margaret certain administrative responsibilities, but only because this delegation of authority suits her and benefits the farm. For another, Kate has long since established herself as the family's moral compass, and this makes all others, including her husband Axel, necessarily peripheral, even dispensable. For a third, "her daughter had grown already into one of the sort of women Kate could never get along with: emotional, large-breasted, hesitant." To the extent that Kate considers her future, it is to "poke at the problem of Margaret," and it does not take long for her to decide that her "kind-hearted" daughter, "fragile, somehow pious, and somehow rather weak" is finally unmeant for the spare discipline of religious orders, let alone any significant responsibility for the farm, but "could be a teacher or a nurse, something helpful and secular, but also somewhat virginal" (32). Hardly successful in hiding indifference while she urges Margaret to return to college—"There's no place here for you anymore" (33)—Kate reveals her true devotion and ultimate agenda. Margaret has been written off, reduced to the consolations of her modest, regimented role and her unexpressed premonition that they are all experiencing in this summer's events "some final version" (52) of the family's story.

Although Kate muses that her daughter might eventually "come to marriage and children," Margaret at this point even seems an unlikely candidate for "marrying off." In responding to the possibility of a relationship with Harrison Randolph, Margaret finds it impossible not to describe herself as simply living "at home"—"Of course, doesn't everyone?" (147). At the end of the novel, empty of tears and hardly hopeful of the future, she can do little more than try to summon "the smooth, shimmering thought of all the things that there were"—and which now seem all but inaccessible to her: "What did people do, after all? More basically, how did they know what there was to do? Muffy (her [college] roommate . . .) was intending to be a curator. How had she found out about that, how had it even occurred to her? Other girls had intended to be other things: an actuary, a kindergarten teacher, a housewife, an archeologist, a newspaper reporter. At the time, such occupations had been merely words to her, phrases whose meaning she had understood, but that meant nothing to her imagination. Mother was none of these things" (184). In the end, Margaret can do little more than comfort silently the equally confused and grieving Henry. "She had done her crying, oddly, for months before the accident rather than since. These days she hadn't any tears left, and she did not feel guilty. Now, however, it seemed to her that she was crying by proxy, and she felt the emotions of tears: relief, embarrassment, the welling up of grief that grieves for itself as well as for the loss" (216–17). Margaret's plight removes her far from Smiley's own experience as a girl, as recalled in a 1995 interview: "Many women spend their lives figuring out what they want because they never had the chance to find out," Smiley recalled. "I don't feel that I've had to summon a lot of energy to write books or do what I wanted to do because it was the most natural thing in the world to me to know what I wanted and make up a plan for getting there."[3]

Henry, the youngest Karlson, is observant but even more innocent, and in the simplicity of his impulses he is a reliable index of the emotional anarchy at work in his older siblings,

John in particular. It is Henry who (in chapter 1) bears witness to John's delinquent nocturnal forays, and it is Henry who seeks escape from Kate's tyranny on the bicycle and the blacktop—and who runs away in search of "everything that could be learned on the other side of the bridge" (126–27). The juvenile inadequacy of his plan for escape and his resources for effecting it (bicycle, layered clothing, inadequate funds) does not diminish the deep seriousness of his plight and purpose. Henry, who has never even thought about the appropriate procedure for crossing a bridge, is simply naive enough to believe that it is still possible for a Karlson to run away. Even Henry's return is telling, since, as he confesses to Margaret, he has come back not to his family per se, but rather to John, the older and adjacent sibling and role model, the one person he understands to be both of the family and outside it. "I really missed him. I mean, he was pretty funny sometimes, you know?" (217) John, an angry adolescent desperately seeking a way to assert his individuality and strike out at his mother, is predictably "funny" in ways inimical to Kate's sense of decorum and form, as Henry has known from early in the novel. John knows full well what it means for a Karlson to be "standing in the moonlit driveway, where he had no business" (1).

John's night rambles are "spectacularly deviant to him, as if his daily resentments gestated something criminal" (3). John is physically and emotionally imprisoned by Kate's regimen; he, like the others, is sexually and socially repressed. He recognizes the dishonesty that tarnishes her "integrity" in dealing with novice horse-buyers and the way she manipulates her story of the "miracle" in trying to gain some advantage in the bargaining.

Alienated by the unrealistic expectations and guilt-laden existence forced on all of them, he has come to hate the waking world of the farm. Consciously or not, he embarks on his rambles because he is aware that Kate, with her belief in the moral significance of training and conformity, abhors aberration and idiosyncrasy. The cool secrecy of darkness gives John a sense of his own significance and potential; nighttime enables him to imagine and feel "about to discover something," feel "so full that with the simple resource of thought he would never be bored again" (3, 5). His initially tentative and later exuberant nocturnal experiments with his mother's car (like his clandestine daytime work with the tractor) find their parallel in Henry's unobserved bicycle escapades and prefigure his own last, desperate ride on Teddy. Kate's oppressiveness has forced her son into a secret life, and for night-lover John, daybreak itself can only mean the onset of the nightmare of his waking hours, a burned-out emotional wasteland of "conflagration" and "glare" (43).

The climax of John's life, then, is not his "accidental" death in chapter 9 (in any case foreshadowed by a series of minor or mock accidents in earlier chapters), but his vision of deformity and waste in chapter 6 when he discovers Queenie's fatally misshapen foal. Crucially, the discovery comes immediately after the unauthorized moonlight drive that, "like skating or sailing or flying," leads to a mere moment of ecstasy. It seems inevitable that John's discovery of the foal—its clubbed hooves bent back at a grotesque angle, its first and last minutes confirmed only by the perfunctory gestures of its mother—would evoke for him his own condition, would prefigure for him his own death because of it. It is likely that this vision, projected on the daylight world, prompts him not much later to tell his brother Peter (during a conversation that reveals deep anger at his sexual repression under Kate's regime), "I think we're retarded. . . . She's done it, you know. The whole family might be normal if it wasn't for her!" (136). John's vision of the doomed foal effectively extinguishes his joy and his hope (inspired by the radio) that, under the right conditions, "any distance was possible in any direction" (113). John's darkened consciousness of "the ghastly and malevolent foal" shadows his life from this point on, as it shadows the remaining pages of Smiley's novel. (John's fate and Smiley's reference to "filthy lucre" [106] recall the desperate, irrational rides in search of love and approbation of D. H. Lawrence's "Rocking-Horse Winner"—not surprisingly, given Smiley's early attraction to modern British fiction.)

Only Peter seems undevastated by John's death and its significance as an indicator of their family's sorry state. In the end Peter, "the creature of her voice and her self-confidence" (97), is doted on by Kate more than ever, though now with an air of desperation. With Margaret marginalized, John dead, and Henry too young and lacking in talent, Peter stays on Kate's agenda by default. He is simply his mother's only likely opportunity to produce a member of the United States Equestrian Team. So even his place and future seem tentative and fragile, and he is riding scared. Peter is both the beneficiary and the object of the series of intense lessons that Kate insists on, displacing mourning with work in clear denial of John's death and its implications for them all. But Peter has long since been aware that he is already too tall for the part, and all his victories are "diluted by growth, the tragedy of his life" (9). The ultimate irony in this, of course, is that Peter inherits his tallness from Kate herself; in effect, his bloodlines are wrong, and she is the natural cause.

It is made clear that Freeway (if not MacDougal) was bred for Peter, but even Peter has reason to wonder if the Karlsons themselves haven't all been bred for the horses. Even Peter is aware that they have been brought up to no purpose other than the one Kate has in mind, trained to share "Kate's vision of what they should be" (14). Kate's dream is to make of her farm a model of the "well-bred establishment" (22), a paradigm for "pastoral order on every hand" (194), an operation to be admired and envied by the less disciplined and self-controlled. With the proper breeding, training, and talent in both horse and rider she might even produce a legitimate Olympian. Control is everything to Kate, and she demands self-discipline of everyone; her most memorable moment of self-criticism arises from her falling into a rage against John for riding Teddy too hard. "It all belonged to mother" (2), Henry says at the outset, and every object on the farm bears the mark of her name. In this context, motherhood always seems for Kate little more than "an eighteen-year surprise" (30), at times merely an afterthought. She sees it as her duty to shape her children to the obligations of the farm and the horses, and believes it necessary to resist their growing complexity and individuality, to deny the vexing idiosyncrasies of character and the ungovernability of their lives. In doing so she creates a narrow, almost ascetic life of tasks and obligations on which her children focus "so hard . . . that they lost any sense of the voluntary" (73). Her dictation of their "leisure" pursuits makes it impossible for them to "choose" to spend their money on anything but boots and bridles. Her intelligence obscured by her obsession, Kate inevitably misinterprets her children's increasingly bizarre and risk-laden behavior—beginning with Margaret's "bawling" and ending with John's mistreatment of Teddy—as mere juvenile aggravation, misconduct that is simply perverse and inappropriate. While others might be ignorant or inept regarding the proper training of horses, Kate is "barn blind" to the needs and possibilities of her own children; she is far from embodying the definition of motherhood set forth by Smiley a little over a decade later in her essay "Can Mothers Think?":

> Successful motherhood is a unique form of responsibility-taking, rooted in an understanding of competing demands, compromise, nurture, making the best of things, weighing often competing limitations, in order to arrive at a realistic mode of survival. A successful mother, we may imagine, is one who actually *looks at* her children and *sees* them, constantly weighing their potential against who they already seem to be, finding a balance that encourages them to live up to their best potential while not destroying them with impossible demands—while at the same time knowing the world they live in well enough to realistically judge how free they might be allowed to be without endangering themselves. Can a culture exist without such a strong model of responsible, realistic care?[4]

Kate Karlson is finally a monster of her presumed virtues, which distort family life and destroy well-being in the obsessed service of "the activity that no lifetime could encompass" (211). At times she seems less a mother and proprietor of a prosperous horse farm than the high-priestess of a hybrid theology in which the Protestant work ethic is driven and kept on track by a Catholic preoccupation with guilt. Life on the farm, infused by her fealty to a vocation that the rest of the family can hardly grasp, elevates chores to the status of so many stations of the cross and the children's infrequently acknowledged successes to simple vindications of the one true faith. That Smiley intends that we see such an obsession with work as the ruination of Kate's family seems supported by her comment to an interviewer that "I've always believed that people act out of desire, so if somebody wants the bathroom clean then they should clean it. I never give the children chores, which is an absolute shibboleth of mid-western life. I don't believe in chores because I think it's the beginning of alienated labour. Everybody ends up giving their children not just the ones that are good for the children but also the ones that they themselves don't want to do. So many things that parents do are covers for tyranny."[5] In an essay on the same subject, Smiley makes it clear that occasions for alienation from work will vary, and that the key issue is not chore, but choice: "Where I discovered work was at the stable, and, in fact, there is no housework like horsework. . . . Minimal horsekeeping, rising just to the level of humaneness, requires many more hours than making a few beds, and horsework turned out to be a good preparation for the real work of adulthood, which is rearing children. It was a good preparation not only because it was similar in many ways, but also because my desire to do it, and to do a good job of it, grew out of love of and interest in my horse."[6] The reader of *Barn Blind* recognizes early on that Kate's interest in the "equestrian growth" of her offspring has less to do with child development than quasi-religious imperatives connected with a private sense of mission. Her purchases of clothing without knowledge of her children's sizes and her inability at one point even to finish making a grilled cheese sandwich are merely comic manifestations of a tragic situation.

Kate's religious conversion seems to have been crucial in having shaped her sense of vocation and dictated the realignment of family relationships and fortunes. Spirituality of a certain kind has become the essence of Kate's distorted sense of life. Her marriage is devoid of intimacy and sexuality, she sees the novices in her riding classes as so many devotees, and views the world with cold abstraction. Every afternoon from one to three she retreats to the living room and shuts the doors behind her. Privacy is her pleasure, and "In her mind's eye she sat there, in the domesticated golden sunlight, on the once cerulean velvet sofa, lapped around by carpets and books and mahogany, solitary and content, as if, in fact, cloistered" (31). Among the projected manifestations of Kate's oppressive religiosity are Peter's turn to daily prayer, Margaret's flirtation with becoming a nun, and John's angry self-flagellation (71) and despairing surrender to being "callous, deceitful, selfish, thoughtless, sneaky, cruel" (131), the Karlson equivalent of absolute evil. In another context, these inclinations might be taken as striking but understandable variations on a family theme, but given the matriarch of this family there is a disturbing energy to it all. Looking backward from *A Thousand Acres* and "Good Will," for example, readers of Smiley can see *Barn Blind* as her earliest full-length study of the damaging power of autocratic parenthood.

Kate is also quite satisfied to relinquish "the possibility of a normal marriage" (128), but Axel's reaction to this decision is vexing, at times difficult for the reader to believe. In chapter 1, with little sense of irony and future implications, he considers himself "a happy man, stupidly happy," both a giant pacing around the farm and "a little boy, who . . . could hardly believe what he saw" (8). Where Kate insists on being the farm's architect, accountant, and taskmaster, Axel is satisfied with his gentleman farmer's panoramic vision of it and the opportunity to see the income from his sixty-hour weeks used to keep it going. In a revealing acknowledgment, we learn that "He was not, he supposed, a man in control of his own life, and yet, straddling one of Miller's soybean rows, he was grinning" (7). To Kate, Axel is "a man without substance" (28), and by the usual standards he is ineffectual to the point of frustration, yet he is as infatuated with his wife as he is awestruck by his good fortune in owning the farm. Axel's love for Kate is genuine, but oddly removed; he carries a torch of "ardent but distant appreciation" (105). His devotion takes the form of passivity, acquiescence, humorous flirtation, and simple hoping for "the second coming of their marriage" (107); in the end, his lack of verbal and physical intimacy marks his impotence as both husband and father. Axel's flirting courtship, subtle and unaccountable, is his own childish and ineffectual reaction to a growing sense of domestic catastrophe.

At times, then, Axel strikes the reader as the family's fifth child, and in fact he is described as "boyish," "youthful," and "without dignity" (28). With his willingness to take passive pleasure in all that is important in his life, Axel finally comes across as something of an irresponsible fool, more a foil for Kate than a partner, let alone an adequate antagonist. When we are told, in chapter 4, that he "feared for his quiet, farmbound children" (67), we see that he does nothing to connect this with his lack of interest in discussing their "equestrian progress" (63). By the end of the novel, when he finally acknowledges the destructive power of what Kate considers "the elegant clarity of the status quo" (29), all is lost, and even then he can only mutter an incredulous objection to Kate's contention that John's death was simply an accident. It is almost too ironic to recall Axel's having earlier observed to Kate, in a rare moment of candor during one of their infrequent conversations, that the farm is "a monument to waste" (107).

In the end, Kate is perhaps too unremittingly formidable and Axel too consistently ineffectual; the imbalance in their positioning within the family makes Kate too much of a villain and Axel too much the fool; while others might remain in awe of the family enterprise this pair has constructed, the reader is left with anger at both parents on behalf of their damaged children. *Barn Blind* finds Smiley well at work on the subject of marriage as a site of power and struggle, but finally without a truly promising combination of compelling characters. Axel's weaknesses overload the equation in favor of Kate, and the youthful inadequacies of their brood include a lack of experience, self-esteem, and coping skills that results in an inability to affect the outcome of their story.

In the long view of Smiley's work, Axel Karlson stands as her first "watcher" in a long piece of fiction—that is, a central point-of-view figure through which the novel's events are taken in. But here it is clear that to witness is not enough, especially when there is already an abundance of repressed points of view in the book, when there is finally no adequate explanation for Axel's passivity, and when the "uninvolved" witness has an ethical imperative to speak and to act for those who cannot. Smiley will eventually transform her passive watchers into vigilant observers, attentive witnesses such as Dave Hurst in "The Age of Grief," Virginia Cook Smith in *A Thousand Acres,* Gunnar Asgeirsson and Pall Hallvardsson in *The Greenlanders,* and Loraine Walker in *Moo*—through whom meditation combines with intelligence to create an alternative form of action.

In addition, Smiley will pursue her interest in a viable, productive maternal sensibility. In "Can Mothers Think?" Smiley recalls that the summer of 1982 found her "pregnant by choice" and teaching the rich but agonized modernism of Kafka. The upshot was a great deal of thinking about motherhood and fiction writing, and about point of view as the key to understanding and expressing a "maternal vision": "For the fact is that, through idiosyncratic voice and point of view, narrative literature highlights the experience of the individual, offers intimate contact with another experience, and circumvents the social differences that inspire hatred and alienation." What we need, she contends, is "a vision of love to set beside all the myths of mother love—

a love that is the particular expression of a particular personality and character, the idiosyncratic, real love of an imperfect self, not the impersonal, vapid ideal based on others' conflicting needs."[7] The fundamental problem Kate Karlson exemplifies in 1980 is that, however capable and satisfied in her accomplishments she might be, she is obsessed with performance and perfection. She neither understands nor loves herself, and is unable properly to love her children and spouse. In the end, then, the emotional conflagration that finally engulfs the Karlsons is too insistently brooding and catastrophic, and overwhelms the key questions of maternal reality. Smiley observes that at the heart of motherhood are two unavoidable issues—and thus, for the novelist, two subjects. The first of these is "the implications of daily power—the way in which one's sense of virtue, and desire to be good and innocent, conflicts with the daily exercise of power over the child. I never understood the interplay of love and power before I had children." The second subject is survival, since survival, not apocalypse, is finally what motherhood is about, and any responsible version of a mother's vision "would encompass survival, as it does in *Beloved* and *Family Pictures,* would encompass the cleaning up of messes."[8]

It is possible to imagine a Karlson family story that begins with John's death and Axel's belated awakening. As an imaginative premise, the Kate-Axel relationship is limiting in its imbalance and can be seen as a product of Smiley's apprenticeship in fictional technique. But a reader of Smiley's work eventually comes to see, through Dave Hurst in "The Age of Grief" and Virginia Cook Smith in *A Thousand Acres,* why survival is not to be taken for granted and what survival means in terms of everyday realities. As her writing progresses, Smiley becomes more ambitious and increasingly incisive in her analysis of marriages and families as sites of contestation and the exercise of power. The broadening of her attention from the manifestation of tyranny to the struggle to survive its impact will prove transforming.

CHAPTER THREE

At Paradise Gate

Smiley's exploration of the dynamics of middle-class American family life, started in *Barn Blind,* continues in *At Paradise Gate* (1981). But whereas *Barn Blind* involves two generations and a single, dominating female presence, *At Paradise Gate* is concerned with the implications and fictional possibilities of interaction across three generations of adult women. The primary male presence, Ike Robison, helps define the circumstances under which the women assemble and interact, but is essentially marginalized by his illness and impending death. By the middle of the novel, the observations that "Men came and went very suddenly" and "If Grandfather dies, then . . . There won't be any men left" can almost be accepted at face value.[1] Smiley's second novel is more concerned with character development and dialogue than plot and setting. Here, domestic conversation is being established as a dominant Smiley mode. Here, too, the key conflicts that engage the female characters seem at times to be inconsistently realized in their own right and incompletely integrated components of the evolving narrative possibilities of Smiley's female (and prefeminist) ensemble. The focused attention Smiley devotes to the thoughts and feelings of the adolescent Karlsons (to some extent obscured by Kate's domination of *Barn Blind*), is given in *At Paradise Gate* to Anna Robison, her three middle-aged daughters, and her adult granddaughter. For Helen, Claire, and Susanna, anticipation of Ike's death is also an occasion to confront current reality and savor old injuries. For Anna herself, personal and family history raise myriad questions prompted by Ike's illness and the family's gathered anticipation of his death. The working convictions of the novel are that to be aware of mortality is to be frightened, that fear and pain trigger memory, and that memory demands a search for explanations.

At Paradise Gate, like *Barn Blind,* is strong apprentice work; Smiley herself has described the novel as having "structure, but no plot," and thus more typical of a first novel.[2] The opportunity to render social texture and to develop character, made possible by a story involving three adult generations, is perhaps the primary feature through which *At Paradise Gate* pushes her forward in the enterprise of fiction writing. As for themes and issues, *At Paradise Gate,* even more than *Barn Blind,* raises questions regarding marriages and families as social constructions and suggests some of the enduring implications for individuals and family relationships of such apparently incidental but eventually definitive characteristics as age, birth order, number of siblings, gender distribution, physical qualities, and "forgotten" but formative childhood incidents. As Valerie Miner observed in a review, this novel contains "genetic mirrors, primal imprints and failed strokes of communication."[3] The long-standing, fundamentally conflicted sisterhood of three adult women, daughters of a domineering father and a passive, accommodating mother, is a configuration Smiley will eventually revisit in *A Thousand Acres.*

In fact, readers can see in *At Paradise Gate* the emergence of several ongoing Smiley themes, early formulations of questions and issues that inform her later fiction. These include the nature, conditions, and costs of marriage; the permanent effects of unexamined choices; the nagging dissatisfaction of women (their accomplishments notwithstanding) with the premises and conditions of their domestic lives; and Smiley's own apparent impatience with received explanations for the way domestic experience is defined, shaped, distorted, and sustained. The presence in *At Paradise Gate* of several generations is crucial, since the inevitable comparing and contrasting of women's lives across time exposes cultural norms and variations that raise important questions regarding gender, social institutions (including the family itself), and individual motive and behavior. For example, Smiley is well aware of the implications of given names—resonant as they are in her own family—and one mark of this is the echoing of Anna's own name in that of her youngest daughter. On one level, then, the social conversation of *At Paradise Gate* can indeed be a headache-inducing "cacophony of her daughters' superabundant opinions" (48), at times an experience (as Miner put it) "like being confined to an endless Sunday afternoon."[4] The interaction of the three sisters is usually such that, as another reviewer suggested, "they are not women one would much care to know," but the complaint that the three sisters are "ciphers" and "indistinguishable" from each other seems inaccurate, despite their shared inclination to retreat to the personas of their girlhood.[5]

Smiley's point, here and later, is precisely that families are the naggingly inescapable, inevitably problematic "givens" of human experience. Families dictate terms and deprive individuals of choices, even as they offer ways to articulate and extend individual identities. At one point early in the novel, as Christine laments the uneventful blandness of married life with Todd Walker, she suggests that his aggravating affinity for routine is a family fault, and something approaching a moral issue: "They don't talk about anything. They don't seem to have any history. At family reunions they get out the old games and play them around the dining room table" (42). For Smiley the key, sustaining family enterprise (and perhaps a moral virtue) may well be storytelling—and retelling. As her career develops, Smiley will become increasingly interested in family stories as history, and history as a revelation of both domestic realities and the larger workings of American culture on the lives of individuals, male and female. Seventeen years later, these concerns will all but define *The All-True Travels and Adventures of Lidie Newton.* On a personal level, Smiley has often spoken and written of the storytelling gatherings of her own extended family, "my mother and her four siblings, their husbands and wives, and many cousins, the thirteen children who made up our generation."[6]

As a protagonist, Anna Robison is a less commanding but finally more interesting figure than Kate Karlson in *Barn Blind,* whose ambitions dominate her horses, her family's fortunes, and Smiley's first novel. Kate's obsessive, controlling presence drives *Barn Blind* toward disaster and resolution, and the thoughts and commentary of other family members prove inadequate to retard this momentum. Anna's position is more expansively central, that of *mater familias* wondering—not without some degree of hostility, longing, and regret—at the pattern of her life. Her life (like the novel itself) seems hemmed in by Ike's weakly urgent cries of "Mother! Mother!" and her daughters' admonishing query, "Is that Daddy?" Ike's illness is the catalytic occasion for the interaction of Anna—who is challenged, vexed, and frightened by her husband's failing health—with Helen, Claire, and Susanna, whose personal domestic losses and disappointments drive them to seek explanations in the final hours of their parents' lives together. Anna recognizes that their collective insistence on "hammering out an agreed upon version of their common history" (11) amounts to a tacit sibling conspiracy, a project doomed from the outset by their disagreement over even the simplest details, their individual resistance to the others' testimony, their "fifty years of prickly rivalry" (47), and the intractable terms and conditions of life itself. As her life with Ike has made clear, some questions are never answered, some explanations never given. Finally, there is Christine, unhappy in her marriage to a man who "is like an open book to me . . . an auto repair manual or something" (158).

In Anna's assessment of the situation, Ike's illness has not only provided an occasion for the public expression of personal laments, but also the potential for frightening change:

> It occurred to Anna that now was the very moment she had been dreading for years, the moment when the voicing of a single word, although she did not know which word, would work like magic to open up everything—Christine's dilemma, her own fears for Ike's condition, her doubts about her marriage and the rightness of her feelings, Ike's self-doubts and dissatisfactions, Claire's resentments of Helen and Helen's of Claire, Helen's contempt for everyone's taste and manner of living. All the compromises they had forged for the sake of companionship and

> daily friendship would shatter . . . the family would end, scatter, disappear as if none of them had ever tried as hard as possible to get along, stay in love, do the right thing, remember what it was that held them together. (137–38)

At Paradise Gate is a study of the painfully earned and often fragile equilibrium that sustains marriage and family life. For one thing, it seems as if the relationship forged by Ike and Anna is a standoff or armed truce between two very different people who have somehow grown to tolerate each other. The novel is also a way for Smiley to posit the question—an ongoing question in her subsequent fiction—of how well people know anything and how much they are capable of knowing about themselves—of whether the explanations for what happens are finally lost in mystery or discoverable by reason, whether lives are the product of accident or design, and whether knowing is better than not knowing.

Anna's self-scrutiny, inspired by both anxiety and amazement, evokes empathy because her maturity makes her aware of and resigned to the limits of her own capacity for understanding, as suggested in Smiley's epigraph from Levi-Strauss: ". . .While I complain of being able to glimpse no more than the shadow of the past, I may be insensitive to reality as it is taking shape at this very moment, since I have not reached the stage of development at which I would be capable of perceiving it. . . . I am subject to a double infirmity: all that I perceive offends me, and I constantly reproach myself for not seeing as much as I should." It is no accident that in the hours between the arrival of the sisters/daughters and Ike's death Smiley places Anna in a psychic fog of emotion and fatigue and a literal nighttime fog that only fades into a "bleached overcast" (155) outside and a "yellow and diffused" light inside the house (161).

Her daughters' efforts to find a common story through which to interpret their individual deprivations merely amplifies the difficulty Anna has in trying to identify and understand the various turns of her own life, beginning with her Wyoming girlhood and continuing with her role as nurse for a dying husband. Anna's effort is a struggle—"She could not follow all the threads through the tangle" (85)—because of the paradoxical nature of family ties. The threads that bind a family together are at once personal and communal, imagined and real, fragile and unbreakable. Names and dates are both recalled and misremembered, long-past incidents are variously interpreted and valued, one individual's dreams and failures are used to measure those of another. Like Ike's storytelling—engaging, entertaining, self-promoting, misleading—what Anna's family knows about itself through these and other stories is highly problematic. Anna herself asks in poignant resignation: "So what if I've felt violated my whole life by Mama's rules and Daddy's demands." For Anna, idyllic, "brown velvet" memories (78) of her early life in Basin are always compromised by the memory of "inhumanly white" curtains, clothing, and gloves (131–32), the obsessive measures of her mother's existence and Anna's womanhood.

The self-serving homecoming agendas of Anna's three spouseless daughters—brought to an oblique focus by Christine's announcement that she and her own husband are planning to divorce—contribute to Anna's resentment and her sense of amazement at having endured a lifetime with Ike, despite their significant differences in personality and outlook. The daughters' own needs to establish a satisfying version of their collective story prove vexing for Anna in part because Ike's clearly irreversible "illness" triggers her memory of a catalogue of the dead, "advance notices of mortality" (79). Ike's death will prove a definitive moment of unavoidable change, and anticipating it evokes memories of earlier moments of transition in Anna's life. The three daughters' agendas also weigh on Anna because their questions and observations concerning Ike, Anna, and Christine invariably carry a note of criticism, if not accusation, regarding Anna's success as a woman, wife, and mother. (It should be noted, however, that guilt is not Anna's fundamental response, nor will it be for Dana Hurst in "The Age of Grief" or Rachel Kinsella in "Ordinary Love.")

For her own part, Anna is furious at her daughters' casual dependence on her as a source of sustenance, even after half a century; by habit they approach her refrigerator "with a ten-year-old's belief in treasure boxes" (48). She finds disconcerting their condescending abandonment of *Gourmet, New Yorker,* and *Archaeology* for *Good Housekeeping, Woman's Day,* and *Family Circle* when they enter their mother's house and what they insist is the quintessential domestic situation. Anna finds intrusive and offensive her daughters' suggestion that she move Ike into the living room or dining room, and resists in this way acknowledging not only the terminal nature of Ike's condition but also the intrusion of his morality into what has become her personal domestic space. Anna sets aside her daughters' judgments and opinions. Since the onset of Ike's decline, Anna has imposed order and coherence downstairs—her own order and coherence—and refuses to consider a regression in which "nothing would have a place of its own" (17), including, presumably, Anna herself. For similar reasons, she refuses to consider bringing in a nurse, whose professional training and competence would imply inadequacies in Anna and constitute an alien invasion of her private domain, her "nest." The advent of an attentive stranger would violate both individual and shared intimacy; after all, only she understands and can respond to Ike's odd fastidiousness concerning the bathroom. In this matter, the daughters' willingness to contribute opinions and money is beside the point. Finally, Anna resists the numerous explicit and implied judgments on her life that come from all quarters, just as she resists Ike's "sentimental and determined rearrangement of what he knew to be her character" (65).

Clearly Anna has a right to feel put upon—by age and infirmity, the self-serving opinions and implied judgements of others, her husband's impending death, her unsought task of addressing her own mortality—and her response is a mixture of pain, hostility, sadness, and fear. This is an earned anger, an assertiveness of spirit validated by a kind of candid self-scrutiny unfamiliar to and undeveloped in her daughters. Anna's kindred spirit in pursuing this task, despite moments of mutual criticism, is Christine. Much of the third part of the novel is devoted to the grandmother-granddaughter kinship (for which Claire's bitterness and "ringing certainty" in knowing and judging constitute an obvious foil), beginning with the morning-sickness revelation that Christine is pregnant. In particular, Anna recalls her own despair at getting pregnant immediately after Susanna's birth, "not only because they couldn't support another child but also because she simply didn't want a fourth baby appropriating her womb, then her breasts and her time and the bits of freedom she would . . . have" (156) as the other children grew. Anna recalls that "her generation had had no choices, only luck, which absolved you from guilt, but Christine could make any choice she wanted, any time" (157). The wishful simplicity of this conception aside, Anna and Christine share a need for autonomy and a fear of relinquishing it in marriage. Anna has no trouble understanding Christine's need for "my own thoughts," ideas following ideas, "moving from revelation to revelation" (140–41). Anna understands Christine's affinity for imagination and intuition (and her aversion to Todd's bland predictability), and the reader sees in Christine's need for autonomy her own mother as a young woman—the runaway Helen who loved art and disorder, who quit college for the army, and who realized her individuality and her dreams in the Alps. Christine finds herself listening to Anna's labored efforts simultaneously to empathize with her and to explain to her the inscrutable dynamics of marriages and families, inscrutable despite a lifetime of apparent facts and clues. Looking ahead to Smiley's subsequent fiction, the restless, independently minded yet family-bound Robison women seem akin to the narrator of "Dynamite," the double-protagonist of *Duplicate Keys,* Dana Hurst in "The Age of Grief," and Rachel Kinsella in "Ordinary Love."

In this context the thematic significance of the bizarre nocturnal phone calls that punctuate Anna's restless dreams and discomforting ruminations becomes clear. "George" is apparently less literally threatening than perverse, given "a tone of voice that implied obscenity, but . . . said nothing obscene"; but his repeated inquisition—"Who is this? Who are you? Hello?" (67)—is, in Anna's mind, clearly the question of the hour for everyone in the house. By the end of part 2 it is clear that Anna must yet experience significant change in order to be released from her season of fear and anger:

> In books and on TV there was always a letter or a dying explanation, but in her experience, motives were never explained. Few people could even remember what they'd been thinking then, and if you tried to remind them or prod them or tell them what you had thought, distance gaped wider, and even rudimentary cooperation came to seem a miracle. There were little burrs she had turned over for her entire life—slights she had been unable to forget, rudenesses unresolved, hurtful remarks that no one remembered uttering, but that had worked their way into her like shards of glass. (104)

As late as the middle of part 4, Anna and Christine share a positive vision of "being alone," Anna's daughters continue to project their own unhappiness into bicker and blame, and Anna concludes that "no conclusions could be drawn" (178). Anna sees no escape from "death and anger and judgment and choice" (183). Ike will die, but his death will hardly assure resolution.

Yet despite the narrow opinions of Helen, Claire, and Susanna—finally an unreliable Greek chorus—and Christine's apocalyptic rhetoric, Anna succeeds in negotiating the territory between "the possibility of failing to survive" and "the habit of going on" (189–90): "Did she have to repent," she muses rhetorically, "because happiness came easily to her, because in the midst of anything, however perilous, a color, a shape, a harmony, or a fragrance was enough, because activity itself was enough?" (187) Her fear of Ike's death and of the autonomy she is about to face is paralyzing, but when language fails her, even when Ike invokes it, she is sustained by memory and yet another story—this one of their trip to Iowa in 1927 and of her being "madly in love for the first time in her life" (209). Ike's death releases her into a despairing sleep but also a dream of grace, in which she is lifted, sustained, "cared for by the whales" (221). She will be able to accept grief and not having love explained, will learn new things and visit Wyoming on her own. Given her husband's straitened circumstances at the end, the embedded commentary provided by the copy of *Winesburg, Ohio* on Ike's bedstand seems clear: In Anderson's book isolated individuals struggle, without success, to express their needs and feelings to others in a claustrally intimate community. (Given Anna's epiphany, a case might also be made that the informing spirit in *At Paradise Gate* is the Virginia Woolf of *A Room of One's Own* and *To the Lighthouse,* the latter of which constitutes an extended meditation on marriage and the family and ends with the unmarried Lily Briscoe's declaration that "I have had my vision.")

By contrast, Smiley provides little explanation for Christine's decision to stay in her marriage and have the baby—and there is scant information to indicate what Todd's own position might be. Since Christine falls asleep during their telling, Anna's stories of her life in Wyoming seems both ambiguous as instruction and unconvincing as inspiration. Clearly, her mother's and aunts' arguments—Helen pleads "companionship," Claire motherhood, and Susanna love—are attempts to use Christine's marriage and pregnancy to redeem their own mistakes and losses. Christine's change of heart could be read as a devotional gesture to "Grandfather" and to the family itself upon Ike's passing, as if to balance the equation with a new life, but the reader can only guess. Given the convincing tone and manner of her previously stated intentions, it is hard to imagine Christine choosing personal unhappiness simply so "the family would go on" (223), and we share Anna's fear of the costly terms under which this will happen.

On a broader thematic level, Anna's forgiving memory of the most painful aspects of her life with Ike is unsettling, perhaps unsatisfying. Tacit reconciliation with Ike or not, Anna still remembers clearly "the times he had hit her, and the times he had strapped the children. With weakness, his impatience had subsided into an old man's crotchets, but once he had beat Claire into a state of absolute silence . . . Helen and Susanna he had knocked across the room, herself he had slapped, pushed, and kicked . . . He had been a violent man" (83–84). The reader recalls Ike's disturbing fascination with Helen's beauty, and the vexation triggered in both Ike and Anna at the mention of Bertha Caldwell and Elinor Olney, both of whom severed their friendships with the couple abruptly and under odd circumstances. It is said that "Susanna got married to get out of the house" (71). There is the stocking tied for the past twenty years to the connecting door between Ike and Anna's bedrooms. And there is the disturbing mixture of fear and resignation with which Anna responds to the harassment calls of "George," at once threatening and laughable, who she must associate unconsciously with the residually threatening presence of her once-abusive husband. It may be possible for the reader to accept, once mentioned, the nagging irritation of slights, rudenesses, and hurtful remarks, but not that "The violence had slid away without a trace" (85), not that "Ike didn't figure in these [irritating] recollections. . . . Things Ike had said or done that hurt shockingly at the time, that she had sworn never to forget, always to take into account, did not affect anymore the mixture of exasperation and custom that was their marriage." Even Anna asks rhetorically, "Did they?" (104). Anna's progression from anger and "extravagant gestures" as an abused young wife and mother to her later rationalizations, forgiving (or failing?) memory, and resignation to sheer fatigue may be at once believable, frightening, and untenable for the reader. Here, resignation leads to silence, and silence accommodates denial, and it is difficult not to recall and continue to resist Helen's assertion, made early in the book, that "Any man is better than none" (42). Whether or not a family history of abusive relationships can finally be accommodated—even in the interest of "family" itself—is a question addressed by Smiley's fiction a decade later.

Finally, the perspective on Anna Robison's long view of her life provided by Smiley's subsequent work enables a reader of *At Paradise Gate* to see the important position Anna occupies in a genealogy of female characters. Anna is at once more complex and interesting than Kate Karlson and less intellectually realized than many of the Smiley women who follow. In the end, the insistent voices of Anna's unhappy daughters—even more than the anticipated death of her husband—compromise her position within the discourse of the novel as a whole. At times she and Christine, the presumptive focuses of much of the sisters' discussion and apparent concern, seem oddly incidental, merely sounding boards for the sisters' laments. But in her need for candid self-examination and her capacity for both anger and reconciliation in the face of limitations and losses, Anna anticipates, among others, Rachel Kinsella in "Ordinary Love" and Ginny Smith in *A Thousand Acres.*

CHAPTER FOUR

Duplicate Keys

The sense of extended social and geographical space that is absent from *Barn Blind* and *At Paradise Gate* is present in *Duplicate Keys* (1984)—Smiley's only urban novel to date. In her first two novels Smiley pays only passing attention to the fact that they are set in rural Illinois and semi-urban Iowa, respectively, the proximate environments of the Karlson farm and Robison house claiming most of her creative attention. But in *Duplicate Keys* Smiley carefully and productively evokes the texture and ambiance of selected segments of New York City in the 1980s, as reviewers in *Newsday, The New York Times,* and *The Village Voice* pointed out. The urban landscape of this novel is affectionately cosmopolitan, containing (in one New Yorker's summary) "the color of dusk on the Upper West Side, the aroma of lilacs in Brooklyn's Botanic Garden, of chocolate tortes at Zabar's, and the bittersweet smell of near success that is perhaps the most pungent odor in town."[1] In fact, for Alice Ellis, Smiley's point-of-view character, the city has become a familiar and comforting presence that embraces the cluster of transplanted Midwesterners whose relationships make up the fabric of the novel. That Alice all but takes her surroundings for granted contributes to the increasing sense of dissonance and disorientation experienced in *Duplicate Keys.*

Alice, like Henry Karlson of *Barn Blind* before her and (among others) Dave Hurst of "The Age of Grief" after her, is at once a voyeur and a Jamesian center of consciousness. Despite her status as one of the group, Alice's role seems always to have been that of a curious and fascinated but essentially passive and uncritical observer of the antic, at times erratic, performances of her friends, a role that seems always to have satisfied her. Her role in her marriage was apparently that of the patient, supportive, and at the same time dependent wife; now that that relationship has ended, she finds herself once more, and by a kind of default, in the ambivalent dual role of community member and outside observer. But then (in what is to become a familiar Smiley narrative trope) an act of invasive violence turns the plotline and the novel's center of consciousness inward—from the city at large to claustral private spaces, from the energetic urban crowd to the semi-functional ad hoc "family" of 1960s expatriates, and from Alice as "accidental" discoverer of a crime-scene to Alice as watchful (if not always perceptive) analyst of people and events. What happens, Smiley asks, when what was "creative and spontaneous" has become risky? What happens when an observer finds herself a witness—and thus, in turn, closely observed in her own right?

Because Alice has been in New York as long as the other members of her group—long enough to have changed in personal and public vision and expectations—she is something of a curiosity in failing to observe, let alone call into account, the changes that have occurred (or ought to have occurred) in people and circumstances since they all met near the end of the 1960s. In her own way she is like Craig and Denny, who perversely hold on to their "beginner's luck" ambitions (and iconic *Rolling Stone* clipping) years after their lone encounter with success, and end up being killed. In Alice readers see an unsettlingly stubborn and insufficiently explained insistence on maintaining an idealized notion of the group's apparent cohesiveness and sense of mutual responsibility, qualities that seem, in fact, never to have been adequately demonstrated. (Denny's fixation on a dreamlike future might be explained by his "golden age" childhood, as reported by Susan in chapter 7; there is nothing similar to help explain Alice's mental grip on their comfortable "Deep Six" idealism, except possibly her only-child upbringing in Minnesota.) It could even be said that the admirable qualities of the quasi-commune were never truly characteristic of the group because they were never explicitly an expectation; it seems that everyone tacitly agreed to share, without claims and complaints, food, clothing, records, friends, beds, and keys. And philosophically, financially, and emotionally, presumably everyone could "afford" the sharing. As Susan summarizes during one conversation, "Craig got out the dope and the unfiltered apple juice, and there was Country Joe and kissing on the Indian bedspreads and discussion of whether marijuana enhanced or dampened sexual desire, and then some friends came over to play music, and that was what really struck me, that friends who rode motorcycles could just walk in at one in the morning. Exotic . . . !"[2]

Having discovered the bodies of Craig and Denny (more than enough evidence that the "exotic" phase of all their lives may be over), and having lost the identity and roles she accepted as part of her marriage, Alice reverts to thinking about herself as the daughter of a hardware salesman from Rochester, Minnesota, for whom everything in New York City is an occasion for wonder. When she becomes Detective Honey's primary witness, she reflexively disassociates herself from the city where she has spent the past six years of her life and is unable to muster, given this withdrawal and resistance, a practical understanding of her relationship to the murder under investigation. In typically unconscious understatement she thinks, "It was not something you learned about, in the end, from reading Kafka, or *The New York Times*" (6). Later on, Alice also apparently misses the ironic coupling of the double-feature she is unable to resist, *Breaking Away* (about a small group of close friends from small-town Indiana) and Woody Allen's *Manhattan.*

At times, such offhand finessing of urgent questions, like Alice's evocation of her Midwestern modesty and her librarian's persona—"mother nurse, father in hammers and hoses. . . . No felonies, no misdemeanors, no car" (7)—is disarming. Increasingly, though, it is an aggravating reminder of her lack of serious self-scrutiny and her reflexive passivity, even in the face of threatening events. When, in chapter 9, Alice finds herself watching her own apartment from Henry's and sees certain signs of an intruder, her urge is "to creep back to bed and snuggle up to Henry's back, to abandon her apartment and everything in it" (185). Even when she continues to watch and later pays more than the usual attention to people and events, it is as if she is "just looking" during one of her window-shopping walks on Fifth Avenue. "None of this really concerns me," she tries to tell her ex-husband on the phone, "except as an unlucky bystander" (227). In murder as in marriage, she thinks of herself only as an object, a victim of chance and whim, an "actor" in a passive role. As the novel develops, however, it becomes clear that Alice's denials of subjectivity and professions of inadequacy do not make her any less involved, and they certainly do not translate into an exemption from thought and action. In fact, Alice's *Rear Window*–like moments evoke a memory of the gradually increasing danger to Hitchcock's wheelchair-bound voyeur, finally unable to dictate the terms of his involvement with what he sees. Smiley's protagonist may also think of herself as an "accidental" witness, but this hardly guarantees her safety.

From Detective Honey's perspective, of course, nobody can ever be "just looking" in New York, and being involved is not a matter of choice. Beyond this, staying alive may require an act of will. Honey's avuncular admonition to Alice late in the novel amounts not only to a lecture on her status in his case, but a teacherly synopsis of the detective novel, including the version in the reader's hands:

> Among other things, a violent crime is the beginning of a train of events, and a sign that whatever balance a given social network has achieved is strained. The crime is a change, and the change is always sudden and profound, affecting every member of the network in unforeseen ways and often violently. Sometimes the murderer kills again, and other times violence simply happens again, through other agents. Something else is always true. The parties to the violence, whether guilty or not, always assume that they know what is going on and can predict what will happen and can make their own judgments about what to do, when nine times out of ten, they don't, can't, and shouldn't. In the end, the investigating officer, whose job is to try and see the larger picture, is blocked and hindered by the ignorant confidence of these parties. (221)

But for Smiley the intrigue and ambiguity of the classic murder mystery are not, in the end, what *Duplicate Keys* is about, and the novel's emotional and cerebral commitments lie elsewhere. As Lois Gould pointed out, "It takes less than a paragraph before we're on to the fact that neither [Smiley] nor we are going to care very much who done it, let alone why. We are all in it for the dissection."[3] Circumstantial evidence aside, *Duplicate Keys* is closer to the familiar Smiley turf of realistic fiction than to that of Dashiell Hammett and Raymond Chandler. Honey, straightforward but somewhat less than hard-boiled, finally gets his killer (the initial clue as to the identity of the murderer appears on page 2), but his periodic, predictably unpredictable reappearances in the novel serve less to demonstrate for the reader his detective skills than to provoke Alice into some higher-level thinking about the group of friends on which his investigation focuses and, more importantly, her own previously unexamined relationship to it. "By relegating Honey's professional activities to the background . . . and recounting the story from Alice's perspective," Laura Marcus observed, "Smiley opens the way for rather different forms of exploration—of marriages, affairs, friendship, growing up and growing older." Marcus was one of several reviewers who noted the novel's foundations in fictional realism as well as other novelistic traditions.[4]

In fact, Detective Honey is one of three people in the novel whose "seductions" quicken her imagination and turn Alice's attention on herself, the others being Henry Mullet and Susan Gabriel. Remarkably enough, Susan's first appearance in the novel is in Alice's bed, anticipating the erotic dimension of Alice's attraction to her, and Alice and Henry literally become lovers in chapter 6. Alice hardly understands the internal effect Honey is having on her, and she resists his investigative moves as she would any perceived intrusion into the comforting "privacy" of the Deep Six group. Predictably, Honey throws her off balance and makes her question herself. "Alice hated her responses to things. Always amazed and respectful, she never managed to find anything out, or even to see what had to be found out." Detective Honey, by contrast,

> could perceive the murderer in everyone, she thought, whereas she was only able to instantly sympathize. He was trained to make judgments, while judgments were the last thing she could make. As soon as anyone spoke she saw his point of view, and it was hard for her to rate points of view or to decide between them. She was a liberal who voted in Democratic primaries, addressed envelopes, and even canvassed from time to time, but she had come to suspect that a vital body politic couldn't really stand such tolerance as hers, widespread. (123–24)

Somewhat later in her periodic musings about Honey's entrance into her life, Alice's response is remarkably like one she might have to a suitor—if not to Deep Six intimate Susan: "Why couldn't she just let all of her fears out, as she had let out all of her suspicions of Rya and Noah? Though she had betrayed their confidence, and the unaccustomed feeling of telling secrets had been demeaning, there was a seductive momentum to it. If she spilled her fears and confusions, he might extend the security of his power over her" (176). Alice wants both to resist and surrender to Honey's seductive ethos of interrogation.

The eventual shift in focus from the streets to Alice's apartment and the stacks of the New York Public Library enables readers to see Alice in *Duplicate Keys* as a variation on what becomes a fundamental Smiley theme, the coming into attentive consciousness of an intellectually capable but previously benighted self. Even the kitchen (a favorite Smiley interior space here and elsewhere) is the site of some revealing dialogue, including a long conversation on the past and the present between Susan and Alice at the beginning of chapter 7.[5] The ultimate focus of *Duplicate Keys* on what eventually proves for Alice to be productive self-examination also accounts for the most striking difference between Smiley's novel and much contemporaneous fiction that records post-1960s disillusionment and malaise—including, for example, the earlier fiction of Ann Beattie and Jay McInerny. In *Duplicate Keys* the disaffection and burnout are articulated and scrutinized more and acted out less, and serve primarily to trigger events and sustain ongoing investigations of character and culture.[6]

Since Alice is both intelligent and no stranger to "ignorant confidence," Honey's lecture has ironic implications for her, however late it comes in the history of the crime and his investigation. When first interrogated, Alice considers Honey pompous, and she is offended when he tells her that "the scene of a crime . . . can be remarkably eloquent, but even the well-meaning presence of an untrained or unobservant person can silence much of what it has to say" (6). Yet prior to phoning Jim Ellis about the murders, she is characteristically unobservant regarding the crumbs on her table, doesn't focus on the fact that she didn't put them there. It is not difficult, at times, to share the detective's frustration with his witness. Arthur Krystal didn't care for Smiley's version of the detective himself, complaining that Honey "doesn't even sound like a cop, but like Smiley's idealized image of one: a cross between a shrink and a systems plan ner. Indeed, Honey is strangely truant from a case that mixes a double homicide, cocaine, the music scene, and some obvious suspects."[7]

A reader can also understand the sentiment of more than one reviewer that Alice is both smart and "scatty," both engaging and "so complex and contradictory, you may well want to strangle her."[8] At times she proves as frustrating for the reader to attend to as the quizzical, lovestruck, and passive Axel Karlson in *Barn Blind.* In Alice's case, intelligence and education are repeatedly compromised by her stubborn belief in the shared history and presumed affinities of her gaggle of Midwestern friends: "'Dinah's Eyes' had brought Denny and Craig to New York, and the rest of them had followed, for various reasons, but mostly because it seemed the natural thing to do, natural even for herself and Jim Ellis to come only out of friendship" (8). It was a life of generous affections, impulsive decisions, and unexamined motives. Such unconditional friendship might have been sustainable in the afterglow of Woodstock, given their ages and the spirit of those times, but (as Detective Honey suggests) in the drug-and-music culture of 1980s Manhattan it might be advisable to change the locks. Yet even when given the chance, the thirty-one-year-old Alice doesn't do this, and for much of the novel she makes a weak witness and even poorer detective because she fails to see how individuals and the group's dynamic have changed since their days in Minnesota. In a particularly revealing conversation with Susan (more revealing of Alice to Susan than vice versa, as it turns out), Alice describes her "favorite former fantasy" but also reveals the engine that made it run: "Didn't you love it, really? Didn't friendship seem like the great immensity that would never be exhausted or used up? There was always someone to talk to, always someone attractive, always someone who had a different perspective on your cantankerous spouse" (133). The murders of Craig and Denny should suggest to her that nothing is now the way it might have been, that the metamorphosis is complete; but it takes her too long, perhaps, to accept the detective's contention that all of her "associates" are now not only strangers, but suspects.

Perhaps the most perverse sign of Alice's loyalty to the vision of unchanging and inexhaustible friendship is her impulse to phone her ex-husband (who has left both their group and New York for California) to talk about the murders. Alice's recollection of their relationship, a relationship sustained primarily by "her wholesale, and possibly demented, adoration of his aspirations" (25), is pathetic enough evidence that it was doomed. Her detailed recollection of the equally pathetic breakup of her marriage (25–26) suggests both its inevitability and her unwillingness to accept it. The fact that now Mariana is "always there," just as Alice had been, would seem to underscore the hopelessness of the whole business. Later in the novel, during one of the candid talks with Susan during which Alice is told more than she understands, Alice acknowledges that "my marriage was just a fruitless attempt to have something I couldn't have, another bent nail in a very ramshackle structure" (101). But typically enough for Alice, this insight hardly leads to productive action, and, as her relationship with Susan becomes increasingly intimate and dangerous, she apparently forgets it altogether.

Another sign of Alice's insistence on making experience conform to her need for "a wealth of friends" is her finger-counting exercise on the bus, in which she pushes aside disappointing realities to arrive at the consoling conclusion that "a dozen acquaintances and one beautiful building might indeed equal a friend" (89). Alice's reflex is still to think of her gaggle of transplanted friends as a safe and stable sodality, discrete from the chaos of New York, even though events have already demonstrated both the group's instability and the intrusion of urban chaos. In Jane Bakerman's reading, Alice's "great goal is to share her life with someone who, like her, will find their mutual history, attraction, interests, and even habits endlessly fascinating."[9] The tangled web of formal and informal relationships—Craig and Denny are partners, Denny and Susan are lovers; Noah and Rya are married, Rya and Craig are lovers; Alice and Susan are "intimate" friends, Alice and Henry are lovers—is only the most overt evidence of this fact. (Smiley further suggests this interpenetration of disparate lives by means of the names she gives to her characters, names that echo oddly to create curious pairings: Alice/Ellis, Honey/Henry, Ray/Rya, Noah/Rya.)

Yet a third indication of Alice's nearly fatal loyalty to the past over the present and the future is her reticence to pursue seriously a relationship with Henry, coupled with her vacillation between Henry and Susan as she watches her "family" disintegrate. As a botanist who works in Brooklyn rather than (for example) a musician who chases a dream in Manhattan, Henry is from the beginning an obvious (and for this reason somewhat resisted) outsider, given Alice's nostalgic construction of relationships. Early in the novel Alice wonders "why, although she had been with Susan for nearly an hour, and on fairly good terms, she hadn't mentioned, or even thought to mention, her walk with Henry Mullet" (87). Thus, while she "adores" Henry and is clearly affected by his entrance into her life, Alice also thinks of him as an interloper, perhaps even a suspect in the crime. "Henry entering her present circle . . . was a complication of cruel proportions. In the first place, she had said nothing to him about Susan or Craig or Denny. He had no idea they even existed." Even Alice herself can recognize this as a misrepresentation and thus a deception of sorts, since, like "presenting herself as any old librarian," it involves leading him "to believe a sort of innocence about her that she no longer believed of herself" (116). But this insight, like others, does not lead to useful conversation.

In fact, Alice's relationship with Henry is one of confusion, denial, disloyalty, and a fortunate recovery, since her post-murder relationship with Susan is one of near-fatal attraction. Divorced and distant from Jim, incompatible with Ray and Noah, and deprived of both Craig and Denny, Alice is thrown into Susan's company. Susan's earlier acts of friendship and her having set Alice up to discover the bodies make this new pairing inevitable. At first, Alice simply luxuriates in having such a long, rich, intimate, and dependable friendship, in which Susan is "porcupine" to her "jellyfish" (89). Vulnerable and malleable, Alice is drawn to Susan's pragmatism, competence, and sheer physical presence. At times she searches, anxiously, for "just the right degree of intimacy," and other times she seems driven by erotic impulse: "Alice could not help staring at Susan, admiring the liquid copper hair that stopped so abruptly at her shoulders, the strong high cheekbones and wide mouth, the eyes set deeply under great arching brows" (99). Sustained from one side by Alice's wish to replace Jim and to retreat from the radical disorientation created by the murders, and from the other by Susan's manipulation of an intimate understanding of both Alice and the crime, a seduction of Alice takes place. She is aware of "a new intimacy between them, not precisely like what they'd had before." Alice's problem is that she is able to describe and luxuriate in this new intimacy, but not think about it critically.

> Part of it was that they spent more time together, of course, necessary time . . . but also idle time, when Alice was more than glad to be a warm comfortable body whose presence in the room might be of some use. Before, Denny would have been that body. Another part of it was that the compelling topics of conversation were new ones, giving their talks a good deal of fresh urgency and, Alice was willing to admit, interest, too. Each evening's conversation held a fascination for her that would be hard to forgo. . . . Now they were talking about their whole lives, and Alice had the sense that they were seeking something, some understanding beyond the solution to the murder mystery, some knowledge of life that only the understanding of an irreducible fact like a murder could give one. This curiosity lent weight to every word they said. Alice sensed that that, too, could be addicting. And Susan needed her. That was most addicting. (139)

Of course, how and how much Susan "needs" Alice, beyond the support of a mutually grieving longtime friend, is an open question. Their conversations, pushed forward as much by Susan as by Alice, reveal Susan's dislikes and disaffections and she becomes (in the reader's mind sooner than in Alice's) an increasingly likely suspect. At times, these conversations between the two intimates are oddly reminiscent of the cat-and-mouse repartee, sustained over several interrogations, between the inspired criminal and the detective who is also a student of human behavior—a trope known to the genre at least since Raskolnikov's extended dialogue with Porfiry Petrovitch in *Crime and Punishment.* In Smiley's variation, the central chapters of *Duplicate Keys* are given over to Susan's "confession" of her anger and vexation at the foolish indulgence and convenient misconceptions that made their collective lives (and, especially, her relationship with Denny) possible, punctuated by Alice's various attempts to deny the implications of what she is being told. The most revealing of the women's conversations might be the one in which Susan recalls stabbing Denny with a fork, an incident that Susan herself marks as premonitory evidence of deep emotional problems but which Alice only vaguely remembers. "Alice, my dear, you amaze me," Susan had said a bit earlier, "You always wait until you think well of something or someone and then you label that the truth" (127).

Once Alice sleeps with Henry, however, her dual needs and divided affections surface as a more than compromising confusion in what amounts to a truly revealing moment. For Alice, still in Henry's apartment, "it was nearly possible to imagine herself across the street, wedded to Susan and as devoted to surviving this crime as the fairy tale princess who must sort seven bags of barley before sundown" (116). This spontaneous projection of herself out of the ambiguities of her new relationship with Henry and into an equally new, but somehow atavistically comforting, relationship with Susan pushes Alice that much closer to the kind of unimagined jeopardy that Detective Honey has been warning her about. The botanist might or might not be a match for Alice, but as a relationship to be worked on rather than surrendered to, he is clearly the safer choice. Later, during a striking window-shopping scene set on Fifth Avenue, Alice's conflict and choice are manifested physically: "Alice realized with a start that she hadn't thought of Henry Mullet in perhaps half an hour. Thinking of him now seemed unaccustomed, alien. . . . Susan drew her attention to a lovely white summer dress . . . but Alice's attention slid off the dress and onto Susan, before whom she stood still in absolute love and familiarity. . . . She could imagine Henry kissing her . . . [but] the sound of [Susan's] voice transformed Alice's memory of her own body into a picture of Susan's" (134). For Alice, the relationship with Susan clearly has erotic dimensions, as well as social and intellectual ones. Alice's reticence to establish a new, post-murder identity through her relationship with Henry is reinforced by the temptation to "complete" her identity by pairing up with Susan. In an interview article published a few years after the novel, Smiley is paraphrased to the effect that Alice and Susan "are based on the two sides of her own personality. In the book, the stronger woman attempts—but fails—to kill the more irresolute woman." (Smiley also indicates that *Duplicate Keys* "includes two male characters based on a former Iowa city boyfriend who played in a band.")[10]

Alice's nearly fatal temptation is to seek in domesticity casually acquired, rather than developed, those qualities she admires but fears she might always lack. "Susan dazzled with her domestic competence, her way with tax forms and vegetables and hospitality and decor. Because of Susan, people always wanted to hang around that apartment, partake not merely of the comfort she had created, but also of the comfort between her and Denny" (14–15). Denny gone is now Denny out of the picture, for Alice as well as Susan, although Alice never quite acknowledges this analysis of the situation. Alice wants a realignment of their lives, "exotically" different from, yet recognizable in terms of, the lives she feels they have all been living for the past decade. "You're amazingly domestic," she insists to Susan, and refuses to accept Susan's rejection: "Now I wouldn't say domestic. I wouldn't say domestic at all. I would say competent, or good at business, never domestic" (102). Nevertheless, Alice presumes the convenient, elegant simplicity—not to mention emotional "desirability"—of her replacing Denny in Susan's life, and Susan replacing Jim (and, before the fact, Henry) in hers. Of course, Susan, at last rid of the endless talk and second-rate music of Deep Six, wants none of it. Susan, a realist with a vengeance, sees Alice as another albatross.

Smiley does not kill off Craig Shillady and Denny Minehart prior to page 1 out of simple deference to the conventions of the murder mystery. She does it so that, through Alice as the discovering consciousness, Smiley herself can explore from the outset the implications of her protagonist's still believing, at the age of thirty-one, in what she believed a decade earlier. In a wonderfully ironic stroke on Smiley's part, Alice finally rejects the services of the "last derelict hippie" (228) locksmith, and not only because she is put off by what strikes her as his anachronistic appearance and manner. In a perverse but clear-eyed moment, Alice recognizes the folly behind all those duplicate keys, and the impossibility now of locking out what killed Craig and Denny and now threatens her. She realizes that not only will Susan always get hold of a key, but that Alice herself will be the source of vulnerability. Of the entire Deep Six group, Alice may be the only one living who still nurtures the ideal of foolish generosity that they were all presumed to believe in. Among the crucial lessons of *Duplicate Keys* is that uncritical intelligence, like an indiscriminate heart, is always a threat to a person's survival.

CHAPTER FIVE

The Age of Grief

In *The Age of Grief* (1987) Smiley continues to develop themes and strategies that have informed her imagination since *Barn Blind.* Her gathering of five short stories and a novella, well received by both readers and critics, reveals Smiley addressing questions of character at a new level and at what could be considered a turning point in her work. As she reported in conversation and recounts in "Shakespeare in Iceland," Smiley wrote the title story of *The Age of Grief* immediately after completing *The Greenlanders,* quite self-consciously pursuing narrative options precluded from her fourteenth-century saga and thematic issues generated and amplified by her nearly obsessive devotion to that massive project.[1]

In thematic terms, Smiley's central concern in *The Age of Grief* is marriage and the family as sites of obligation, distraction, catastrophe, and hope. As in *Duplicate Keys,* she also finds herself examining some practical consequences of having to move on after the 1960s and early 1970s. She is interested in the back-and-forth passage of individuals, particularly women, between the social and the domestic, between public and private spheres. As a fiction technician, Smiley becomes adept here at modulating point of view so that cultural issues and moral questions resonate through personal perspectives. In particular, she gathers in *The Age of Grief* a cluster of stories that develop from relationships between "watchers" and "doers," passive and active characters whose relationships distill the essence of the disjunction between personal vision and the realities of domestic life. The quintessential *Age of Grief* story is sustained by a relatively passive point-of-view character and an active, even provocative, friend, partner, alter ego, or confidant(e). The book offers several variations of the paradigm, culminating in the title piece.

Smiley first used the watchers/doers paradigm in *Barn Blind,* where Axel Karlson proves a too-diffident lover of his wife and both are tragically detached from the plight of their children. The strategy reappears in muted terms in *At Paradise Gate,* where Anna Robison is relegated to waiting and watching by anticipation of her husband's death—but also drawn into a new self-awareness by her granddaughter's problems. Alice Ellis, the witnessing consciousness of *Duplicate Keys,* finds herself close to, but at the same time outside of, the apparently fulfilling relationship of Susan Gabriel and Denny Minehart, a relationship that provokes Alice's ardor, envy, and curiosity. Just in time (perhaps a bit slowly, from the reader's perspective) Alice comes to understand her own capacity for misperception in observing the affairs of others and the impact of this misperception on her own life. In *The Age of Grief,* the paradigm is expressed in "The Pleasure of Her Company," "Lily," "Long Distance," and the title story. "Dynamite" and "Jeffrey, Believe Me" provide instructive variations on the dominant theme.

In "The Pleasure of Her Company" and "Lily" Smiley develops successful short studies on the passive/active theme as rendered in *Duplicate Keys.* That is, in each story a passive point of view reveals its own shortcomings and errors. In the former story Smiley uses limited omniscience to create in Florence a sense of wonder and surprise at what "love" can entail; in the latter Smiley uses point of view to postulate a critique of the passive life as haven from the world's squalor. In "The Pleasure of Her Company," the opening story of the collection, Florence, in the midst of a series of tentative relationships, is hardly a casual observer of Philip and Frannie Howard—and what appears to be their successful marriage. As a nurse, Florence (the name Smiley gives her can hardly be a coincidence) is by vocation trained to vigilance and caregiving. But as competent as she might be among children and newborns, she consistently misinterprets the signs and symptoms of the Howards' situation and the reasons for it. She is enchanted by the large, "lovely" Victorian house and the stained glass she wishes she could see further into, failing to register that Philip's preference was for the house owned by the couple with the new baby and "the chance to live their life better than they were doing it."[2] She attends to the details of the Howards' lives in the context of her own unspoken needs ("a white dress, perhaps a wedding dress"); when they move in she sees and envies the abundance and variety of their possessions, but fails to understand the strained insistence of Frannie's laughter. Florence recalls as little more than a curiosity that "her best friend in college was the most mysterious and beautiful woman she ever met, and the only man who ever treated her friend badly was the one she married" (8). She mistakes Philip and Frannie's tolerance of her neighborly "invasions" and "bribes" as a sign that they welcome the pleasure of her company. She sees the evenings she shares with them as infused not with boredom and distraction, but with "companionable silence." Only on the brink of their separation does Florence allow that

"Philip and Frannie are not perfect" (11), and even this observation is idle rather than incisive. There is more than enough evidence here that "Marriage is something Florence doesn't understand at all" (8).

From the reader's perspective, of course, Florence's hovering attentiveness to her neighbors—in effect, a kind of courtship of the couple that elides into a courtship of Frannie—is an unconscious way of excusing herself from just the kind of candid self-examination that might prove useful in developing her own relationships, whether with "the medical student," "the photographer," or Bryan. This is evident in Florence's confused handling of her most recent relationship, despite her appreciation of Bryan's attributes and her "new mother's" excitement over being in love. Obtusely uncritical herself, she is annoyed at Bryan's reserved response to Frannie, and attends to his stories only when they are unthreatening: "When he talks about his ex-wife, she can't keep her attention on what he is saying" (15). On the few occasions when she has doubts or questions, Florence does not pursue them. It is no surprise that she acknowledges yet again that "Marriage is such a mystery to me" (15). She is at once so noncommittal and so blissfully ignorant of the possibilities of relationships that, like John Marcher in James's "The Beast in the Jungle," she is in jeopardy of overlooking the obvious, and losing everything.

Given all this, it is no wonder that Florence lacks even a distant notion of the true nature of the change that has occurred in Frannie's life—"importing exotica, exporting domestica" (7), Philip might put it—the result of a deliberate, eyes-open understanding on Frannie's part that reveals just how skewed Florence's own vision and expectations regarding Frannie have been. (Here and elsewhere in her work—*At Paradise Gate, A Thousand Acres,* and *Moo,* for example—Smiley demonstrates an interest in gender and androgyny, including the various and complex nature of women's relationships with other women, as well as with men.) Of course, Frannie anticipates this change in her declaration that "I haven't had a really intimate woman friend since the day Philip and I got married, though I'd had three or four the day before. There's a friend I've had since grammar school, who must know more about me than my mother does, and yet . . . It seems like once I let her in, even her, the door will be broken open forever, and Philip will be the loser" (10). But Florence, who, on a superficial level, "wants Frannie, Frannie's delight, conversation, thoughtfulness, all to herself" (17), can hardly understand what the loss would mean to Philip, and is far from recognizing how much of a loser she herself might be.

That Florence has some distance to go to appreciate properly the possibilities of her relationship with Bryan, let alone to "penetrate the marriage mystery at last" (18), is obvious from her comment that his perceptive thoughtfulness "is rather thrilling. It's almost unmasculine!" (16). Her confusion regarding gendered expectations, domestic tranquility, habits of mind and behavior, individual needs and ambitions, and the admixture of all of these in longterm relationships nags her to the end of the story. Because she dotes on Frannie and writes Philip off fairly early, Florence pays little attention to the remodeling of his house, the phases of his personal transformation, and the lessons they might have offered about endurance, if not change. Her stubborn nostalgia for "rusty-red sofa" evenings ("don't you think it was nice to just sit around in the evening with most of the lights off and drink brandy and talk?") is reminiscent of Alice Ellis's mindset during her least perceptive moments in *Duplicate Keys*. In the end, Florence, to whom hours of watching but not truly *observing* the actions of her friends hardly reveals the secret of marriage, is possessed only of the indulgent wisdom of Philip, a helpful neighbor after all. She is at least on the verge of her own active engagement with the possibilities, her own "spirit of remodeling" (25).

In "Lily" Smiley comes closer than elsewhere in *The Age of Grief* to a kind of sardonic narration and nervous tone more typical of Ann Beattie and Jayne Anne Phillips, among other contemporaries. Since the reader is told from the outset that the Humboldts' relationship is in trouble, the story's ironies turn sharply against Smiley's protagonist. Beautiful, talented, accomplished, and without companionship much of the time, Lily only (and finally) wants to ask Kevin and Nancy "why, in fact, no one was in love with her" (29). Self-consciously fastidious, Lily fears that "life itself was to be found in dirt and disorder, in unknown dark substances that she was hesitant to touch" (30–31). Devoted to her writing and teaching, she fears that she is "turning back into a virgin" (43). She breaks off a relationship by not answering her mail. Like Florence prior to her belated enlightenment, Lily is convinced that what she wants exists in some essential form, and Lily assumes that the Humboldts will be able to tell her what this is. She is at once attentive, speculative, reticent, and usually wrong.

Lily also embraces as a given the harmony that, in actuality, is missing from the Humboldts' relationship when they arrive at her front door. When she hears Kevin's lament regarding "dumb cowboy" Hobbs Nolan she fails to understand that Nolan is not a cause, but a symptom, and she is repelled by precisely the kinds of "confidences" that might put her on the verge of answers to her larger question. Annoyed by visitors' belongings scattered about, she interprets the evidence of distraction (if not disregard) as a sign of intimacy, and her misreading of just such signs keeps her from seeing, until too late, why the occasional messiness of her friends' marriage (petulance, taunts, hostile glances, innuendo, gestures of placation) might be preferable, in their eyes, to brutal truth and violent squalor.

In fact, there is nothing new in Nancy's "disorderly" (38) presentation of self—"dropping things" has been Nancy's way as long as her hip-length hair has been her glory—and her insistence on it is her way of asserting her identity in the face of Kevin's overprotective, controlling behavior. Nancy is the actor in this situation, literally and metaphorically, whose work is appreciated by her husband only if it translates into income and whose initiatives in other directions upset the "balance" achieved through mutual silence. Kevin, it should be noted, is essentially a practiced showman on the diving board and only a risk-taker at work because Nancy, with her unglamorous but steady job, is his insurance policy. Kevin's scissor-wielding is properly read as a *re*action to what he has seen and heard, hardly an initiative taken to change his life and finally a simple matter of assault and abuse.[3] Lily's intimidated confusion at the crucial moment—"No, it doesn't seem to me that she loves you anymore" (51)—derives from her inclination to ally herself with neatness and order, with resolution. In addition, her growing sense of what marriage might really offer in its "attractive complexity" can't catch up with the pace of events. She has sought new knowledge, but is far from prepared for the moment that will "draw her into the Humboldts' marriage and . . . implicate her in its fate" (43). Her romantic hopes dictate that she misread the warnings, inevitably to assume that "something dramatic had been averted" (47). The love she is after and the love of her writing are apparently far removed from the *eros turranos* reality to which she bears witness—the brutal facts of life with love the tyrant. At her more naive and comically self-confident moments of match-remaking Lily, like Florence, recalls Austen's Emma Woodhouse, prior to her social education.

Through Lily, Smiley demonstrates that love can be freighted with old baggage and new revelations in a mixture that resists not only equilibrium, but also analysis and understanding from outside the relationship itself. Here, as later in "Ordinary Love," Smiley reminds us that human affairs do not always pursue lines of logic and that, in addition, they may violate expectations of dramatic conventions and literary forms. And finally, where Florence remains essentially unmarked and little blamed despite her lack of perception and understanding—in the end, the pathos of her silliness protects her—Lily is confronted, scolded, and presumably changed by what she says and learns concerning love during the visit of her old (and now former) college friends. The final paragraph leaves Lily frightened and confused, but her final words to Nancy can be read as either consoling or radically enlightened. In the end, though, Lily realizes not only that "finding out for yourself" has its risks, but also that the price of finding out for yourself might not be any greater than the price of trying to find out by using others.

The blame avoided by Florence and somewhat buffered by Lily's bewilderment falls hard on the protagonist of "Long Distance." Because the point of view of this story is that of a male character, and because the principal female character is "absent" and from another culture, it is possible not to see that the story picks up thematically where "Lily" leaves off. But from even before the phone rings, the author's ironic judgment on a person who tries "to get something for nothing" dogs Kirby Christianson.

The early paragraphs of "Long Distance" reveal not only Kirby's self-absorption, but his habit of avoiding rather than engaging responsibilities. "The thoughts of Mieko are accompanied by a feeling of anxiety as strong as the sensation of the hot water, and he would like the water to flow through him and wash it away" (71). When Mieko calls, he shrinks from an active role in what he knows will be their final conversation—wishes even to escape the ceremonial level of "tedious apologies"—and would like to hang up on her and blame the disconnection on faulty technology. In Kirby's simultaneous consideration of his hot water complaint and the dilemma presented in Mieko's planned visit, we see his tendency to give as much thought to workaday discomforts as to central issues in his life—often letting the former displace the latter from his mind. Later on, he will retreat into big chairs and quiet corners at Harold's house, in an attempt to sulk his way through discomforting guilt and general disappointment over the state of his life.

Given his understanding of both Mieko and Japanese culture, Kirby's behavior in Japan is particularly reprehensible. In light of her gender, her age, and a culture that expects women, even educated women, to aspire only to modesty, deference, and self-denial, it was a remarkable leap for Mieko to seek personal fulfillment in the first place. Even in his own telling, as self-protective as he tries to make it, Kirby reveals that he understood, however imperfectly, how "one by one, I broke down every single one of her strengths, everything she had equipped herself with to live in a Japanese way" (91). Mieko was very pretty, he was lonely, and he understood her history and environment enough to find ways to offer her little doses of emotional sustenance in exchange for her devotion. Given this, Kirby's focus on the word *pleasure* is oddly selective and particularly revealing. Mieko uses the word in referring to what she must now permanently relinquish—and which certainly involves more than sensual experience and intellectual exhilaration combined. For her, this "pleasure" was an intimation of fulfilled identity and escape from a repressive patriarchal culture. On the phone, even Kirby "understands at once from the hopeless tone of her voice that to give up the pleasure that Mieko has promised herself is harder than to die." Kirby encouraged her to assume she might achieve both identity and escape, but all of the risk, public and private, was to be hers, not his, and in "Long Distance" there is little sympathy to spare for a man who "understands that in his whole life he has never given up a pleasure that he cherished as much as Mieko cherished this one" (73).

The immediate measure of Kirby's "permanent smallness" (92) is his need to blame fate or other people for what happens, and when possible to blame them in the same breath: "In a just universe the father would rather die alone than steal such a pleasure from his daughter" (73). Kirby seems unaware that a reconstruction like this radically distorts the reality of the situation and the roles of the players, including the one he does not mention. Another measure of his character is his tendency toward overdramatization and self-pity, which causes him to resituate events in the context of disaster, such melodramatic scenarios apparently making moot the real-world decisions and actions that make him pathetic. His drive to Minneapolis is dangerous, to be sure, but the reality of danger seduces him into memories of others' winter tragedies and self-serving fantasies of his own death. At one point, thinking of Mieko's grief, he thinks that "She might never weep like that again, even if she heard of his death" (76). All of this marks a denial syndrome in which Kirby's words and actions are presumably irrelevant, in which "inertia carries him onward" (76–77) so that when he nonetheless arrives safely for Christmas, "His car might be a marble that has rolled, only by luck, into a safe corner" (78). Kirby, however, is less lucky than careful, protective of his own well-being to the point of disengagement from others. Because to stay on the phone sustains his self-image and takes less initiative than hanging up, we see him as less sympathetic than cowardly and patronizing in listening to Mieko's grief, and he compounds his crime by doing so. Kirby is merely relieved that he will not have to face the music and so, before fleeing his phone for the holidays, is willing to "give her a little company after all" (73).

But in the end, when he seeks sympathy, if not absolution, from Leanne, he gets only hot cocoa and judgement. Until this moment Kirby is nothing but patronizing toward Harold and Eric, in spirit if not in voice. He believes his own conduct somehow superior to the stolid, bourgeois predictability of the one and the "Nordic primitive" pretensions of the other. He is repulsed at the furniture in Harold and Leanne's living room. He mocks Eric for his politics, especially his insistence on oldest-brother prerogatives and his conservative think-tank spin on "the family." But Kirby lacks the generous spirit that informs his relatives' Christmas gifts to him; there is scant evidence that he could claim solid Socialist credentials, were he to answer young Anna's query, and it seems clear that he is a man of modest possessions more by virtue of personality than commitment. An "armchair facing the television, which sits on a spindly coffee table" (81) is not an inaccurate measure of a man of such spiritual deprivation.

Kirby comes to know that he is not a man like Eric, "who votes, owns property, has a wife, worries" (84), or like Harold, who, without self-consciousness, can say, "Principles are principles, any day of the year" (86). Kirby's disinterest in his brothers' wives as individuals, joined with his handling of himself with regard to Mieko, suggests that he will never have a family of his own. Finally, he is a man of failed sensibility, and we see his life as a series of wintery journeys between cold and sparsely furnished rooms. He is not the villain that Larry Cook is in *A Thousand Acres,* but he is a scoundrel, nevertheless. It is hard to forget that during his long drive Kirby seeks comfort in remembered "images of Japan and southern China," pleasant distractions from the overlapping anxieties of storm and guilt. "They seem like postcards" (77), he thinks. Mieko, similarly commodified, and like the gadgets he brings back from Japan for Christmas presents, will now fade into memory as just another souvenir. Kirby is Lieutenant Pinkerton to Mieko's Madame Butterfly—though it is clearly a realist rather than an operatic spirit that governs Smiley's story. In fact, one of Smiley's intellectual links to the realist tradition of modern fiction is her Jamesian attention to the subject of ethical behavior when cultural borders are crossed. (While James offered his own share of troubled observers, from Daisy Miller's Winterbourne to John Marcher in "The Beast in the Jungle," he also created several memorable scoundrels—in particular, observers who lack vision—including the "literary scoundrel" of "The Aspern Papers.")

"Jeffrey, Believe Me" and "Dynamite" constitute another, differently conceived set of stories concerned with active and passive personality. Both stories are told in the first person and involve women capable of carrying out spectacular covert initiatives; in fact, both protagonists have already done so once and neither is finished with her work. Both women have engaged in extraordinary acts for reasons that would strike most people as bizarre if not outrageous, and which remain mysterious even for them. Both women are quite intelligent, but neither understands herself, and neither monologue is as much an attempt to understand a life as to explain it. Both women are activists who have, for the time being, become subversives-in-waiting whose potential for further activity only expands as their stories end. On one level, both stories seem to be strikingly successful exercises in the writing of fiction in order to postulate, if not fully to explain, the connection between the extraordinary and the everyday world: Why and how would a woman, absent marriage and a viable male partner and without the aid of artificial insemination, become pregnant? Politics and ideology aside, what kind of person would construct a bomb and blow up a public building? On another level, the stories together show Smiley exploring in increasingly complex ways the dynamic relationship between action, observation, and vigilant meditation—intelligence put to work on the anarchic tendencies of life itself.

In recounting to Jeffrey the manner in which she maneuvered him into impregnating her, Mary also reveals something of her motivation. It is a blend of biology and belief, and the calculated and the quirky. For example, her newly achieved condition apparently owes something to her concern for "Humanity and, specifically, the gene pool" (59). Having always found Jeffrey both physically and intellectually attractive, and embodying the right blend of talent and temperament, she considers him the perfect sperm source for helping her sustain the human race in what she considers its optimum form. Her reasons for the elaborate and apparently successful conception scheme also have to do with Mary's rejection of marriage as the locus of her fulfillment. She sets aside the domestic ethos even as she employs domestic skills in her plan, "as if I had wanted marriage rather than motherhood" (62). Further, the source and conditions of Mary's pregnancy apparently have everything to do with the fact that Jeffrey is a confidant and an intimate friend—"You do like me" (63), she is convinced—finally more reliable than her sometime partner Harley. In light of Jeffrey's reticence to push their intimacy further, Mary is happy enough to take the initiative for them both. Given her self-defined mission, the shape of her plan and the manner of her pregnancy are also driven by her belief that, lacking Jeffrey's conscious cooperation, subversion and seduction will best enable her to avoid a "cacophonous conception" (60). Finally, Mary's pregnancy also owes something to her interest in controlling her own body and her belief that it is possible to dictate the direction of her life. She takes Jeffrey up on his assertion that "if you can't create your own life-style in the twentieth century, what consolation is there?" (61–62). All of this and none of it is enough to clarify the situation. (Mary proves as elusively anticonvention as Roland Barthes, whose work she is reading during breaks from her elaborate preparations.)

In the telling, then, Mary's story takes on a curious integrity, a not-incredible coherence. Her explanation is oddly akin to the perverse, reactive word game she and Jeffrey play "when I want to inform you tactfully that I am strong enough for the urban nightmare" (64), and which works according to its own internal logic. It is oddly related to her orderly, elaborate, ritual-like preparation (cooking, washing, sewing, cleansing) for the critical moment. In an important sense, the "how" of her impregnation—in effect, the explanation of how the ship gets into the bottle—is simpler and much less important to Smiley than the fact that it is part of the elusive larger meaning of life itself. The explanation tells us "everything," which is not enough to dissipate the wonder. "The masts stood up and the sails spread and the bottle filled with wind," Mary recalls. "Won't you believe the lifelong importance of this mystery to me?" (65) "Jeffrey, Believe Me" is a story about storytelling and its role in the human effort to understand life itself, often at the expense of mystery. The story of Mary's elaborate conception is at least in part a mystery for which the explanations reveal more about the nature of explaining than what took place. At the same time, it could be said that "Jeffrey, Believe Me" is like Mary's successful brownie gambit, at once imaginative and perhaps too clever.

Michiko Kakutani, for example, reviewed the story as "a silly, mannered monologue."[4]

For the same reason, it is hardly enough to dismiss Alexandra Day in "Dynamite" as simply a fugitive radical who has successfully abandoned her bomb-making days in New York and started a "new life" in the Midwest. To think of her as just a dormant activist, a quiescent bomber, is only to raise more questions. Why did Sandy Stein become Alexandra Day? What is the connection between violent activity and everyday life? Why does she fear contact with her family? What next?

Sandy Stein is still "underground" because she is at last trying to live the one life she has been given, and (like Mary) she remains a mystery even to herself. Sandy's story—"I am still known as Sandy," she reminds herself and the reader—demonstrates the simultaneous presence of order and anarchy in both private and public affairs, and the way storytelling attempts to create a system to accommodate paradoxes and extremes. Sandy is a shift engineer at a fertilizer plant in rural Missouri, a "glamourless" job for a chemical engineer that is based on a simple formula: "from air and natural gas we make ammonia" (96). Her preoccupation is now with safety questions, and all the mundane procedures and equipment checks that mark her workdays have to do with avoiding disaster in the form of poisonous emissions and catastrophic explosions. At one time she shared with her grandfather his anarchist hero, Kropotkin, and his impatience with meetings; the urge to do "the most extreme thing I could think of" (114) prompted her to quietly do research, woo Maury Nassiter, infiltrate the radical movement, and blow things up. She did all this for personal reasons, apparently (leftist ideology is never mentioned), her selfish, destructive impulses having emerged as early as her tulip-picking days in Brooklyn. "It is the itch to do the most unthought-of thing," she says, "the itch to destroy what is made—the firm shape of my life, whether unhappy, as it was, or happy, as it is now" (115). Now Sandy lives a quiet rural life, and "every day, with every safety check, every cost-benefit analysis, every decision about what maintenance to order first, I consider the comparative value of life, money, and time" (104). She is fascinated by Michael's ingenious idea for detecting ammonia leaks through acoustical monitoring. After the visit of the unmet couple she takes to be "the representatives of blame," she is capable of self-criticism and remorse, "the conviction that I might have understood more, acted less ruthlessly" (115). The sustained contradictions of Sandy Stein/Alexandra Day's life, like those of her grandfather before her, determine the parameters of her existence.

Her focus on trivia throughout "Dynamite" is Sandy's way of acknowledging the resistance of myriad experience to needful connections and logical schemes. "I open my eyes," she says, "and I am in Missouri, and everything is collecting in my head, light and heavy, animate and motionless, bright and dark. Of my life it could truly be said that all is lost, except these things" (114). "These things" are undifferentiated and unordered, and she conveys the frustration of having little more than names, dates, and unanswered questions to work with in coming to terms with a life without pattern, network, or helpful genealogy. Looking to others, she sees more of the same, especially in her grandfather and her non-Jewish, jazz-singer, antidomestic mother. "My grandfather would have said that the life of the individual is trivial indeed" (98–99), she says, and marvels at his ability to live, happily, a Socialist-American-Yahnkih self-contradiction. Even so, while living with contradiction is being able to accommodate the trivia and tolerate a sense of "devaluation," it does not impose meaning, or restore value. "It sounds to me now," Sandy says, with reference to her constantly distracted mother, "that the trivia she didn't like to talk about was her life." Her mother is, of course, idiosyncratic, but thinks perhaps that in a life of unanswerable questions, reasoned responses hardly matter. "Don't we have cousins down south?" Sandy once asked, thinking of family connections, only to be told, "There must be, somewhere. . . . Everyone from around there is related" (99). The story, it seems, is always "very sketchy."

For Sandy, anarchy is real, a felt presence in the unpredictable everyday. It lurks in the possibility of ammonia leaks, in the chance that blowing up a building might also claim an innocent victim, in the stupidity that results in her falling into a well. It takes the form of accidents—the crushing of her father by one of his own trucks, the motorcycle death of Scott. Above all, anarchy is demonstrated in the disintegration of her family and her own ties to it, and in Sandy's constantly jeopardized relationships with Scott and Michael. In ways she can describe, but for reasons that Sandy can't explain, her family falls apart; they move frequently, lose track of relatives, take on curious manners and habits. For reasons that elude her, Sandy is unable to get close to people. In her experience, personal quirks have been a form of self-assertion, and the doing of violence once brought her into feeling and being. "I don't think we're having anything as promising as a fight" (113), says Michael, and it is clear that, in

Smiley's estimation, the quintessential danger, the ultimate explosive potential for mayhem, lies in human personality.

But so does the countervailing need for order, the urge to make sense of things, the impulse to connect and reconnect. Sandy laments the loss of Scott, his war wounds and post-traumatic outbursts notwithstanding. She embraces Michael's genius even as she withdraws from his efforts, physical and intellectual, to get closer to her "inner life." Her post-dynamite years continue to be punctuated by incompleted gestures to contact her mother and siblings. She offers up her notes from underground, trying in this way to answer the question, "Why are you this way?" (116). And nothing brings home the paradox of order versus anarchy and watching versus doing than her final, contradictory thoughts. "The fact is that I am a happy person," she offers. "I feel the love that I feel every day for the simple objects of this solitude, for the spacious silence mid-continent, and I think, that's one price to pay for this, that life for this one" (104). Her job at Farm Services is to seek out signs of a threatening situation and keep it from occurring. But Sandy ends her monologue with the promise that, presumably in an effort to verify herself and confirm her contradictions, she will once more turn activist. She will reenter the public world, stealthily but without a plan, this time not to blow buildings but "to ambush my mother in some act, any act, to see her as she has never been seen before" (117). She intends once again to jeopardize the tranquility she has achieved, by doing the outrageous and unexpected. That Sandy Stein (in 1986 or thereabouts) has graduate-level scientific training and that she works in a fertilizer plant eerily anticipates such notorious 1990s incidents as the "Unabomber" attacks and the fertilizer-bomb destruction of the federal office building in Oklahoma City. But in "Dynamite" Smiley is more analytical than prescient: Sandy's bombing days are far behind her, and risk management has become her vocation. In the end, Smiley turns attention away from specific acts and back to the problem of the relationship between public identity and private motive.

Nor are the outrageous and unexpected what Dave Hurst, in the title story, considers life to be about. Before Dana's affair initiates him into the age of grief, he is a believer in planning and predictability. He sees his life as a logical sequence of events—college, dental school, marriage, children, and professional success—and is happy with the way things have turned out. For him dental school was a large meal, and "I took my spoon and went at it as deliberately as possible" (122). Accustomed by culture and training to compete in the world, he is also prepared to settle into a life of relative comfort and advantage, proprietorship and inheritance. (In this respect he is like several other Smiley males, from Axel Karlson in *Barn Blind* to Larry Cook in *A Thousand Acres* and Lionel Gift in *Moo.*) Now, he and Dana have two solid careers, three healthy children, and a vacation house. Their dental practice—with its gender balance, scheduling efficiencies, cast of interesting patients, and humane and dependable staff—is a model of equilibrium. Even the occasional "aberration" can be accommodated in the overall equanimity: They have three girls, but "Stephanie is our boy" (128); there are two Daves in the office, but some clever distinctions in name usage keep confusion at bay; the Hursts carry too much mortgage debt, but have no reason to believe that, with their combined incomes, they can't handle it.

But for Dana, life is a succession of personal challenges, even confrontations, beginning with her approach to dental school as an adventure rather than a career path. She is the only woman in her class, she is determined to get perfect grades, she "crushes" school between her fists "like a beer can" (124). Later, the unorthodox husband-wife dental practice, the huge loans and mortgage payment, pregnancy and childbirth, and "the drama of motherhood" (125) are merely additional adventures for Dana, personal challenges that, particularly when they can be made to impinge on each other, nourish her need to lock horns with life and do everything in the most difficult way. Where Dave is by nature cautious and thoughtful, Dana is "defiant": "When she came into the lecture hall every day she would pause and look around the room, at all the guys, daring them to dismiss her, daring them, in fact, to have any thoughts about her at all" (122). Married, Dana grows restless with tranquility and routine, responds to the perverse itch to destroy the firm shape of the life that she and Dave have put together. It is the itch that, beyond thought and reason, upsets equilibrium; it is, Sandy Stein would say, what puts bombs in banks. In an explanation of Dana in the context of gender, it might be offered that a bright, capable, and ambitious woman could view equilibrium and routine as tools of a patriarchal social order—that is, business as usual that is worth avoiding. In a 1995 interview article, Smiley is quoted as saying that:

> If I'd had a father I might not have married so many times. But I think it's important for people to recognise who has power over them so they can fight against that! But for

> women, their determination to fight against power in later life is undercut by the fact that they're drawn to their fathers, who symbolise it. If you're a woman who has no father, all you recognise is the imposition of power . . . I was never trained by family life to give special consideration to men because they were men.[5]

In love and surrounded by potential competition, Dave once took on a challenge of his own: "I used to meditate over my patients in the dental school, but it wasn't enough," he laments ironically. "I wanted to be a dentist and have drama, too" (125). But clearly the daring Dave of their courtship was a Dave Hurst out of character. The Dave Hurst determined to win Dana by scaring her on midnight bike rides down the longest and steepest street in town was a possessed lover, willing at that point in life to do "anything for this thing" (212). "It was like falling in love with Dana," he says. "I couldn't stop doing it and I was afraid she could" (123).

For Dave, the prize was worth such risk, particularly because he seems to have believed the prize to be permanent and the risk to be a onetime thing, like taking a final exam in a course he didn't like, or dental school itself. That Dave misguided himself in this assumption makes him immediately vulnerable to his knowledge of the affair, an explosion that alters every element of everyday reality—distorts schedules, skews routines, engenders fears, triggers fantasies, raises questions, and affects the emotional chemistry of everyone involved. This is a test of a different order. That Dave initially resists the truth of the situation is consistent with his personality and his need, and confirms that he is human. But that Dave's visceral resistance and denial give way to productive acceptance of his altered condition lifts him above all of Smiley's other passive observers in *The Age of Grief.*

> I am thirty-five years old, and it seems to me that I have arrived at the age of grief. Others arrive there sooner. Almost no one arrives much later. I don't think it is years themselves, or the disintegration of the body. . . . What it is, is what we know, now that in spite of ourselves we have stopped to think about it. It is not only that we know that love ends, children are stolen, parents die feeling that their lives have been meaningless. It is not only that, by this time, a lot of acquaintances and friends have died and all the others are getting ready to sooner or later. It is more that the barriers between the circumstances of oneself and the rest of the world have broken down, after all—after all that schooling, all that care. Lord, if it be thy will, let this cup pass from me. But when you are thirty-three, or thirty-five, the cup must come around, cannot pass from you, and it is the same cup of pain that every mortal drinks from. (154)

This is wisdom emerging from suffering; it is sober testament rather than simple grievance, the insight of a man who might yet make it.

It bears observing here that in the early Smiley novels, and in preceding stories in *The Age of Grief,* a defining mark of flawed character is comfort with or indifference to not knowing. "I don't know" is inevitably a disclaimer, indicating a desire for intimacy but not involvement, risk, or responsibility. Axel Karlson's failure to acknowledge the damage being done to his barn-blinded family and Alice Ellis's obtuse rejection of murder clues are discussed in earlier chapters. In "Lily," Lily Stith says "I didn't say I knew anything. I never said I knew anything" (54). In "Long Distance," Kirby says of Mieko's loss, "It isn't important, exactly. I don't know" (90). Florence finally has to be lectured at, albeit amiably, to consider finding out about life for herself. Dave differs from all of these in being willing from the outset to know himself rather than spend too much time and energy scrutinizing and judging others. Perhaps not surprisingly, Smiley has explicitly linked "The Age of Grief" (and "Ordinary Love," which followed two years later) to what she learned from the "unexpected but inevitable" dissolution of her second marriage.

> It was painful for everybody but it was clear that it was especially painful for the children. And I think everybody feels this, that when it's that painful there's only suicide or mass murder as an option. I wrote "The Age of Grief" and "Ordinary Love" directly as a result of that break-up and they express the pain that I felt then. But then it's also true that we all survived it, and I couldn't forsee that at the time. Times like that draw on your imagination because you have to imagine ways of surviving that are tenable for everybody.[6]

Dave Hurst's burden is to acknowledge the unimaginable and go on. He must do this because, having invested far more in his family than he ever realized, he loves them enough to hope for the future despite the present, and hope can only be sustained if he avoids the defiant, definitive confrontation that he knows Dana will inevitably seek. Hiding, with cricketlike instinctiveness, outside the vacation home, he says, "It seemed to me that if I could stay outside forever she would never tell me that she was going to leave me, but that if I joined them inside the light and the warmth, the light and warmth themselves would explode and disappear" (158). He is at once desperate, pathetic, and smart enough to realize, as Lily Stith did not, that where love matters, anything uttered is permanently said. This does not keep him from jeopardizing everything when his darker side—manifested by the garrulous and hostile Slater—"invades" him and he tells Dana that he could kill her. But here, on the brink, Slater/Dave has the sense (or perhaps just the redemptive instinct) to step aside and offer his loudest screams to a chilly night that offers back the glory of the stars. "They lay across the dark blue sky like sugar and diamonds sprinkled together. And Lord, how they shamed the flesh" (176).

Dave embraces awkwardly the painful knowledge of Dana's affair, his effort hindered by confusion ("perfect sight and perfect mystery at the same time") and desire, and his frustrating, ungovernable, bombastic loquacity. But mercifully enough the flu arrives to fell everyone in turn and take the edge off ego and complaint; he is finally able to absorb the impact of events as purposeful, vigilant grief, and thus avoid a definitive catastrophe. This is not a typical "male" response that derives from a traditional male point of view, as Smiley's observations in "Can Mothers Think?" would suggest. Dave's interest is in survival, "rather than the grand gesture of tragic death that ends so many masterpieces. There is, in western literature, what has to be interpreted as a refusal to go on, a willingness on the part of the larger heroes to vacate the mortal world through conflict, suicide, or a failure of the will to live."[7] But for a man who truly loves his wife and children, conflict joined in words or deeds would only compound disaster; the implications of legal remedies (separation, divorce, custody) designed to address the social contract but not the grief are, like those of Solomon's solution, too dispassionately efficient even to voice. Dave's story is that of a man who once thought of himself as having everything forever, but who is now trying to save as much of it as he can. "You can't grieve for every tooth, every mouth," he says. "You can't even grieve for the worst of them; you can only send the patient home with as many of the teeth he came in with as possible" (137). Here it is as if someone asked Smiley, "Can fathers think?" and she offered David Hurst as her answer.

The reader is convinced that Dave loves his family because he demonstrates the depth of his investment in the content, tone, and compassionate flow of his narration—its measured cadence, its humor, its affection for nuance, its chastened self-deprecation. His feelings for himself are always leavened by irony, sensitivity, and awareness of everyday needs and ultimate possibilities. He demonstrates the depth of his investment when he describes with affectionate precision the differences among his children. He demonstrates it in the domestic detail he provides, in the parenting skills he shows, in the schedule-juggling he undertakes to sustain a joint dental practice and three children. He demonstrates his love in the candor with which he considers his own actions and degree of responsibility; "I took on Dana," he says, "I felt about her the way she felt about dental school" (123). He demonstrates his love in the fairness and humor with which he considers Dana's personality and perspective on life: "Dana would say that she loves routine. That is how she got through . . . dental school, after all, with an ironclad routine that included hours of studying, but also nourishing meals, lots of sex, and irresponsible activities with me. Her vision of routine is a lot broader than most people's is. You might say that she has a genius for knowing what has to be included" (126). We hear in this sensitive, supple first-person narration a resilient intelligence in the process of coming to terms with reality.

By inclination and experience Dave knows that routine is the curse and blessing of family life, and that while, in a sense, routine was the culprit, the context of Dana's transgression, routine can carry them through the worst moments and buy the time he and Dana need to make the survival of their relationship possible. Dave's monstrous pain must be stared down, granted some space, and outlasted. Both the family and the dental practice require that Dave's vigilance and grief take forms that make it possible for both the fixing of teeth and the feeding of children to continue. Marriage lives or dies in the "ironic middle," and surviving the age of grief depends on how intelligently people respond when ambitions have to be readjusted and understandings renegotiated, and where there is no map, script, or plan. "Every feeling is in the mind as well as in the body" (158), Dave says. His is the vigilant sensibility of a capable mind, and it is enough to carry them through. Referring to her own experience as a parent, Smiley writes, "I never understood the interplay of love and power before I had children. I never knew what it felt like to have my actions magnified so enormously by the dependency of another. The intensity of my feelings, both positive and negative, was a certified surprise to me. In bad times, the strength I found to maintain some kind of stable routine, the faith I had in the simple value of survival, all of this came to me through my children."[8]

Dave Hurst's love for Dana and his children fits Smiley's definition of maternal love in "Can Mothers Think?" It is "a love that is the particular expression of a particular personality and character, the idiosyncratic, real love of an imperfect self, not an impersonal, vapid ideal based on others' conflicting needs."[9] It is tempting, in recognizing this, to argue that in writing "The Age of Grief" Smiley simply recast the familiar straying-spouse plot and created in Dave a clever displacement of the female situation and point of view—that is, father Dave is basically a brilliantly realized mother in disguise. But the temptation will be resisted by any admirer of Smiley's creation of (for example) Rachel Kinsella in "Ordinary Love" and Ginny Smith in *A Thousand Acres*. The temptation should be resisted by any reader who has pondered the possibility of sustained nurturing qualities in a male protagonist. More to the point, then, is Dave Hurst's modeling of stable parenting in the face of melodramatic temptations and his continuing belief (now with a more unwieldy and more precious object) in "anything for this thing." In all respects, Dave Hurst takes Smiley far beyond Florence's "almost unmasculine" Bryan of "The Pleasure of Her Company."

In "The Age of Grief" (and, later, in "Ordinary Love" and "Good Will") Smiley makes it clear that every marriage and every family, however comfortable and secure, harbors the potential for its own destruction. A family is comprised of individuals, and, frequently enough, the compulsions, needs, dreams, ambitions, and unfinished business of individuals often emerge, express themselves, and jeopardize the whole. Early passion often gives way to familiarity, predictability, and anomie. But in "The Age of Grief" she goes far beyond the kind of situation witnessed by Florence and Lily in the broken marriages of their friends, and the vision of a permanently diminished life given to Kirby Christianson. In her brilliant novella she demonstrates through Dave Hurst what it really means that (in words from one of Raymond Carver's marriage stories) "anything could happen now that we realized everything had."[10] In leaving the reader Dave makes no claim to understanding marriage, whether "small container" or "not a thing at all." But when he says "I don't know, but I can't help thinking about it" (213), we know that he understands more than most, and why the understanding will stay with him for the duration. "The Age of Grief" is, in the judgment of many readers, a contemporary classic, a brilliant execution of the novella form that may eventually stand with *A Thousand Acres* as one of Smiley's most successful longer works.[11]

CHAPTER SIX

The Greenlanders

The Greenlanders (1988) occupies a crucial position in Smiley's academic and private lives, as well as her career as a writer. Her massive rendering of the declining decades of a long-vanished Greenland colony is a synthesis of years spent in the formal study of medieval literature and language, and it is also Smiley's first significant attempt to reach beyond her formal training in fiction writing by working out a variation on an established (but now largely unread) genre and developing an unconventional narrative voice.

Smiley had been introduced to medieval English literature as an undergraduate English major at Vassar; immediately after graduating in 1971, she traveled to Winchester, England, where she worked as a digger at a medieval archaeological site. While pursuing her Ph.D. in English at the University of Iowa (beginning in the fall of 1973) and studying Old Norse under John C. McGalliard, Smiley translated and read, among other texts, *Njáls saga,* "the longest and grandest" of the Icelandic sagas, "detailing the ramifications of a marriage and an ever-widening feud while at the same time depicting the panorama of life in Iceland." Smiley was "not a good student of Old Norse." Nevertheless, in her second year of graduate study she absorbed the sagas, as they "dripped very slowly into my brain, and the images that they made there were ones that I pondered over and over."[1] Her intention was to write a doctoral dissertation on Icelandic sagas, and she sought and was awarded a 1976–1977 Fulbright-Hays study grant with this in mind. In Iceland Smiley was told about the Greenland settlements that had been founded (circa 985) just prior to the imposition of Christianity in Iceland and several centuries before the sagas were recorded—but which had died out by the mid–fifteenth century. "I just thought, boy, what a great subject," Smiley was to recall. "That was about 1977, so I had it in my mind for a long time, but I knew I didn't have the skills as a novelist to do it justice. I had some other ideas, so I decided to write those novels first and learn my craft."[2]

Returning from Iceland having conceived a novel she could not yet write and with no thesis topic, Smiley renegotiated the final project for her degree, and in 1978 submitted for her dissertation the nine short stories collected as "Harmes and Feares." In 1981, following several temporary teaching appointments, Smiley joined the faculty at Iowa State University. In February 1983, having published *Barn Blind* and *At Paradise Gate* and having completed *Duplicate Keys,* she began immediately what became months of background research and reading for *The Greenlanders* and started to turn her thinking and her Fulbright experience toward the writing of the novel.

Smiley's challenge was less one of research than one of conception and execution. The colony began with Iceland's outlawing of Erik the Red and his apparent determination to turn exile into opportunity in Greenland. Greenland's status as an "exile" settlement that maintained necessary—but uneasy and intermittent—contact with Iceland and Norway apparently defined the island's relationship with those countries for generations. Greenland, like other European colonies, cherished its own resources and production, but was inevitably considered by Europe itself as just another resource for the accumulation of wealth and building of power. (The founding of the Greenland settlement also anticipated the long project of Western Europe to colonize and exploit the world as they knew it—the early settlers of various colonies often including individuals banished from mainstream society.) Yet, the controlling fact of the Greenlanders' story was its plodding grimness, ending in wholesale death brought on by implacable forces—external forces certainly, including the harsh climate and undependable sources of food; internal forces quite possibly, including internecine conflict and social chaos. Of course, the Greenlanders themselves could not know the end of their story, but could only suspect it, and then only by anticipating apocalypse in defiance of the simple hope that earthly redemption in the form of a stranded whale, a successful hunt, a visiting ship, human affection, an early spring, or a mild winter might put off the need for the ultimate salvation.

From a twentieth-century perspective, the fate of the Greenlanders was overwhelmingly pathetic rather than tragic or ironic. Further, the emotional extremes of late-medieval Nordic culture, as recorded in the sagas and chronicles, resulted in brutal and sensational events that made for starkly rendered melodramatic tales rather than nuanced stories driven by character and idea. The Greenlanders' vision of human experience was dictated by their medieval version of Christianity, so when they considered their lives in terms of "story" they saw themselves and others in terms of moral exemplars or emblems rather than characters. As for "literary" voice and style, the dominant mode of the sagas and chronicles was a direct and dispassionate "plain style" rather than the reflexive discourse of irony, commentary, and subordination familiar to the twentieth century.

But Smiley emerged from her research with some useful answers to a central question:

> Why did the Greenlanders disappear after centuries of relative prosperity? There are some theories: that the northern climate grew colder, that there were attacks by English and Basque pirates. Some people think that the skraelings—Eskimos—laid waste to the settlements. The most general answer is that the Greenlanders were so blinded by their own cultural prejudices that they were unable to adapt when conditions changed. They never stopped looking to Europe for succor, long after Europe had abandoned and forgotten them. Though they could get along fine with a thin lifeline, they could not get along with no lifeline at all.[3]

It is known that the Greenland colony died out, but what can be understood of individual lives requires informed extrapolation from a sparse written record and a gathering of silent artifacts. What must the Greenlanders have been thinking and doing in the years of their decline, when they were an outpost of their civilization and on the cutting edge of oblivion?

Smiley discovered in the surviving Icelandic records real people and events that she was eventually to incorporate into the book. "Because a lot of the characters were historically attested, they really seemed to come to me as living things outside of myself. I felt as though I were bringing to light the story of a lost people, as if I'd known those people and was finally telling their tale to the world in the ways that they deserved to have it told . . . I really did feel a responsibility to make their way of life and their agonies and passions known, these people that fell through a hole in history and disappeared."[4] For Smiley the disappearance of the colony eventually raised social, economic, political, and even environmental questions for her own, equally unstable postcolonial world. "The whole time I was writing [the novel], I felt very socially responsible," Smiley has said. "One of the first things that intrigued me about it was that it was the only attested case of an *established* European civilization or culture falling apart and vanishing. There's the sense that if we in our time knew how they in their time somehow managed to let go, somehow managed to lose control, then it would help keep us from losing control of our own situation."[5] Given Smiley's subsequent studies of "losing control of our own situation"—most consistently with respect to land use and environmental issues in such otherwise dissimilar works as "Good Will," *A Thousand Acres,* and *Moo*—it is useful to think of *The Greenlanders* as her first sustained interrogation of the relationship between the ideology of ownership and longterm catastrophe.

Smiley's preoccupation with explaining Greenland's collective, catastrophic death seems to have had a nagging analog in her personal life: an extraordinary preoccupation with fear—of accidents, of random violence, of nuclear annihilation—and therefore an almost overpowering sense of mortality. Smiley's contention is that her generation, born immediately after World War II, always had two main preoccupations: "We were the generation that grew up with the pill and the atom bomb. I don't think our concerns have changed, although they may be dissipated by getting to work on time. But if there is a single person in my generation who doesn't deeply believe that they and their families could be blown to smithereens at any time. . . ." The anxiety is sustained, Smiley maintains, "because we're constantly barraged with the ends of things: planes blowing up, governments falling, famine overtaking Ethiopia."[6] That these comments could emerge in an interview given *after* the fall of European Communism in 1989 reinforces the notion that Smiley's has been more than a single-issue anxiety—as does the essay "*Puissance,*" in which Smiley recounts major bouts with fear in 1973, during a visit to the intellectual fundamentalist L'Abri Fellowship in Switzerland, and in 1980, when the threat of nuclear war became for her a specific focus for anxieties triggered by hostage-taking incidents and American anti-Communist drumbeating. In "*Puissance*" Smiley stresses the way the "unexpected" termination of her first marriage helped end her first bout with fear, and that, in the second instance, the fear dissipated when she made herself write a story about nuclear war, "The Blinding Light of the Mind," and "resolved the narrator's situation well enough to end the story and publish it" (in the December 1983 issue of *Atlantic*). She also reports that a third major confrontation with fear occurred in 1992, upon the birth of her third child. Smiley confronted fear this time by resuming her girlhood passion for horseback riding and embracing the joys and fears of jumping.[7]

The Greenlanders, then, develops from the fusion in Smiley's imagination of two radically different fin-de-siècle sensibilities, those of the late fourteenth and late twentieth centuries. Near the end of the fourteenth century, human will, expectations, understanding, and "reality" supposedly counted for little in the face of divine intentions. Near the end of the twentieth century, human imagination and inventiveness—at once valorized and commodified by science and technology—presume to define reality and in fact are implicated in the threatened condition of the planet itself. (For comparative purposes, it is worth noting that, in 1985, Smiley was writing a thousand years after the founding of the Greenland colony and six hundred years after intimations of its death might first have been felt.) At the same time, the "ways" of twentieth-century fictional realism could not be casually imposed on fourteenth-century reality. In order to write her Greenland novel, Smiley needed a narrative style that would do justice to the Greenlanders' failure by enabling her to render not only event, but also a way of thinking *about* event that was fundamentally preliterary. Not only was Smiley writing about people whose story had ended well over five centuries earlier, she was writing about what was predominantly an oral enclave of a minimally literate late-medieval civilization. For the Greenlanders, reading and writing were available only in certain quarters (such as government and the church) and otherwise pursued by rare individuals (for example, Smiley's Gunnar Asgeirsson). Theirs was a culture whose literacy was much different in capacity and function from the literacy that printing would eventually make possible (beginning about the time the Greenland colony disappeared).

"I found the sagas fascinating as examples of absolutely pared-down narrative," Smiley has said. "I decided that they were really about cause and effect more than anything else, because some little tiny cause would always lead to cataclysmic effects, and the saga would map out these effects, both geographically and historically."[8] Yet what were cause and effect in the mind of the fourteenth century? Smiley was writing about a people who, on the whole, accepted the will of God—accepted that their lives were governed more by inexplicable natural phenomena (including the Great Death), and vaguely understood social and political forces and events (the schism within the Catholic church, for example) than by the exercise of individual will and choice. Even when they were in some way attentive to the more conspicuous factors that affected their lives, the Greenlanders were essentially resigned and passive before them. They saw their condition as fate-driven and narrowly determined, yet at the same time barely coherent in terms of direction and intention, and mitigated only by the pathos constructed by their faith. Their usual mode was not action, but reaction. "There were some things I noted about the typical medieval or Icelandic voice," Smiley recalls in a 1988 interview.

> One of them is they almost never used subordination in a sentence. They almost always used coordination—and this happened, and this happened, and this happened . . . I'd always envisioned them as seeing the world as some kind of phenomenal movie that's just rushing past, that they don't particularly understand but they are very present in. So that's what I tried to achieve in the style. For us, everything is subjective. It's all a projection of one's own personality. So you don't know what's real. For medieval

> people, it's just the opposite of that. One's own personality is not very well understood. And so everything seems to have objective reality—dreams, visions and prophesies or whatever.[9]

As for direct literary influences beyond the Icelandic sagas and chronicles themselves, there were Sigrid Undset's *Kristin Lavransdatter* (1923), a three-volume saga of life in medieval Norway, and the later fiction of Icelandic writer Halldór Laxness, in particular *Independent People* (1946) and *The Happy Warriors* (1958), in their own right inspired by the chronicles and sagas. Closer to home, Smiley had, some years earlier, found "magical" and compelling Conrad Richter's use of "a very archaic language" that evoked his sense of the speech and thinking of early nineteenth-century settlers in his Ohio Valley "Awakening Land" trilogy, *The Trees* (1940), *The Fields* (1946), and *The Town* (1950).[10]

Smiley began the actual writing of *The Greenlanders* in May 1984 and the first complete draft emerged on 24 June 1985, the product of a furious and obsessive creative period during which Smiley did research in England, Denmark, and Greenland. "I couldn't get it out fast enough," she later reported. "I ran to my word processor; I adored writing it. At the end it was coming out 12 to 20 pages a day. It was that classic experience where it seems that others are speaking to you, you're not really creating them. And I don't know where it came from."[11] The final *Greenlanders* manuscript exceeded 1,100 pages; it was the product of a novelist's imagination probing the oblivion into which the lost colony had fallen, and working hard to make the theories take human form. At the same time, whatever its origins, Smiley's inspiration had its price. In an interview given just prior to the book's publication, Smiley observed that "the book about the Greenlanders changed my life forever, in ways that I didn't expect it to . . . I won't say that it caused my [second] divorce. But I will say that it revealed emotional terrain to me that could not be accommodated by my marriage."[12] Several years later, in "Shakespeare in Iceland," Smiley added that

> I was convinced that [*The Greenlanders*] was my masterwork, and that the process I was going through was a necessary process for such a work. I also have to say that I didn't like it, that what it had done to my life, my routine, and my sense of myself appalled me, and I thought, though I loved *The Greenlanders* itself and still do, that I never wanted to go through that again, even for another masterwork. I learned my lesson, and the lesson was that literature wasn't everything, didn't deserve to be everything.[13]

Her response to this insight was to begin, the day after completing *The Greenlanders,* to work on "The Age of Grief," a story in which she would consciously explore some of the more immediate and personal "issues of balance of parents and children [in a domestic situation] . . . How do you balance the claims of the children against the claims of the parents?"[14]

The Greenlanders' story emerges through emotionless declarative sentences that report the violent episodes and intimate interludes that define their life. Smiley presents a harsh tale in which debilitating minor incidents and destabilizing larger events combine with ungovernable internal and external forces to ensure that the Greenlanders' history will be relatively brief. In the novel itself, the pathos of the Greenlanders is that all but the most intuitive, imaginative, or astute—such as Birgitta Lavransdottir, Gunnar Asgeirsson and Sira Pall Halvardsson—lack any understanding of their condition and fate beyond the demands of everyday routine and seasonal need. (For this reason, Smiley's occasional use in the novel of parenthetical commentary for confirming psychological texture or revealing meditative capacity in a character may strike some readers as stylistically anachronistic and intrusive.) The pathos of the Greenlanders is that of those few whose intelligence and vision may have enabled them to understand the larger implications of their shared condition, none was able to produce an enduring final record; at the end of Smiley's novel, the true priests are all dead and Gunnar Asgeirsson is virtually alone as a weaver, parchment-maker, and scribe. The pathos of Gunnar, Margret Asgeirsdottir, and Sira Pall is that they are people attempting to realize their humanity but whose fate is merely to illuminate the terms of a fatal melodrama. *The Greenlanders* conveys the bewilderment of a slowly weakening, steadily fraying civilization in which meaningful conviction, civil obligation, and the skills of everyday life endure from year to year but decline over the decades.

In a reading of *The Greenlanders* the effect of Smiley's relentlessly flat and passionless narration ("Now it happened that . . . And so it happened that . . . It was the case that. . . .") is a sense of irreversible, long-accomplished events before which human efforts were doomed from the start. The paradoxical effect, even when sequential paragraphs begin with "Now . . . Now . . . Now . . . ," is that everything being shown to the reader is immediately and irrevocably appropriated into "Then." The prose style of *The Greenlanders* is direct, terse, measured, and unforgiving—and it reinforces the reader's sense of the Greenlanders' tendency to treat even memorable events not as compelling and defining moments, but simply as markers of time and the handiwork of fate. The arrival of a ship from Norway or Iceland, or a notably successful or unsuccessful seal hunt, or an eventful session of the Thing (Nordic Greenland's judicial forum), or the most recent time of hunger merely offers the Greenlanders a way to mark the passing of their lives. Their habit is to pursue on a daily basis the obligations of long-established steading routine and, within the limits of climate and chance, to wait for the ice to break up and blow out of the fjords, for the next shipment of tools and supplies and fashions to arrive from Europe, and for the appearance of the next bishop and the latest emissary from the Norwegian court.

The fumbling administration and untimely death of Kollbein Sigurdsson are symptomatic of the progress of North Atlantic civilization in Greenland. Kollbein wears bright clothing and considers furs a matter of style rather than warmth; with his retinue of courtiers and sailors he is a man preoccupied with status and show. Yet he manages Thjodhilds Stead poorly and fails to maintain its prosperity, and as a governor his response to shortages is to expect more sacrifice from the governed. Crucially, Kollbein is an indecisive and unimaginative man living in an unstable time and place; he is an easygoing and slow-moving administrator among people accustomed to inherited enmities and hardly averse to impulsive reaction. As is also the case later under the status-seeking Bjorn Bollason, Kollbein's is not the controlling hand the Greenlanders need if their society is to function and their collective enterprise is to endure. The key test for Kollbein Sigurdsson is the disposition of his suit at the Thing for the killing of Skuli Gudmundsson, "hirdman and representative of Kollbein Sigurdsson, himself direct representative of the king,"[15] in the wake of Kollbein's own perfunctory and ineffective efforts to control the proceedings. His case is fundamentally weak (given Greenlander protocol), and he is outmaneuvered by those he has habitually treated as inferior; he has no recourse but disgruntlement at the summary dismissal, citing "what he called outmoded practices, for the Thing had long wielded no power in Norway or even in Iceland, where the power of the king ruled" (120).

But in Smiley's larger perspective on the fate of Greenland, the victory of Gunnar Asgeirsson and Olaf Finnbogason over Kollbein Sigurdsson and his ego is hardly a triumph to be savored by the colony at large. Margret Asgeirsdottir's brother and husband feel they have received justice at the Thing, but the perfunctory rejection of Kollbein's case merely nurtures disregard for central authority and contributes to further destabilization of the civil polity. Manipulation of the Thing for personal gain and as an outlet for Greenlander-Norwegian tension also contributes to the court's progressive devaluation over time. Eventually, the deaths of various lawspeakers and the loss of collective legal memory, both formal and informal, cause the corpus of law itself to be lost; eventually, Bjorn Bollason uses the shield of pragmatism to pack a truncated court with his own judges. By the end of the colony's productive life, the Thing has been reduced in duration, jurisdiction, and authority; a seven-day civil obligation withers to an affair of three days or less, a token and ineffectual gesture at protocol and coherence, and finally falls into disuse altogether. Not surprisingly, Kollbein Sigurdsson's foolish death due to his unnecessary participation in the swimming contest evokes more cynicism than agony in the settlement, with the Greenlanders concluding that "with Kollbein Sigurdsson and Skuli Gudmundsson both dead, there was little to make of King Hakon and Queen Margarethe in Greenland" (142). But the further weakening of government brought on by this death eventually makes it possible for outlaws such as Ofeig to go unchecked, for desperate people to embrace the religious fanatic Larus, and for the Bristol men to loot and kill in the absence of organized resistance; the Devil enters Greenland through the door of disorder. In Smiley's novel the life and death of Kollbein Sigurdsson serves as one of numerous reminders that decisions and events that would have little impact in another setting invariably affect the longterm viability of the Greenland colony—that in this time and place, small personal gains almost always lead to large public losses. Greenland is hardly a place that suffers fools; it is a place that allows little margin for error in human affairs.

Lacking faith in the secular order, the Greenlanders wait for signs and portents, and for dreams and visions to interpret. That the plague has not visited Greenland is taken as a sign that God may, after all, be looking after them. When a wounded reindeer disappears into a willow thicket in a time of meager hunting, the Greenlanders consider the event "a sign of the future" (295).

The ultimate hope of the Greenlanders is to be deserving of the salvation for which they hunger, a hope sustained in earlier days by Bishop Alf and later on by the Greenlanders' anticipation of his successor, but kept alive in the final years of unanswered waiting only by a sad procession of the unordained, self-ordained, tentative, and unstable. "The Fate of men," says Sira Jon, "is to yearn for an answer from the Lord" (148).

Sira Jon's description of his own spiritual condition shows him to be a lost soul among floundering spirits. He tells Sira Pall Hallvardsson:

> I am humiliated to be here, at Gardar, when I should be at Nidaros or even Paris. I have been trained for that, not this. Oh, brother, what means it that just before sleep, or just waking, I often see myself in such a cathedral as at Rheims . . . and the great space of the cathedral is filled with the glory of God, and . . . the stony gloom of Gardar and its turf smell seem paltry to me, a shame to God and His Son, this crude altar and these ragged tapestries! Thus pride and humiliation partake of each other, and the thing that I long for seems at times pure and at times defiled by my longing. (106)

Sira Pall's grounded wisdom concerning the burden of all Greenlanders, cowherds and clerics alike—"In the fertile soil of the Greenland fjords, there is an eighth mortal sin that sprouts, and that is the sin of yearning" (106)—is resisted and dismissed by Sira Jon. Similarly, Sira Pall's description of the Greenlanders themselves reveals not only their uniqueness as a culture but also why Sira Jon's disdain for them and for the church's "work in the western ocean" makes his ministry fail: "They are half-wild, like horses left in the mountains to fend for themselves. They have made their own paths through the wilderness, and they balk at being led. And anyone who would lead them must sometimes confess that the paths they have made are as good as or better than those he would bring them to. They are not, perhaps, men of our world, as men in France or men in Flanders or Germany are, though they seek after the fashions and ways of the world and consider themselves like us. But they are new men and Vikings at the same time" (148–49). It is significant in this and other scenes that Sira Pall speaks from a humble stool, as an inferior; Sira Jon pontificates from the "high seat" that he has inherited through the death of Bishop Alf, and he desperately seeks refuge from the realities of Greenland life in his office, his magnificent vestments, and the lurid illumination of whale oil lamps. (Later, in another distancing gesture, Sira Jon will refer to the Greenlanders themselves as "a devilish lot" [308].) Sira Jon's decline from angry cynic to insane recluse grotesquely anticipates the implosion and disappearance of the Greenland settlement itself.

It is also significant that Sira Jon's revelations (tantamount to confessions) are offered to Sira Pall during their periodic debates over the meaning of church doctrine and policy in Greenland. Pall Hallvardsson is himself part Flemish and part Icelandic; like Hauk Gunnarsson, Margret Asgeirsdottir, Finn Thormodsson, and Kollgrim Gunnarsson, he is sustained by skills and a sensibility born of the "western ocean" as well as the Continent. "It seems to me that the Lord asks two things of men," he tells his bitter colleague, "and one of these is penitence, devotion, and sacrifice, but the other is the wise husbandry of the goods of the world, for the care of His servants and their charges" (181); and later we are told of Sira Pall, "He saw that he was a man made for this world" (357). He is, in short, one of several Greenlanders who have the potential to put a supple mind to work on their situation and enable them all to survive it. But in Sira Pall's case, reason is required to sit below pride, marginalized by the prerogatives of nepotism and hierarchy. In a world in which superstition and spiritualism are the dominant (indeed, "correct") responses to hard times, Sira Pall is a thwarted realist.

Sira Pall is the priest as social pragmatist in a struggling culture driven by desperate needs and selfish appetites, restricted by dogmatic religiosity, drained of resources by the home country, and constantly jeopardized by an all but suicidal clan structure (marked and reinforced for the reader by the patrilineal Nordic naming system). Sira Pall's dilemma is nowhere more evident than in the middle of the novel, when he examines Sira Jon's meticulously kept account books for Gardar, books in which "Each year had a single finely written-over page, and at the end of every quarter, numbers of goods for use and for the archbishop at Nidaros were totted up. Sira Jon's hand was so fine that Pall Hallvardsson could hardly make it out, and . . . Sira Jon's method for coming to the figures he wrote down escaped Pall Hallvardsson completely" (266). Sira Jon's account is, in one reading, simply a version of what was called a "Domesday" or "Doomsday" Book, a survey of properties and values and a census of people and livestock. (Such periodic surveys are sprinkled throughout the novel by Smiley, and they tally the gradual decline of quantity and quality in settlement life.) In another reading, though, Sira Jon's neurotic record is little more than data amassed obsessively and without context or meaning. Like the philosophical treatise and fastidious but pathetically irrelevant records of Joseph Conrad's Kurtz in "Heart of Darkness," Sira Jon's jottings are a testament to the abandonment of ethos and failure of vision in a place of immense spiritual deprivation. Late in the novel, the spiritual abandonment of Greenland is confirmed when a demoralized Sira Pall (the last cleric to know the full liturgy) finally relinquishes the religious life of the colony to its two spurious and fanatical "popes," Larus the Prophet and Sira Eindridi.

The death of Bishop Alf in 1377 follows by precisely a year the death of Kollbein Sigurdsson. This coincidence stresses the Greenlanders' dependence on equally fragile secular and religious lifelines—and marks in unmistakable terms the onset of the colony's progressive disintegration. Smiley makes this awareness tangible in her periodic descriptions of the Gardar church itself, as when, perplexed by the state of the written record, Sira Pall examines the tattered tapestries and hangings. "Here and there the tatters were neatly stitched, but not everywhere. Even from where he was sitting he could see that repairs of some of the hangings would involve stitching stitches to stitches, and the best needlewomen in Greenland could not necessarily make such repairs handsome. Some of the tears offended the sight" (267). Even the most sacred symbols seem beyond salvage, and even the stone of the church's walls shows signs of weakness. The sense of disrepair in the religious fabric of settlement life is expanded through references to weak candidates for the priesthood, the cessation of manuscript copying, and the gradual loss of the liturgy because of merely sporadic and perfunctory attempts at pedagogy. Outside the church, the tattering of Greenland is seen in the wearing out of metal tools and weapons, and the almost useless state into which the reindeer-hunting pits have been allowed to fall. The Greenlanders' decline is also evident when their transformation from warriors and hunters to herdsmen and farmers is followed by their becoming scavengers, looters, and petty thieves during times of sickness and famine. It is worth noting that the Thing, the Greenlanders' fundamental tool for articulating and distributing justice, is without a legitimate lawspeaker from the time Gizur Gizursson dies, very early in the novel.

Well beyond Gardar, of course, the cycle of neglect, disrepair, failure, and abandonment of steadings afflicts enclaves throughout Greenland. "Steinstraumstead [the refuge of Margret Asgeirsdottir, Asta Thorbergsdottir, and Sigurd Kolsson] was falling down" (259), and everywhere there is a sense of "too few servants and too much land" (260), whether steadings are large or small. The failures are quantified; at one point alone reference is made to "three or four in the valley leading to Isafjord, two more in Isafjord itself, and two on the way to Solar Fell" (271). It becomes clear that the failure and abandonment of any steading—whether in parable or recent memory, and whatever the benefit to more powerful or opportunistic neighbors—ultimately contributes to the failure of the colony as a whole. For no matter how large a given steading and rich in potential, its viability for supporting life depends upon competent neighbors, adequate administration, and a critical mass of labor to do the work. More land in fewer hands is a sign of failure, not an enlightened response to it—let alone an answer to the problem of not producing enough food. As Smiley later argues in *A Thousand Acres* and reiterates in *Moo,* failure-and-consolidation is highly questionable as a longterm policy for the distribution and stewardship of land.[16]

The Greenlanders' preoccupation with property rights strongly determines their imaginative limits and their sense of their basic enterprise as survival (if not prosperity) through the acquisition and retention of both real property and portable "wealth"; at the beginning of the novel, a mere splinter of land is the tangible source of Asgeir Gunnarsson's resentment of Thorunn Jorundsdottir. Territoriality and possessiveness make the Greenlanders stubborn in their refusal to imagine alternative configurations of property allocation, not to mention land use, or to adapt to altered fortunes and circumstances, whether of patronage, climate, or natural resources. Even when change occurs, it is grudging change and always within familiar parameters of thought and practice—as when sheep and goats replace horses and cattle on many steadings. The Greenlanders' resistance to change is, Smiley suggests, as telling as any other factor in causing the failure of individual farms and, eventually, whole steadings and the colony itself. The earliest presentation of this theme appears in Ingrid the nurse's traditional tale of Thorgils nursing his children after the murder of his wife by cutting into his own nipple, thus discovering "what is possible in Greenland, where folk must learn new ways, or die" (15). A later articulation and thematic companion story is the inset tale told by Lavrans concerning the Norwegian-style steading at

Hvalsey Fjord. The insistence of the folk at Thorbjorn's steading "to live in every way as they live in Norway, with hangings on the walls and lots of chairs and the livestock scattered all over the countryside" (171) lasts for only two generations and two winters—until the supplementary income of seafaring wealth and warriors' pay disappears, household reserves are squandered, and the shortsighted, profligate lifestyle bankrupts the family. The piecemeal burning of the steading's furnishings and stripping for firewood of the magnificent, ornately carved woodwork is yet further testament to the need for more flexibility and less pride in Greenland. "My Thorbjorn," says the Devil, "the light of your pride has been like a beacon in the darkness to me, and I have come to take you for my own. You can go with me now. Your folk, I assure you, will follow shortly, one by one" (173). This story—apparently based on fact but now transformed into a cautionary tale—is hardly embraced by its auditors, particularly Olaf Finnbogason, Asgeir Gunnarsson's foster son and the quintessential Greenlander. Yet, in time, all the Greenlanders prove to be "Thorbjorn's folk."

The Greenlanders' resistance to change also makes them suspicious of, if not hostile toward, anyone different from themselves, beginning with the skraelings, and intolerant of nonconformity within their own community. The skraelings are demonized, in a manner consistent with the Greenlanders' Manichaean, good-or-evil dualism, and are the object of race-conscious ethnocentrism. The skraelings, whose occasional gestures to reassert their claim to Greenland are dismissed as enigmatic primitive behavior, become objects of ridicule, taunts, anxious curiosity, and occasional violence, an "evil" presence relegated to the lawless northern regions of Greenlander consciousness. Although they are constantly aware of the skraelings' presence, the Greenlanders scarcely ponder the larger possibilities of coexistence on the edges of arctic life. The skraelings' evident well-being in defiance of the elements is merely ascribed to their "demon nature." Gifts from the skraelings are thought to be transformed into "crawling and corrupt objects" (186). The patience and intelligence shown by skraelings when hunting seals and whales are considered humanly impossible: "Some of the Greenlanders were much envious of this sort of hunting . . . but this sort of hunting is not in the nature of men, and whales come to Christians only by the grace of God" (168).

A particularly revealing paradigm of the Greenlander-skraeling relationship emerges when, for the second time, Finn Thormodsson tries to trade his cleverly designed arrows for seal meat, only to find that "the skraelings he had traded his arrows to in the summer had learned how to make their own, and taught everyone else the same trick" (330), and that now they are hardly dependent on him, as he still is on them. The inversion of this paradigm, in which a Greenlander might consciously learn from skraeling culture (and thus add to his resources for survival) is beyond the curiosity, imagination, and pride of most Greenlanders, even when conditions prove particularly hard on the steadings. This is true even of Finn Thormodsson, who has not anticipated being snubbed by skraelings. The few among the Greenlanders who are open to skraeling ways and teaching—Hauk Gunnarsson and Kollgrim Gunnarsson among them—are typically mistrusted, alienated, or rejected outright by their peers. Even Asgeir Gunnarsson "joked more than once that he was not going to be the one who probed into what skraeling tricks his brother might have taken up. There was no telling what a Christian man could learn from the demons of the north" (17). At the beginning of part 2 ("The Devil"), the narrator reports a "diabolical" skraeling attack on Ragnvald Einarsson's steading; but for the most part—and with the striking exception of Quimiak's symbolic reclaiming of Sigurd Kollson after Asta's death—the skraelings seem content to bide their time and watch the Greenlanders blunder toward oblivion. Finally, Smiley does not propose armed conflict with the skraelings as the pivotal factor in the Greenlanders' disappearance; instead, she stresses the Greenlanders' cultural myopia, the constant toll taken by accident and illness, the enervating impact of weather and climate, and the debilitating effects of internal discord. In her interview of Smiley, Marcelle Thiébaux reports that "She thinks cultural rigidity prevented them from adapting completely and choosing to dress like the Eskimos and live in tents. This could account in part for their downfall."[17]

It is also worth noting that even the Greenlanders' fascination with visitors from Iceland and the Continent is ambivalent, even paradoxical. The arrival of Icelandic and Norwegian ships, naively anticipated by many Greenlanders as a source of replenishment of food, culture, gossip, and faith, is never more than a mixed blessing, since ships that replenish supplies and replace tools are also a means to exact "tribute" and thus drain the settlement of resources it needs to survive. Further, the polish, prosperity, and vitality of men such as Bjorn Einarsson Jorsalfari—the cosmopolitan "Jerusalem traveler"—create an awkward and at times demeaning contrast to the impoverished circumstances and plodding character of the Greenlanders. The arrival of "a large, richly painted vessel with a beautiful red and gold sail" and passengers such as Jorsalfari's "richly and fashionably dressed" wife (195) reduces the gray fabric of Greenland life to little more than a faded backdrop. The Greenlanders are drawn to the vigor and color of a homeland that has all but forgotten them, even as their simple loyalty, passive devotion, and hope-driven lives are seen as naive and archaic (when recognized at all) by emissaries from a late-medieval Europe undergoing rapid transformation.

The relationship between Greenlanders and nonconforming insiders is no less obtuse than that between Greenlanders and outsiders. Independence and nonconformity that result in notoriety within the community invariably heighten the anxiety brought on by constant external threats and it is typical of the Greenlanders to find ways of distancing themselves from the dissonance created by the idiosyncratic. Individualizing difference is dismissed as cultural quirkiness (Hauk Gunnarsson, Finn Thormondsson), social deviance (Thorunn Jorundsdottir, Ofeig Thorkelsson), behavioral aberration (Vigdis in her gluttony, Sira Jon in his insanity, Larus the Prophet in his fanaticism), or life as a morality play (St. Olaf the Greenlander, Larus the Prophet, the skraelings as demons). The Greenlanders' anxiety regarding difference is heightened by a bewildering, unvoiced fear that perhaps their traditions and habits are somehow failing them because of the subversive and heretical conduct of peers. The response to this anxiety is control, justified by consensus and habit as necessary conditions of order—especially when a particular transgression can be "understood" and dealt with as an aberration in the context of Greenlander religion and law. The discomfort of the community is manifested in the repression of autonomy, innovation, and passion; the tools of repression are rejection, punishment, banishment, and death. This is the cultural dynamic, the social context, in which the lives of Asgeir Gunnarsson, Margret Asgeirsdottir, and Kollgrim Gunnarsson are played out. In Smiley's chronicle-as-novel, their story explains the story of the Greenland colony itself as one of stubbornly embraced cultural reflexes and habits of mind—shared convictions, behavior, and fate.

Asgeir Gunnarsson's killing of Thorunn Jorundsdottir (in reaction to her begging, whispering, and vexing presence in his life) demonstrates the Greenlanders' compulsive inclination toward violence as a response to enmity and injury (real or imagined), or even to a period of bad luck. Asgeir's being called before the bishop and stripped of his second field fourteen years later illustrates the endemic nature of revenge-seeking and favor-currying within the community, neither of which is subdued by the problematic, temporary success of Erlend Ketilson's scheming. Still later, Sira Pall tells Birgitta Lavransdottir that "The race of the Asgeirssons . . . is known to be a wayward and self-reliant lineage. In addition to this, many in the district speak of the enmity between Gunnar Asgeirsson and Erlend Ketilsson, and say that this enmity is cherished more carefully in the heart of Gunnar Asgeirsson than it is in the heart of his neighbor. . . . Have you become as folk to whom gall tastes as sweet as wine?" (110) Indeed, Gunnar exacts revenge on his tormentors, but for Asgeir Gunnarsson's progeny the end of enmity is that the family steading is confiscated and Gunnar sentenced to lesser outlawry. Such instances of almost random violence and retribution are all the more lamentable since many in the colony are simply struck down by blind circumstance itself, as when Hauk Gunnarsson is killed by the ice, and many others die of illness and accident. As Birgitta Lavransdottir later observes, "There is always a jest to be played upon the Greenlanders" (351). Sira Pall—on many occasions Smiley's voice of unheeded insight and intelligence—is right about the debilitating effects and larger costs of enmity among families. One of the basic costs of internecine violence is a reduction in critical mass that the community can ill afford, and another is the occasional loss of an individual uniquely gifted or otherwise suited to lead the Greenlanders through difficult times.

The visits to Greenland of well-traveled, cosmopolitan men such as Nicholas the monk, Thorleif the Magnificent, Bjorn Einarsson Jorsalfari, Thorgrim Solvason, Skuli Gudmundsson, and various other captains, sailors, retainers, and tale tellers fascinate most Greenlanders. They also contribute to the seduction of Margret Asgeirsdottir, in whom difference, defiance, and autonomy seem the essence of life. Margret's culturally designated teachers and role models are the Gunnars Stead and Siglufjord women, such as Ingrid the nurse, but her kindred spirit and true mentor is her uncle, Hauk Gunnarsson, the survivalist loner. Margret's culturally approved space is the steading house, but her emotional home is in the hills above it. (As a romantic spirit surrounded by convention and repression—and truly free and happy only in the natural world—Margret invokes the memory of Cathy in *Wuthering Heights* and Hester in *The Scarlet Letter.*) Thus Margret's seduction actually begins before her twelfth birthday, when she first meets Skuli in his role as a ship's boy and he hands her the bird cage made of willow withes, in which her beloved uncle Hauk later places a songbird. Once Skuli returns from Norway with entertaining descriptions of Queen Margarethe's court and his gift of needles carved from bird bones, it is only a matter of time before the melodrama of the red gown is played out, with the drab and predictable Olaf as a foil, and despite the object lesson of the willful and "bad" Freydis Eridsdottir in Gunnar's cautionary tale.

Smiley's strategy for developing Margret as an introspective romantic figure within a narrative form that resists internalizing and introspection is consistent with the culture against which Margret struggles and the literary tradition on which it builds. When Margret first reveals herself in the red gown, to Skuli's "perfect admiration and surprise," she "knew this as sin and vanity [and] she also fell into the terror of never seeing such a look on his face again" (101). Later, on the verge of what is to be her final meeting with Skuli, Margret's thoughts on the conduct of her life are presented as a moral struggle between innocence and guilt, a dialectic in terms of which an adequate sense of her humanity is impossible.

> She thought . . . of how miserably she had given herself to temptation, and how little she had resisted at every point, but gladly had gone into his arms the first time, and more gladly each time since. She thought what a sinner she had become in the eyes of the Lord, and how gaily she had embraced her sin, so that the last year had fled by so quickly that time seemed really not to have passed at all, and she seemed to herself exactly the same guiltless soul that she

> had been. At once she hungered for the year not to have passed, for herself to be again the truly guiltless person she had been, but not, she realized, so that she might resist temptation, only so that she might have again each moment of the last year. (117)

Margret is consciously and unrepentantly sinful, her "fever" overwhelming the tenets of a cold faith and the rigid morality that will inevitably reclaim her. Later, Smiley reinforces this sense of her as simultaneously in rebellion against and inextricably caught up in her culture's ethos, when, as Asta Thorbergsdottir's servant, Margret recognizes in Asta's perverse embrace of the skraeling Quimiak the self-destructive power of her own earlier passion. Smiley makes Margret's capitulation to "sin" consistent with the fatalism that is her Greenlander legacy, an ability at once to act and to consider oneself helpless before inscrutable forces and witness passively what is happening.

The courtship-seduction is mutual; Skuli is the handsome, colorful, and clever suitor, and Margret the strong and graceful, aloof but finally accessible Viking princess. Skuli beguiles Margret (and himself) with stories, and with the observation that "in the court of Queen Margarethe . . . it is not considered ill for a man to admire a married woman" (92); she answers with red Bergen silk, defiantly displaying her "fever" in the Vatna Hverfi hills. Both the killing of Skuli and Margret's castigation are justified at the Thing, but Margret's homeless internal exile and overpowering grief isolate her for life and rob the colony of the gifts of an imaginative sensibility and resilient spirit. Smiley makes it clear that private, self-sustaining passion is at once vital and alien in that time and place—"The red dress was too long, and fell in folds over her shoes, a good fashion for court ladies with nothing to do, of little use in Greenland" (101)—and a source of dissonance that the colonial mind refuses to tolerate. In a culture driven by moral melodrama, Margret and Skuli can hardly be left alone as people, but rather must become object lessons, and finally emblems. Greenlander morality, like Greenland itself, eventually subdues even the strongest will. But again, while violent retribution and cruel punishment are consistent with local custom, custom's self-righteous destruction of the defiant lovers proves costly to Greenland itself in the end.

The Margret-Skuli pairing has its counterpart in the next generation, in the love affair of Kollgrim Gunnarsson and Steinunn Hrafnsdottir. In this case the man is the provocative, exotic figure, with Steinunn, the Icelander, drawn beyond caution to the brooding passion of Kollgrim and the overwhelming landscape of his fjords. In this case it is characteristic of the enforcers of convention and order that they are unable to imagine Steinunn, a woman of status and means, violating her marriage vows for a Greenlander (let alone the enigmatic Kollgrim Gunnarsson) without the intervention of diabolical forces. To implicate witchcraft as the power behind the adultery, rather than human passion and will, serves their purposes. It draws upon the neurotic and fading power of the church to demonize Kollgrim (in part by linking him to the skraelings), justify his immolation, and rid the settlement of his inscrutable integrity, independence, and pride. Sira Eindridi's angry and bombastic rhetoric of damnation and despair fills the vacuum created by Bjorn Bollason's ineptitude and cowardice as lawspeaker to eliminate yet another

Greenlander capable of surviving the effects of the culture's repressed imagination. Kollgrim's defenseless "I don't know" (482) while under interrogation constitutes his bewildered capitulation to a way of life that, as a free spirit of the northern places, he will never understand; the counterpart of this surrender is Steinunn's madness and catatonia.[18] Finally, in trying to defend Kollgrim, Gunnar Asgeirsson is, like his own father, defeated by manipulation and cunning, in this case abetted by Icelanders whose intention is hardly to assist the Greenlanders to survive, let alone flourish. The bitter irony of Gunnar losing his only son to what has become a hysterically retributive ethos is that in the twilight of his life (and that of Greenland civilization itself) he finally seeks "a kindness between men" on the grounds that "each man knows the suffering of others through the suffering he feels" (443–44). The irony seems small consolation, as does Gunnar's knowledge that the Greenlanders, now without one of their best hunters, live to regret their actions.

The fate of Asgeir Gunnarsson and his descendants is, in Smiley's telling, more striking and individualized than that of the Greenlanders as a whole; Gunnar and his progeny are individually rendered "characters" in a novel that is itself absorbed into an epic of catastrophe. "It seems to me that we have come to the ending of the world," says the visionary Birgitta, "for in Greenland the world must end as it goes on, that is with hunger and storms and freezing, though elsewhere it may end in other ways" (320). For the Greenlanders collectively, the smaller incidents that exact large prices and the larger ones that do likewise quietly add up to apocalypse by attrition—the gradual and irreversible loss of food, heat, shelter, clothing, and light. Such pathetic closure for their story is particularly poignant more than five centuries later to a technology-driven culture that understands how the Greenlanders' orality-dependent, highly subjective, and fallible memory does more to sustain the debilitating enmities of clans than to nurture a sense of shared experience and a productive understanding of the world. The primary narration aside, numerous instances of oral storytelling (in tale, song, and verse) are scattered throughout Smiley's novel, as if to prove the contention that poor folk "have words for meat and little else" (275). But the sheer number and variety of narrators and stories also reveals how inconsistent and vulnerable oral storytelling is as a record of who the Greenlanders were and how they lived. As Gunnar recognizes upon examining the writings of Einar Bjarnarfostri the Icelander, his countrymen's written record might be better served by a Greenlander than an outsider who is "little interested in such tales, about men no one knew" (227). It is one of the frustrations of Gunnar's life that he must struggle to write his own version of their story, an impassioned and imperfect search for the truth of their humanity.

Bereft of sister, wife, and son, and lacking the resources to sustain life, Gunnar is the quintessential Greenlander, reduced to hopeless grief in a very lonely place. "He saw what he was, an old man, ready to die, pressed against the Greenland earth, as small as an ash berry on the face of a mountain, and he did the only thing that men can do when they know themselves, which was to weep and weep and weep" (555). This gives Smiley's book its historically dictated moment of closure. All the same, it is difficult not to recall as well the defiant and doomed love of Margret Asgeirsdottir. Margret's spirit dies with Skuli, long before she is cut down by the Bristol men, and so does the (symbolically rendered) regenerative capacity of the colony. The end of Greenland itself is prefigured in the death of Margret Asgeirsdottir's passion and the repression of her vitality: "The red silk gown disappeared" (121).

Smiley's epilogue, then, seems an instance of postmedieval authorial surrender to benevolent impulse in an otherwise unforgiving book. The Greenlanders, having squandered both human and natural resources, face the prospect of starving and freezing in the dark. Gunnar alone has been responsible for the deaths of eight fellow Greenlanders, while he himself is without a male heir and his lineage is reduced to a single, tenuous thread. The great loom of Margret Asgeirsdottir and her female forebears casts a motionless shadow, the colors, patterns, and craft of even a modest domestic life having died with the weavers. Nevertheless, Smiley in the end offers her reader the stubborn voice of Gunnar Asgeirsson in the increasingly frigid air, providing, in the absence of other kinds of nourishment, food for his children's imagination: "'My father, it is very silent, except for the wind. You might enliven us with a tale.' And the children peeped out of the bedcloset, and Gunnar told his tale" (558). In fact, in an interview statement shortly after the novel's publication, Smiley acknowledges another defiantly humane gesture: "Packed as her book is with brutal acts, it isn't nearly as violent and cruel and the original sagas," the interviewer observes. Smiley's response: "I had a failure of determination."[19] Smiley's novel is, five centuries after the fact of their living, the Doomsday Book of the first European Greenlanders' tenure on the earth. *The Greenlanders* is a vast reckoning of stories concerned with both the Greenlanders' life and storytelling itself—the difficulty of storytelling under certain conditions, the problems inherent in storytelling when the facts and the telling are separated by centuries, and the need to make the effort, after all.

CHAPTER SEVEN

Ordinary Love and Good Will

In the two novellas published together as *Ordinary Love and Good Will* (1989), Smiley is concerned with the themes and issues at the heart of her experience and her oeuvre in the years leading up to *A Thousand Acres*—that is, love, marriage, power, and their disposition in middle-class domestic life. Like "The Age of Grief," both "Ordinary Love" and "Good Will" are stories about families that, at one point, are well, happy, and secure. Also like "The Age of Grief," the novellas that follow are stories of what happens when (in Dave Hurst's words) there is a breakdown of "the barriers between the circumstances of oneself and the rest of the world."[1] The paired 1989 stories oppose each other conceptually and thematically, beginning with radical differences in point of view (one male, one female) and in the handling of plot (one traditional, one innovative). Both stories find Smiley continuing to explore the narrative dynamic of observing versus acting that informs her fiction from the outset but that receives increasing attention, most notably in *Duplicate Keys* and *The Age of Grief.* Particularly in "Ordinary Love"—as, soon after, in *A Thousand Acres*—Smiley deploys a strong, ironic voice for the candid reassessment of events that are well on their way to playing themselves out.

That Smiley more than succeeded in satisfying appetites whetted by *The Age of Grief* was confirmed by uniformly positive reviews of *Ordinary Love and Good Will,* including Michiko Kakutani's summary observation that in the 1989 volume Smiley again focuses with great success on "the evanescence and mutability of love, the fragility of illusions, the elusiveness of emotional safety." These concerns, considered by many to be quintessential Smiley themes, emerge in "the closed circle of marriage and family that excludes others and that can sustain or suffocate those who live within its bounds. And like her earlier fiction, the stories pivot around a moment of revelation that will forever alter her characters' lives"[2]

Both "Ordinary Love" and "Good Will" are successful ventures in a genre many writers and publishers consider troublesome; novellas are usually considered too long for use in a magazine and too short for a book, and therefore not commercially viable. But as one reviewer observed in praising Smiley's stories, "Novellas are more than just scaled-down novels for people on the go. As a narrative form, the novella gains a kind of intensity and gravity from compression, and it may be the perfect vehicle for the subtle dramas of home and family." And, he adds, "the novella form serves Smiley well because of the long, deliberate scrutiny she wants to give to matters close at hand."[3] Difficult both to master and to market, the novella is nonetheless a form with which Smiley has an intellectual and imaginative affinity, and this affinity is a key to understanding what Smiley the writer is doing with the form.

In her "Shakespeare in Iceland" paper Smiley highlights the potential for narrative to give "direct access to the inner life" and allow a writer "to reveal the disjuncture between what is felt and what appears." In "Can Mothers Think?" she cites as crucial to narrative prose the role of point of view, which "highlights the experience of the individual, offers intimate contact with another experience." And in an interview that followed the publication of *Ordinary Love and Good Will* she described the novella as "a concentrated thought, or a concentrated meditation on one theme," as in a play, and aiming at "the same cohesiveness, the same concentration . . . the same thought orientation."[4] In each of her novellas, Smiley strives for direct and revealing access to the concentrated mental workings of a unique first-person narrator's mind. She catches Bob Miller and Rachel Kinsella at definitive moments of personal understanding—following what may have been long seasons of benightedness or denial—when not to address their worst moments as parents would be to deny the depth and significance of their losses.

In deliberate, analytical fashion, Smiley conceived of and approached "Ordinary Love" and "Good Will" in somewhat different terms from those of "The Age of Grief" and in contrast to each other. "Good Will" does share with "The Age of Grief" the point of view of the father/husband (though neither is, in any responsible reading, just the father/husband's story). In both of these narratives the point-of-view character recounts his earlier sense of self-confidence and domestic security, the disruption of this comfort and order, and his reaction. As narratives, both develop in traditional linear fashion, from introduction to denouement, and Smiley even recalls that Bob Miller's story emerged for her as a single draft that required few changes.[5] In part because of its linearity, in part because of the tenacious ironic shading that helps us anticipate Bob Miller's downfall, "Good Will" is finally more clear but less satisfying than either "The Age of Grief" or "Ordinary Love." But "Ordinary Love," which proved quite difficult for Smiley in the writing, departs sharply from the other two novellas in intention and effect.

> The form I wanted to use was not linear. The most secret and dramatic section occurred halfway through, not at the normal time of climax. And the story was not complete, I thought, until the children's voices came back to the mother, until she had been forced to hear their responses to her assertions. And the fact is, it was not just that my editor was stubborn and, I thought, untrained to read this sort of text, it was that through many drafts I did not know what I was doing. I did not know how to make this unfolding form of secrets and surprises work. I was forced to write at the outer edges of my powers of *formal* invention, though I could actually hear my narrator's voice very clearly. The models for "Good Will" were all laid before me, as old and venerable as literature itself. The models for "Ordinary Love" were not even within me. I had to think them up as I went along. It was hard work.[6]

"Good Will"

The Bob Miller being interviewed in the opening section of "Good Will" has consciously and successfully erected barriers between himself and the rest of the world. With planning and control, he has shaped his farm and his family into a back-to-the-land existence that he characterizes as "self-contained, not isolated and hostile."[7] He has been so efficient and so undemanding of outsiders in accomplishing this that he is typically treated as an odd but principled fringe member of the Moreton community, always considered a possible barterer for the useful cast-offs of the region. Because his minimalist lifestyle seems to be a successful one, he is considered locally as more than an inventive eccentric, and he himself considers the arrival of the visiting writer-interviewer a confirmation rather than a surprise. "The fact is that years ago . . . I used to imagine some interviewer just like Tina passing through, showing just her degree of dignity, respectability, and knowledgeable interest . . . And here she is, though I stopped looking for her long ago, right on schedule, reacting as she was destined to react. The pleasure of that is a private one, not one Liz would share, but not one I am inclined to give up, either." Even this early in the story it is difficult not to read this as egotism rather than simple self-confidence expressing itself, especially when Bob claims that back then he even "foresaw that she would focus on the money," since that was his own focus in interpreting—without apparent irony—his lucky estate-sale purchase as "a good omen, a substitute for knowing what I was doing" (99). The precisely reckoned figure of $342.93 reveals the vigilant obsessiveness with which he approaches daily life, and it testifies to his position as the ultimate point of authority for all of the family's plans and decisions. His apparent ability to live without capital hardly leads to the conclusion that he is able to do without the exercise of power—according, of course, to his own good will.

The selective and presumably uncritical ear and eye with which Tina Morrissey responds to the Millers' story during her interview (the published book chapter suggests otherwise) causes the reader to wonder from the outset whether the key concerns raised by the family's lifestyle might have to do with something other than cultivation and penny-counting. In fact, all of the apparently self-effacing comments Bob makes are inevitably supplanted by assertions of possession, dominion, and control; while his wife and son are often referred to, "we" inevitably segues into "I," and "our" into "my"—my land, my house, my workshop. His description of Tommy's room amounts to a catalogue of Bob's own accomplishments, and he tells us that "my pleasure is the knowledge that I have brought all of my being to bear here. . . . If he were really afloat, his bed would bump against the window, and he could look upon the orchard I planted, then bump against the shelves I built, where he could snatch down tops and cars and blocks and tools and dolls we've made him; this is a lovely sea, I think, tiny, enclosed, friendly, all his and his alone" (102). Bob's granting of possession is never anything but rhetorical and brief, and it is never assumed that anything in or of the Miller house ultimately belongs to anyone but him. In this respect Bob Miller recalls Kate Karlson, the possessive and domineering matriarch in *Barn Blind.* With respect to Smiley's use of male characters specifically, the largely passive proprietorship of Axel Karlson is well on its way to becoming the arbitrary and tyrannical rule of Larry Cook in *A Thousand Acres.*

In fact, the sustaining ironies of "Good Will" emerge from Bob's irrepressible revelation of his need to control everything in his purview, even as he makes claim after claim to doing everything in the least intrusive, least coercive manner. Some of these ironies literally concern the origins of their house and its relation to the land. Bob tells the reader, for example, that his owning the property in the first place owes something to the original house burning down generations ago—"good fortune" on which later events will cast further ironic light. He also mentions, in a matter-of-fact but obviously gratifying moment, that "My land is laid out rather deceptively—the smallest part is open field, valley floor, but all of these acres are visible from the house, and all of them are flat" (105). He is able to survey at a glance all he is master of, and that the eye can easily take it all in is apparently a part of his good fortune. And Bob also acknowledges, in a perversely self-deprecating (and revealing) moment, that the siting of the house itself was a mistake, based on his interest in reusing the old foundation. "I resent its lack of grandeur," Bob says of the house; "sometimes I can see the structure I might have built so clearly that the frustration of what I've done is explosive. Here we live, here we will always live. No gardens, barns, sheds will ever mitigate the permanence of this mistake" (107). Yet while Bob has made a fundamental error in founding his project, in the flush of prosperity and recognition he is oblivious to the ironic resonance of such an admission, such claims. Bob Miller's self-centered and shortsighted comments are bound to be nullified by events.

Of course the discussions of home schooling and Tommy's apparent enthusiasm for everything about the farm are further occasions for Bob to reveal his pride in being able to control not only his son ("his schooling is my decision to make"), but also his wife. Bob relishes the moment when he overhears Liz using his own arguments—arguments she herself once resisted—in justifying home schooling to Tina Morrissey. Liz's understated observation that "This was not how I intended to spend my life"

(108) is a comment she reiterates through increasingly obsessive behavior if not words, an insight confirmed by future events. Bob is, not surprisingly, patronizing, resentful, and dismissive of Liz's increasing need to "be saved" and to express her identity and independence through church attendance and prayer. He never sees himself as a cause of her search for society as well as salvation, and when she finally chooses a Pentecostal congregation—"this collection of the rural poor, the badly educated, and the nakedly enthusiastic" (112)—he speaks condescendingly of nothing but "sect" and "dogma." In November, when Liz declares herself saved, Bob sees her action not as a form of self-assertion or a survival strategy, but rather as a "taking off" or "divergence" from him (130–31). He resents more than fears the implications of her new distance, but feels and understands nothing of the unmet needs in her that are splitting them apart.

As for Tommy, whose troubled mind is already finding expression in "stray sounds that simply escape his lips, from grunts to hisses to yells" (105), he is considered by his father simply to be an interesting, lively "organism," like much else under Bob's jurisdiction. Bob claims that Tommy is not subject to the same yearnings "for doing something you needed to do" (109) that Bob himself felt at the same age and on several later occasions; the boy's eager volatility (as revealed in "the look") is likewise set aside as having been significant only in its earlier expression through Bob himself as a child. Bob Miller's belief in his own "genius," reinforced by those around him, makes him oblivious to his potential for flawed thinking and catastrophic failure, particularly as a parent; in these respects, too, he reminds us of

Kate Karlson in *Barn Blind.* Finally, of course, Bob is unable to recognize Tommy's increasingly deviant behavior and its potential for becoming disturbed criminal conduct. He will misread his son until their "paradise" is permanently lost, and he never seems fully to accept his own responsibility for what happens to the family.

Bob Miller's determination to control the conduct of others and to avoid conflict, dissonance, and sustained ambiguity has several sources and effects. One of these is his obsessive need to demonstrate Thoreau-like self-sufficiency and to withdraw and achieve a separate peace after his tour in Vietnam; another is his egotism and sense of moral rectitude. Similarly, there is Bob's professed deism, which is hardly militant but clearly assumes a microcosm in which he is the prime mover, in effect winding up his little universe and then claiming just to watch it work, glorying in "the rightness of every thing that is present expressing itself through my appreciation" (115). Later, when Liz's churchgoing initiative ends in capitulation, he is both relieved and confused by her ironic comment that "There wasn't room in my life for two of you . . . You and God" (183). Bob is in part the smug product of a culture in which male prerogatives are privileged as often as not, as is suggested in his occasional invocation of his own father's and grandfather's rules and pronouncements. Near the middle of his story, Bob says that

> My grandfather, who had five sons and many dogs, always swore he treated boys and Saint Bernards the same way. He convinced them when they were small that he was bigger and knew more than they did. Even when they

> outweighed him and had more schooling, they were so in the habit of obedience that he didn't have any trouble. My father and his brothers all had jobs and families whom they supported. This was the fundamental test of my grandfather's method. Were they happy? Did they drink, harbor extreme political views, display long-standing anger, treat their wives well, live up to their potential, contract cancer or heart disease? My grandfather was untouched by these issues. . . . He did not think of problems as effects he might have caused, more as afflictions. (145–46)

A reader who has been paying attention sees this as unexamined faith in a world view that is both repressed and repressive, and finally little more than wishful thinking. Smiley has said that her own "irreverence" and directness are due to growing up in the absence of a powerful male figure like Bob Miller and his father and grandfather, given her own father's illness and parents' divorce. Concerning her father, she recalls that it was "clear to me that he was an authoritarian man and that, in order to do what I wanted, I was better off without an imposing, controlling figure in my life. . . . I think it's important for people to recognize who has power over them."[8]

Smiley gives Bob Miller a past, an ideology, something of a belief system, and male cultural baggage, and these help explain the person he is—a man who believes in luck, ambition, and his own "genius." But both here and in "Ordinary Love," Smiley is also concerned with the countervailing motivations that lead to conflict with the "givens" of control. For Liz, intelligence and sympathy lead not only to religion, but also to several direct (if finally ineffectual) efforts to question and counteract Bob's treatment of their son. When she suggests Bob take a more nurturing and positive approach to parenting, he rejects praise and occasional rewards as patently inappropriate. For Tommy (as for Rachel Kinsella) Smiley postulates the fundamental motive that is also the extraordinary one—that is, the powerful presence of human "yearning," "need," "desire," "passion," or "appetite" to assert the self in the world outside of the secure and ordered family unit. As Tommy's destructive behavior finally makes evident, he is emotionally abused, resentful, and hostile—far from serene and happy. He has no useful reference points or connections to society outside his own family and the farm, and even within the family has little experience with true decision-making and responsibility. He has only the social perspective his father has granted him, and his anger at being deprived is expressed as displaced hostility toward Annabel, one of the many who participate freely in the larger world from which he has been excluded, and at the same time the one peer who is most clearly different in appearance and thus easy to objectify. Bob and Liz believe they have not taught racism to their son, but even Bob finds this conviction difficult to reconcile with their awareness that "Annabel could be the first black person Tommy's ever seen" and that life with his parents is "all he's ever known" (170). Tommy's ignorance of what being "different" does and does not mean is a blank page on which he can impose his personal needs. In addition, Bob in particular is not without palpable prejudice of his own toward Lydia, and Bob and Liz have developed in Tommy the personal deprivation, low self-esteem, confused anger, and unfocused resentment that lead to abusive behavior once an object for his attention appears. It is not necessary for Bob and Liz to strike out at Annabel because she is black. They need only to have created the social and psychological preconditions for their son to pick a scapegoat for his displaced anger. As Lydia Harris puts it, "Terrifying is when the parents are the source of the trouble, not the kids" (141).

Once Tommy attacks Annabel Harris and the two families are forced into a relationship, Bob's own prejudice against Lydia and hostility toward the black girl emerge—when they skate together, when he does compensatory work at their "Russian Easter egg" home, during his nighttime conversations with Liz. Even to acknowledge this much reveals Bob to be more bewildered than wise, as accustomed as he is (in Lydia's words) to put more stock in "who you know" and "what you know" than in considering "who you are" (150). (One of the central ironies of the Millers' failed friendship with Lydia Harris is that, as a woman and an African American, she could offer them more than a little wisdom concerning what it means to truly understand "who you are.") Bob is more concerned that Tommy used the word "Nigger" in public—and that this will lead to "disapproval of us and this setup we have" (120)—than he is in pursuing the domestic causes of this effect. For her part, Liz too eagerly joins in wordplay denial (as in the "Miller takeover bid" game) of their influence on Tommy's behavior, and later admits envy of her own, and wanting to have Annabel's lavender coat herself. Outside the farm as well as on it, Bob's passive-aggressive conduct and his evasion of even Liz's pleas for tolerance make Tommy's fire-setting inevitable. Interestingly enough in this respect, it is after the attacks begin and Bob is thrown off balance by the "mystery" of his son's behavior that he begins to refer to him as "Tom" rather than "Tommy," as if to imply, by abandoning the child's name, that he expects more responsibility in the boy for what is happening, and less accountability of himself as a parent.

To the end, the abiding issue for Bob Miller is the "triumph of my will" (120). He is a bewildered and pathetic tyrant whose references to "mystery" when power fails him reveal a desire not to know or be responsible; he is unwilling to alter vision or gain understanding in time to redeem his situation. In her *Belles Lettres* interview, Smiley explains that in "Good Will"

> I wanted to write about trying to be God. Bob creates his world, and I wanted to write about what the creator learns from the rebellion of the created. His son's problem is that he can't find a niche in his father's world. Everything is either something his father has made or done or something his father knows all about. I wanted that story to be about someone who very laboriously learns that the world he has created is not what he thinks it is. And I could only do that, I thought, from a man's point of view.[9]

Yet even in chastened circumstances, when Bob recognizes the ignorance and pride that brought him down, he seems fundamentally unchanged, as Liz predicts even before the fire. He refuses to grieve their losses, claims that it is "without question too soon for the truth," and stubbornly "loiters" behind Liz's efforts to work toward recovery (195–96). As parent and partner he is still only marginally functional, still the megalomaniac Liz once called him, able even at the end to feel slighted because Tina Morrissey's chapter "about me" is a short one and to take perverse pride that the liability case could set a precedent "that might refer only to me" (193). Bob Miller may not be God, but he is still a certain kind of man.

"Ordinary Love"

Because "Ordinary Love" was, like "The Age of Grief," written in direct response to the pain Smiley felt upon the breakup of her second marriage, the similarities between the two novellas should not be surprising.[10] For example, both stories have to do with extramarital passion and its effects on spouse and children. But in the later novella the point of view is that of the woman whose impulses and needs break down the barriers, who makes time and room enough in a crowded but coherent domestic life for passion and transgression, and thus brings on immediate discord and a lifetime of questioning. Beyond this, in "Ordinary Love" Smiley explores further, directly through a female narrator, the notions of maternal vision and mother love. While "The Age of Grief" provides an analysis of Dave Hurst's parental response during the six-week period of Dana's affair and his helpless knowledge of it, "Ordinary Love" focuses on the moment of reassessment when Rachel Kinsella and her children examine the impact of her passion and Pat's dramatic reaction to it. As Kakutani notes, "Ordinary Love" is a story of two climaxes, the melodramatic one in which Rachel tells Pat of her affair, and the more psychologically driven "epiphanic moment" twenty years later. Kakutani is also quick to clarify that "melodramatic" here is more a descriptive than an evaluative term: "Though many of the events in Rachel's story are startlingly melodramatic . . . Ms. Smiley writes with such perception about the emotional perversities that assail the human heart that she manages to utterly convince us of her characters' actions—and the lasting consequences of their choices."[11]

In writing this story, Smiley again creates "the particular expression of a particular personality and character, the idiosyncratic, real love of an imperfect self, not an impersonal, vapid ideal based on others' conflicting needs"; but she also addresses the theme of survival and "the cleaning up of messes" long beyond the moment when a marriage disintegrated and a far different family dynamic came into being. "I find marriages very interesting to observe," Smiley once told an interviewer. "To other writers, maybe, love affairs are more interesting, but I am fascinated by marriages, because they're the relationships in which love and power co-exist for the longest time." In fact, "Ordinary Love" is as conscious an effort to study marriage and the individual as exists in Smiley's *oeuvre.* Perhaps more than any other Smiley story, "Ordinary Love" stands as a testament to her analytical agenda regarding American families as social units. In the same interview, Smiley said that

> I think what has happened in the twentieth century is that all the forms of systematic thought about society and culture have failed. They have proved themselves to be brutal or ineffective. Right now writers are trying to come up with some other system for thinking about individuals as social beings and society as formed of individuals. Clearly

> the intermediate form between the individual and the society is the family. Writers feel that they will figure something out if they explore the cruelties of the family as a microcosm that will lead to some understanding of the individual on one side and the society on the other side. That's certainly the way I feel.[12]

In writing "Ordinary Love" Smiley sets aside the received form and pattern for narrative fiction that shape "The Age of Grief" and "Good Will." Using an approach also to be taken in *A Thousand Acres* and *Moo,* Smiley makes events themselves less important than reflection on them; cognitive work displaces action as her dominant mode. Rachel knows that neither the *what* of her affair nor Pat's violent reaction to her announcement of it could be considered familiar or "ordinary" in the experience, memory, and ongoing lives of her children, and she knows that her absence has long since created in them the need to know more than they have been told and been able to imagine. That her relationship with Ed Stackhouse was short-lived and that the decree that gave Pat sole control over the children yielded rather quickly to de facto joint custody are among many realities that are now beside the point. For Rachel, who has always been a close observer of her offspring as both individuals and parts of a larger pattern of family life, the perceived obligation to testify at last is also a personal need for storytelling and response. "Reunions are fraught with echoes," she tells us, and she knows that truly to begin speaking about decades-old matters she will have to conquer "an ancient wave of terror" (7–8). The immediate occasion of the storytelling is Michael's homecoming from India, but the partial family reunion that develops also takes place on the anniversary of the family blow-up many years before. The mode of the telling is what some rhetoricians would call exploratory discourse, but what Smiley would, in an honorific sense, call "gossip," and to the extent that reunion is possible for the Kinsella family, it takes the form of this dialogue. If "Good Will" is driven by the rhetoric of possessiveness, "Ordinary Love" is sustained by—perhaps more accurately, consists of—the rhetoric of domestic conversation.[13]

In "Can Writers Have Friends?" Smiley redeems gossip from its humble status in social discourse, describing it as the pursuit of understanding human motivation. "Gossip," she says, "is about the understanding and assimilation of daily events," and she defines it in terms of five stages: information, amazement, fascination, speculation, and understanding. Smiley's contention is that

> every pair or group of gossipers is constructing a piece of fiction by making a logical character out of a mysterious person, or a logical story out of an untoward event. The story that emerges after all the facts are known and fitted in is, in my opinion, often a work of collaborative oral art, which I would define as life reworked by thought. I frankly can't imagine how people could have moral lives without gossip . . . discussing incidents and motives refines moral decisions and makes one's moral life participatory rather than reactive.[14]

For Rachel this means that she is obliged to describe Pat as a partner in marriage without depending upon this description to justify her affair. She says that Pat is by temperament and training a clinical researcher who worships Piaget and believes that "the mind . . . doesn't create order, it *is* order" (12). She recalls that Pat functioned in terms of theories and explanations, and believed in schedule and protocol, but that he also had a true-to-stereotype Irish temper. She reports that "his enthusiasm for family life was the passion . . . of a true egomaniac" (93), and recalls her own "peculiar and suffocating feeling" (14) in the face of all this regimentation and power, a feeling that only grew with their relationship.

For Rachel, as for Tommy in "Good Will," life cannot be fully realized only in reaction; the need for personal independence from limits and expectations must express itself, and the very irrationality of this need is the key to its validity and power. Passion is the response to passion. "In my experience," she says, "there is only one motivation, and that is desire. No reasons or principles contain it or stand against it," as the long-remembered stories of her mother's strong-willed cousins verify. "Even as a child, I never questioned the power of desire" (33). This is why, for example, Rachel tells her children what attracted her to Ed, but finds it beside the point to go very far in discussing her feelings after losing him. This is why she describes precisely but does not dwell on the violence with which Pat greeted her announcement; she was aware of this potential in him but ignored it. Passion drove her to tell Pat about the affair during a quintessential domestic moment and in the kitchen, the symbolic center of their tranquil new "domestic container" (40). Years later, neither the man she left nor the man she left him for is really the point, sufficient to explain all that damage, neglect, and permanent loss. "I wanted him to know I wasn't his" (78), she ventures at one point, but later: "Certainly I had no intentions, only appetites." In the end, Rachel acknowledges "I was a slow-burning fuse, but a fuse nonetheless, who could not fail to blow up the little gathering around the table" (93). In other words, she loved her own possibilities, or as she says of Ed, "what I really wanted was not to love him but to be him" (48). Yet a third way to put this is that there is no such thing as "ordinary love," or as Smiley put it, "All love is extraordinary or it all isn't."[15]

A feature of Rachel's personality that helps convince the reader that she was capable of the passion for which she once lost a family, is her ability to view her life ironically, as during the picnic at Eagle Point Park. "I could say that the terror of my divorce and its aftermath tamed me, made me an accountant to my very soul . . . [but] the truth seems to me more delicate, having more to do with how lovely this spot is, how I need to see it develop through the seasons. . . . The joke is on me, who has turned out to have that farmer's attachment to familiar places, after all" (36). Rachel is a realist. (In this respect she recalls Sandy Stein/Alexandra Day, the former homeward-bound bomb-maker, in "Dynamite.") So now, of equal importance to her telling of her own story is her listening to the stories of others—beginning with talks after Joe's return for the summer and continuing through the conversations on Ellen's back deck and in the car on the way home—the stories her children tell and which would be unnecessary if not for her actions two decades earlier. Since Rachel wants her children to respect her explanation of what happened, she must in turn embrace the individual (as well as collective) stories of their lives after that, however ruthless or painful; and, as the stories reveal, the children's lives *have* developed in partial, recognizable response to that traumatic moment in their experience. The result is a variously rendered yet commonly focused circle of stories that fits Ursula Le Guin's definition of fiction as a carrier bag rather than a linear tale of (male) heroic violence: "I would go as far as to say that the natural, proper, fitting shape of the novel might be that of a sack, a bag. A book holds words. Words hold things. They bear meanings. A novel is a medicine bundle, holding things in a particular, powerful relation to one another and to us." It is a mistake, Le Guin says, to reduce narrative to heroes, conflict, and killing. "Conflict, competition, stress, struggle, etc., within the narrative conceived as carrier bag/belly/box/house/medicine bundle, may be seen as necessary elements of a whole which itself cannot be characterized either as conflict or as harmony, since its purpose is neither resolution nor stasis but continuing process."[16] Le Guin might find it appropriate that in "Ordinary Love" Smiley created her own carrier bag, a discursive network to contain domestic conversation, the narrative manifestation of gossip.

As needful of their own telling, but also as tentative initially as Rachel, all of her gathered children probe, jest, question, circle, and retreat from the subject, hesitant to ask questions—particularly the one question that, if answerable, might help them understand why Rachel left them. "I think humans are genetically programmed to stay in one place all their lives," says Michael, physically and emotionally battered by his life in India; "Then why is the history of mankind the history of travel?" (73), counters Ellen, fearful of leaving home and married to a risk-taking man. But every gathering of the family is a potential occasion for questions and revelations, and for the Kinsellas the catalyst for epiphany is Rachel's smile on hearing Ellen's declaration that "I don't have time for another man" (69). In response to Rachel's story of the affair that broke up the family, and the "reasons" for it, Ellen unloads on Rachel the story of their six-day abandonment, and Michael finally tells of his disastrous love for both Margaret and Lucie. Candid gossip is never easy, especially where families are concerned.

And Rachel must listen patiently despite her foreknowledge that these stories will finally explain nagging behavioral patterns (Ellen's domestic closeness, Joe's summer home-stay, Annie and Daniel's constant phoning), confirm familiar plotlines (Michael has lived the kind of exotic life toward which Rachel's affair turned out to have been an isolated gesture), and confirm as well her worst maternal fears (for example, the children abandoned in a London apartment while Pat acts out his anger and responds to his own passion). "What they say creates a vast and complicated but vividly articulated new object in my mind," Rachel says, "the history of my children in my absence, at the mercy of their father" (86–87). This oral history—a cantata of points of view—is at once punishment and conciliatory gesture, a cathartic declaration that falls something short of forgiveness or pardon, something short of a master-narrative. "We survived, Mom," says Joe; "Oh, I don't know," says Michael (88). The stories are, collectively, the history of the clan in perhaps its most useful narrative form—the family as collaborative oral performance, now more or less together, soon to be apart once more. And, of course, the telling, like the reunion, is inevitably incomplete: "It is as if, in our family, the one necessary presence that each of us fixes on is the one presence each of us cannot have" (92). In particular, Daniel, Pat's scapegoat in the wake of the divorce, is missing from the reunion group, and Pat's absence is as palpable now as Rachel's was so long ago.

Ordinary Love and Good Will is a provocative yoking of novellas—point and counterpoint, theme and variation—that finds Smiley testing the imaginative possibilities and narrative potential of first-person point of view. "Ordinary Love" explores the revelatory potential of collaborative voice. Successful in their own right, the book's paired stories anticipate in rhetoric and theme the coercive male tyranny and the long-silent female voices of *A Thousand Acres.*

CHAPTER EIGHT

A Thousand Acres

Long before writing *A Thousand Acres* (1991), Smiley was aware of the environment as a central issue in American life. In the eighth grade she had read John H. Storer's *The Web of Life,* and this "reinforced that sense I had of the variousness and interconnectedness of land, animals, plants, people, town and countryside, prairie and civilization." Later,

> as it turned out, all sorts of agricultural issues and environmental issues became a part of my daily life once I moved to Iowa [in 1971], lived in small towns, started reading the *Des Moines Register,* began to know people who lived on farms or had been raised on farms. My absolutely first ecological concern when I got to Iowa was to wonder, as a result of reading Barry Commoner's *The Closing Circle,* whether the well water on the farm we were renting was contaminated with nitrates, and whether, if I got pregnant, I would be able to carry the baby to term. My second one was to wonder how often over the years the bees who were living in our house had been poisoned with DDT. A lot of times, as it turned out.[1]

By 1987, when Smiley first mentioned to her husband the idea of rewriting *King Lear,* during lunch at a McDonald's restaurant in Delhi, New York, she recognized that the relationship linking the American land, American agriculture, and those who depend on both was problematic from the moment of America's "discovery" by Europeans.

Beginning in the summer of 1987, a series of chance occurrences led to Smiley's conception and development of *A Thousand Acres.* In the Delhi McDonald's, "decorated with pictures of the Midwest" that included one of a man standing in a barn, Smiley mentioned rewriting *Lear,* and her husband suggested that she could set it on a Kansas farm. Shortly after, Smiley met the actress Glenn Close, who had written her after reading *The Age of Grief,* and in after-dinner conversation Smiley began to describe a hypothetical production of *Lear* "done as if from the older daughters' point of view" and possibly starring Close. In the late winter of 1987–1988, driving with her husband from Minneapolis to Ames, Smiley "looked out the window somewhere around mile 170, and said 'You know, I could set that King Lear book around here, I know about this area.'" And finally, Smiley was teaching a course in world literature for non-English majors that included (among other works) *Don Quixote, Candide,* and *The Metamorphosis,* involved some reading in and discussion of economic historian Fernand Braudel's *Civilization and Capitalism,* and contained threads of feminism, environmentalism, and "a vaguely Marxist materialism. . . . By the end of three semesters teaching this course, I had a much clearer idea of how our times have evolved out of Shakespeare's times, and how ideas and questions posed in his works have been answered and modified by history. I developed a thought or two about the intrusion of notions of ownership and commodification upon familial and romantic relationships, and a thought or two about the specificity, as opposed to universality, of Western European ideas of family order, of ownership and exploitation of land, resources, and the services of other human beings, of conflict, literary form, ego, power, gender, and the finality of death. . . . While I was teaching this class, I was writing *A Thousand Acres.*"[2] Embedded in the course was Smiley's understanding that the dispossession and eradication of indigenous peoples and the subsequent occupation and "taming" of the land—agricultural production serving as both premise and confirmation—anticipated the ownership of property as a condition of American identity. Smiley's reading and teaching were revealing the subtext of agrarian American culture to be conquest, possession, and control.

For Smiley, to live and write in the heart of the country late in the twentieth century was to be aware that American farming has become both a business and a way of life, an enterprise that powerfully controls the land and defines the lives of those who depend on it. Economic and political forces engendered far from the farm itself—government subsidies and price supports, policies on wetlands and erosion, legislation (or lack thereof) regarding fertilizers and herbicides, taxes on gasoline and regulations on shipping, federal manipulation of interest rates, foreign policy and overseas markets—are in crucial ways more powerful and less predictable factors in the farmer's life than ambition, sweat, weather, and luck. Over time, farming has grown less visibly brutal, at least to the outside eye, but it remains deeply problematic. The design of *A Thousand Acres* is to reveal how owning land and operating a farm are the matrix of a harrowing way of life. Smiley's novel should be seen as a contribution to the literature of ecological vigilance, notably the numerous "green" histories and commentaries on the environment, and the literature of agricultural reform, which includes the essays of Wendell Berry, feminist histories and sociological studies of agrarian culture (at times critical of Berry's male-centered "agrarian ideology"), various analyses of the social and economic causes and consequences of the American farm crisis of the 1980s, and ecofeminism.[3] Smiley's own 1991 Iowa Humanities Lecture, "A Thousand Acres: How Much Is Enough?" provides a focus for this wide-ranging discussion. Her lecture title is not only an allusion to her novel, but also a fundamental query regarding what Smiley sees as an "infatuation with scale" that characterizes late-twentieth-century agricultural theory and practice. Smiley's achievement in writing the novel was to fuse her established skill at revealing the dynamics of domestic space with her awareness of the economic, social, and biological forces that drive agricultural production.

In *A Thousand Acres* farmland itself—and everything that stands and moves upon it—speaks the language of ownership. Of course appropriate and timely planting, a successful crop, and an efficient harvest are the most obvious signs of possession and control. But so are well-maintained property and occasional new construction; so are Harold Clark's enclosed, air-conditioned tractor and his new planter. The meaning of such cultural markers is internalized by Virginia Cook by the age of eight, when she recognizes that for her father a Buick sedan with gray velvet seats is a way to proclaim both the birth of his third child and his ownership and successful stewardship of six hundred forty unencumbered acres. "The Ericson children and the Clark children continued to ride in the back of the farm pickup," Ginny says, "but the Cook children kicked their toes against a front seat and stared out the back windows, nicely protected from the dust. The car was the exact measure of six hundred forty acres compared to three hundred or five hundred."[4]

Larry Cook's Buick is an extension of his land, just as his land has become an extension of him; it signifies security and power, and pride in both. Years later, Ginny remembers "the hot musty velvet luxury" of riding in that car as "a pleasure like a secret hoard of coins" (5), and she recalls how possession, privilege, and her coveting of Dinah Ericson's window seat led her to the "appropriate and desirable" conclusion that the Cook farm should eventually total a thousand acres. "It was that simple" (4). Ginny remembers living "on what was clearly the best, most capably cultivated farm. The biggest farm farmed by the biggest farmer. That fit, or maybe formed, my own sense of the right order of things" (19–20). She also recalls Larry's contention that the Ericsons, with their emotional (that is, impractical) fondness for animals rather than machines, exemplified the wrong order of things. That the Ericsons have to sell their farm and endure exile to the city confirms for the Cooks that cows with fancy names, dogs that do tricks, and farmers who make ice cream represent an unacceptable way of life. As a child Ginny seemed able to block out any recognition that the Cooks' thousand-acre logic, reinforced by the laws of agricultural economics, would cost her her friendships with Dinah and Ruthie Ericson. But years later, in acknowledging her own complicity, she reveals that even as she became a beneficiary of the ideology of accumulation she was also becoming one of its victims.

Her father's devotion to both size and thrift—"the purchase of more land or the improvement of land already owned"—is inseparable from what Ginny remembers as "his lust for every new method designed to swell productivity." And, she adds, "We might as well have had a catechism":

> What is a farmer?
> A farmer is a man who feeds the world.
> What is a farmer's first duty?
> To grow more food.
> What is a farmer's second duty?
> To buy more land.
> What are the signs of a good farm?
> Clean fields, neatly painted buildings, breakfast at six, no debts, no standing water. (45)

This catechism of the good farmer was already time-honored when embraced by Larry Cook. In particular, the conviction that water in a field will both look bad and compromise production was behind the founding act of John Cook, who, in an early commitment to innovative farming, laid the first drainage tile in 1891. "Tile produced prosperity," Ginny tells us, "a floor to walk on" (15). The floor on which the Cook family grows and prospers is ultimately one of ownership, production, and what Smiley refers to in her Iowa Humanities Lecture as "a blank perfection of fields." (It is worth noting that "Cook" is one of numerous names of European and American explorers and discoverers used in *A Thousand Acres;* others include Cabot, Carson, Clark, Ericson, Fremont, LaSalle, Lewis, Pike, and Zebulon. The act of naming or renaming land and environment is, of course, central to the explorer's project of claiming it.)

For Smiley, the catechism of the good farmer is as fundamental as (and not unlike) the catechism of the good king, adumbrated by Shakespeare throughout the histories and several of the tragedies. And, as in Shakespeare, and *King Lear* specifically, the fundamental question is, "What is a good king?" How does the king stand in relation to his power? What prerogatives and freedoms does power give? What obligations does it entail? What are its limits? Where, in the end, do the king's responsibilities lie? Smiley has said that Larry Cook's consummate paternal villainy emerged from her

> longstanding dissatisfaction with an interpretation of *King Lear* that privileged the father's needs over the daughters'. Right before I started the novel, I felt a growing sense of a link between a habit of mind that perceives daughters and children as owned things. I felt, viscerally, that a habit of mind exists in our culture of seeing nature and women in much the same way. In fact, they represent one another in a lot of writing. That's a strong element of *King Lear.* Lear's always talking about nature and his daughters, conflating the two. Thinking along those lines, I went back to the play and reconsidered my dissatisfaction with the order of the universe the play proposes, which is that the daughters have a certain relation to the father that the two older daughters betray but that Cordelia lives up to.[5]

In another interview, Smiley recalled that the "somber game" of transforming *Lear* into a novel made the writing "laborious and exhausting. Two pages and I was wiped out. I could hardly drag myself back to the typewriter. . . . Despite all the success the novel has had, I still feel alienated from it. My monster child."[6]

Larry/Lear takes his landowner's prerogatives for granted and exercises power without considering consequences; even when dividing his "kingdom" he does so less because such a move is carefully considered and responsible than because it is his to make. Dividing his land among his daughters is, like abandoning new cabinets in the driveway, an arbitrary, autocratic demonstration of power. Like Harold Clark, who tries to control his sons by manipulating his will, Larry knows how an act of giving can be an exercise in control.

Smiley does not, as Faulkner did for the McCaslins and De Spains, explicitly trace the family history back to the founding assumption that the land was created to be bought and sold. She does, however, trace the Cook patrimony back to John Cook's Godlike resurrection of the land itself, land "created by magic lines of tile my father would talk about with pleasure and reverence" (15). In redeeming the marshy land from mosquitoes and "disuse," John Cook was, in his own sense of things, improving it; he was making it useful and putting it "into production." In the mindset of Western "progress" the labor that goes into such improvement becomes "sweat equity," and with the commodification of labor the spirit of amelioration becomes a devotion to ownership, privilege, and control. A latter-day sign of the agricultural production ethic at work is ambitious capital, embodied in Marv Carson—no less threatening as a banker and promoter because of his farcical wealth of misinformation on toxins, nutrition, excretion, and exercise. Peter Conrad (a British observer) sees Marv Carlson as "a prophetic figure," and observes that "Smiley astutely relates [Shakespeare's] play to the social and economic circumstances of rural America in 1979, the year of Larry's fatal decision. . . . The Iowa land-owners are themselves held hostage by the banks which lend them money and which later, calling in these loans during the Reagan decade, ruined the country's agriculture."[7]

Perhaps the most telling early manifestation of this ethic of ownership—one chillingly replicated in the lives of Larry Cook and his daughters—was John Cook's consolidation of his partnership and hold on the land by forming a union at age thirty-three with the sixteen-year-old Edith Davis. Two generations after the Davis-Cook union, the Cook family's success at accumulating land and making it conform to human wishes has turned Larry into a millionaire. Larry Cook is a canny, ambitious, and successful farmer, and considers it appropriate that all things come to him. "However much these acres looked like a gift of nature, or of God, they were not," Ginny tells us. "We went to church to pay our respects, not to give thanks" (15). In Zebulon County, production confirms possession, and possession confers status and nourishes pride. In Smiley's reworking of *King Lear,* the ruin of the Cook family derives from more than investment blunders of fatal magnitude.

The tile worked. But where, Smiley asks, did the water go? The answer, of course, is "Nowhere." Water, at once absent and omnipresent, pervades *A Thousand Acres.* Water is the essence of filled-in wells and the drained depressions of pothole ponds; of the old quarry where Ginny and Pete seek respite from domestic catastrophe and into which Pete later drives his truck; of the slough where Ginny finds the water hemlock for poisoning Rose's sausage; of the drenching rainstorm into which Larry/Lear wanders and howls; and of the rainy days and moisture content that threaten the final Cook harvest. Ginny says that she was "always aware of the water in the soil . . . endlessly working and flowing, a river sometimes, a lake sometimes" (16), and she recalls that "water trickling in the blackness" has become a constant in her life, the medium through which "nameless and unknown children who may have lived and may have died . . . have vanished into the black well of time" (47). *A Thousand Acres* is concerned with numerous ways in which life on the land ebbs and flows, like the land itself as it changes hands and like the water table beneath it; Smiley contends that all life dependent on the soil is both sustained and threatened "below the level of the visible" (9). "The grass is gone, now, and the marshes," Ginny tells us, "but the sea is still beneath our feet, and we walk on it" (16).

In addition to hidden water, "A farm abounds in poisons, though not many of them are fast-acting" (310), Ginny says in recounting her search for a way to kill her sister. And she offers a catalogue of examples: chlordane, arsenic, insecticides, kerosene, diesel fuel, paint thinner, Raid, aerosol degreasers, used motor oil, atrazine, Treflan, Lasso, and Dual. Later, on the day of the Cook estate auction, she notices stacked cans of DDT in the barn. Not only is Ginny's poisoned sausage a too-clever homemade time bomb that she may not really wish to go off, it is, in the face of so much invasive chemistry, simply redundant. "You didn't have to bother," Rose reminds her. "All that well water we drank did the trick" (355). Rose's breast cancer—like the cancers that killed her mother and Verna Clark, and like the gynecological problems that cause Ginny's miscarriages—is yet another reminder that the conventional tools and procedures for running a farm seem to constitute a "logical" and therefore necessary extension of the premise that the land should be possessed and controlled by any available means. The Cooks' Iowa farm is contested territory, under assault by agricultural chemistry and technology, and the bodies of Smiley's female characters become contested objects within that territory. At one point in her 1991 Iowa Humanities Lecture Smiley cites the chemical contamination of human breast milk: "Without my having bought [toxic chemicals], I now have possession of them. They have come to me by secret paths—through the air and the water and the food chain." And later she adds, "this contamination above all things strikes me as a metaphor for evil."

As Rose and Ginny come to know, for Larry Cook the logic of drainage tiles, herbicides, and the casual killing of birds and animals in the fields (235) is also the logic of incest and rape. For Larry Cook, control has become abuse, and abuse has become routine. That Larry's destructive habits—including the sexual abuse of his daughters—should not be considered anomalous becomes clear when Rose reminds Ginny that "He fits right in. However many of them have fucked their daughters or their stepdaughters or their nieces or not, the fact is that they all accept beating as a way of life. . . . This person who beats and fucks his own daughters can go out into the community and get respect and power, and take it for granted that he deserves it"

(302). Eventually, Rose's argument becomes a crucial subtext of the novel when Ginny herself takes it up during her last conversation with Ty:

> You see this grand history, but I see blows. I see taking what you want because you want it, then making something up that justifies what you did. I see getting others to pay the price, then covering up and forgetting what the price was. Do I think Daddy came up with beating and fucking us on his own? . . . No. I think he had lessons, and those lessons were part of the package, along with the land and the lust to run things exactly the way he wanted to no matter what, poisoning the water and destroying the topsoil and buying bigger and bigger machinery, and then feeling certain that all of it was "right," as you say. (342–43)

Ty's response is understatement that emerges from denial: "I guess we see things differently" (343). But the truth is not lost on Rose and Ginny. In the end, Larry Cook is both a poor custodian and a failed father—self-centered, tyrannical, arbitrary, and destructive.

For Rose and Ginny the truth is that by their father's standards and their father's community's standards "woman" (wife or daughter) is merely generic female, a domestic fixture with no identity and status of her own. On Larry's farm, a model of success and source of social standing in Zebulon County, women's roles are dictated by the patriarch, and women are a means to maintain, consolidate, and legate property, objects to be used rather than subjects capable of volition and will—inheritors of a long tradition of socially constructed roles for American prairie women.[8] When his wife dies, Larry hardly misses a beat. The church club ladies come in to sort, pack up, and distribute her personal possessions, and she "disappears," like water drained from a pond. Ginny recalls that "Nothing about the death of my mother stopped time for my father, prevented him from reckoning his assets and liabilities and spreading himself more widely over the landscape" (136). Later, Rose's recollection of their abused adolescence could fit them all, mother and daughters alike: "We were just his, to do with as he pleased, like the pond or the houses or the hogs or the crops" (191). In the words of Smiley's 1991 lecture, "the habit of ownership requires objects." For the Cook family the story of their thousand acres is part of an agri-cultural tragedy. For the Cook women—relegated to received roles, domestic space, and cipher status—their family drama is despair-ridden domestic tragedy.

Larry's possessive mindset and mindless abuse of his daughters are signaled in his tendency, especially when challenged, to address and claim each as "my girl"—a verbal habit he shares, revealingly enough, with the daughterless Harold Clark, whose facile use of the phrase reveals its cultural embeddedness. (The sisters' troubled emotional development and bewildered capitulation to Larry's proprietary behavior are revealed in their continuing to call him "Daddy," even as adults.) Larry's characteristic disdain for his "girls" as holdings no more significant than his livestock is revealed in his outburst on the verge of the storm in chapter 23. In a venomous tirade, Larry shifts quickly from a scoffing reference to "you girls" to a divide-and-belittle focus on Ginny as "my girl," after which he assaults her, almost uncontrollably, with expletives: "bitch . . . barren whore . . . slut . . . dried-up whore bitch" (180–81). At such moments, Larry Cook seems an ideological heir of Faulkner's Thomas Sutpen, who simply thought of women as breeding stock necessary to his founding of a dynasty. In *A Thousand Acres,* Larry's sexual and emotional outrages against Rose and Ginny ultimately prove as self-destructive as Sutpen's against the women of Sutpen's Hundred, and they create psychological poisons as devastating as the water-borne chemical contaminants that invade his daughters' body tissues.

As surrogate mothers Rose and Ginny seem successfully (and perhaps unconsciously) to have protected the adolescent Caroline from abuse by their father. But this has created in her an innocence of family experience as shared by the rest, and thus a stubborn innocence regarding the others' deepest motives and commitments. This innocence, made possible by their efforts to give Caroline "a normal high school life" and her own long-standing disinterest in farming, has helped make her a "better" daughter than her sisters, "neither stubborn and sullen, like me, nor rebellious and back-talking, like Rose" (64). She is a "Loving Child," Cordelia to Larry's Lear. The ignorance born of innocence and her move to the city make Caroline a creature of unexamined loyalties and affections and a defender of the world of appearances that Ginny and Rose know to be corrupt. Like her husband Frank, Caroline is not *of* the farm, so she defends both it and Larry; having been given an idyllic rural childhood, not to mention an atypical Cook girlhood, she protects its memory at all costs and against all intimations of needful truth:

"You're going to tell me something terrible about Daddy, or Mommy, or Grandpa Cook or somebody. You're going to wreck my childhood for me" (362). She believes that "things generally are what they seem to be" and that "people are basically good." She sympathizes with the apparent suffering of the good father-farmer-king and criticizes the "evil" actions of her sisters.

It is left to Rose to insist that Larry is the dysfunctional father of a dysfunctional family, whose history is family chronicle to outsiders and grotesque nightmare for her. By extension, *A Thousand Acres* becomes the story of a dystopian agrarian culture. It is revealing that Rose herself is the initiator of the Monopoly tournament that occupies the family's leisure time almost nightly for two weeks, a competition over real estate that seems natural enough to all concerned, having been brought up on an ethic of land ownership. Ironically, Rose herself proves the shrewdest and most successful player: "Rose, by slowly and steadily accumulating money, buying properties only with a certain percentage of it and hoarding the rest, managed to move toward a million dollars without ever actually winning a game" (78). It is a telling moment, because it shows Rose to be a true child of her father; she is at once more deeply, fatally injured by both his farming practices and his behavior as a father, and more like him in her own right than either of her sisters. At different moments in the novel Rose is variously motivated—by fear, frustration, jealousy, selfishness, sibling rivalry, and a need for revenge and to tell the truth. But her clever success in the Monopoly tournament anticipates her eventual recognition, and later revelation, that "I *want* what was Daddy's. I want it. I feel like I've paid for it, don't you? You think a breast weighs a pound? That's my pound of flesh. You think a teenaged hooker costs fifty bucks a night? There's ten thousand bucks" (303). Having been objectified, she is still a prisoner of the ideology and the language of commodification; her furious retribution must be retribution in kind. When Rose brings the monopoly tournament to a violent conclusion, her declaration that "I'm tired of this game" (140) is an angry gesture toward both closure and disclosure, an expression of frustration at the lifelong game they have all been playing and the denial and silence that have become a Cook family way of life.

In the end, complete closure eludes Rose. Anger and awareness of her suffering at Pete's hands enable her to understand what she suffered under Larry. Her brazen exhibition of her cast ("Pete did this") marks a crucial stage of her struggle for selfhood, and it anticipates her all-out attack against her father. Rose then moves beyond self-defense to self-possession. "Her idea was that there was no such thing as provocation," says Ginny, "that no matter what she did, Pete simply should not hit her, and therefore if he did hit her he was entirely wrong" (141). Rose's working out of this issue with Pete would seem to anticipate a confrontation of Larry. "He's got to repent and feel humiliation and regret. I won't be satisfied until he knows what *he* is" (216), she tells Ginny. But Rose's response to her abuse is increasingly one of expressed anger; her need and purpose are to turn the family story into a revenger's tragedy. Ginny recalls being fascinated and frightened (and, initially, puzzled) at Rose's vicious outbursts. Neither of them seems aware that, in the absence of an appropriate object against which to direct itself, such a hatred will become self-consuming.

When Larry Cook's progressive disintegration and eventual death cheat Rose of a healing resolution for her incest experience, it becomes clear to her that there can be no confrontation of the evil-doer, no disclosure and acknowledgment of crime. "Now there isn't even a chance that I'll look him in the eye, and see that he knows what he did and what it means. As long as he acts crazy, then he gets off scot-free" (235). Pete, in his own right marginalized by Larry because he had only ideas and musical talent (but not land), becomes a casualty of Rose's frustration, eventually "overwhelmed and crushed" (304). Rose herself dies consumed by both cancer and cynicism: "We're going to be angry until we die. It's the only hope" (354). Such melodramatic tendencies in *A Thousand Acres* have evoked strong responses in some readers, including Katie Roiphe's judgment that the use of incest as a theme is at best a "literary vogue" and at worst "a cheap trick," a "kind of bargain-basement epiphany."[9]

It remains for Ginny—for years a repressed and (like Caroline) silent believer in existence-as-appearance—to acknowledge, confront, and reveal the Cook family's secrets and betrayals. As a narrator Ginny claims no point of view; this assertion reveals her highly compromised and confusing status in a family and community where women are given clearly defined, nominally valued, and in certain respects rewarding domestic roles that have no social or economic power. The assertion also places Ginny at the center of a pervasive metaphor of vision and silence (or, more precisely, muted and refracted speech) that Smiley develops in *A Thousand Acres.* Smiley has acknowledged not particularly liking the novel while writing it, or even when finished, in part because *King Lear* as a literary point of reference meant that "I was writing to it rather than it coming from me." In addition, though, her point-of-view character was necessarily "talky" because of social and psychological restrictions on Ginny's physical movement and because drama was being transposed into narration; Smiley had to make Ginny "smart and meditative." Smiley "had to substitute revelation for action," which finally "makes the novel contemplative." (Smiley also recalled that "sustaining the 'I' point of view was very tedious. At one point I thought, 'If I have to write one more sentence that starts with "I" I'll kill myself!'"[10]) In Ginny's case, feeling, seeing, and speaking lie on a continuum of past action, current perception, and potential discourse, a continuum both defined and short-circuited by her incest experience. Smiley chose Ginny as her narrator only after careful consideration, making what she calls "a craft decision": "In my experience of pairs of daughters, the older one is often more anxious and tends to wring her hands. The younger one is often more certain of everything. From a narrative point of view, it is much more interesting to have a narrator who is uncertain of what she thinks or what should be done or what the future will hold."[11] (In the action-driven *King Lear,* of course, Shakespeare offers no explanation for the behavior of Goneril and Regan.)

Sexual violation and physical abuse by her father make Ginny a self-less person. Overpowered as a girl in order to answer to Larry's needs and wishes, she, like Rose, enters adulthood in a state of both physical and emotional self-denial. She lacks a clear sense of identity and the capacities to feel, to see, and to speak. When, at nineteen, she marries Ty (perhaps a half-conscious strategy to escape from Larry), she is unable to ask and to give, unable to love. Perhaps nowhere is this more evident than in her dissociation from her own body, of which she is sometimes obsessively aware but through which she cannot feel. In Ginny's recollection, innocent childhood episodes of body-consciousness shift quickly to a memory of obsessive cleanliness and her wedding night, her unconscious effort to discard her memories of midnight violations, and her ongoing touchiness regarding sex and its "contradictory little rituals." "I didn't want to see my body," she says. And then: "One thing Daddy took from me when he came to me in my room at night was the memory of my body" (279–80). Ginny's affair with Jess Clark is both exhilarating and frightening because it puts her back in touch with her physical self. The affair evokes in her both "a goading, prickling pleasure" (161) and an obscene and frightening image ("my back came to seem about as long and humped as a sow's") of her own sexuality.

Beyond this, Ginny finds herself locked in a troubled pattern of enduring Larry's outrages and catering to his wishes. "When we are good girls and accept our circumstances, we're glad about it," says Rose, "When we are bad girls, it drives us crazy" (99). When Ginny makes a pathetic spectacle of herself in order to fetch eggs for his six o'clock breakfast, she associates this being "good" with her body as an observed object and her father as voyeur. Her body was "graceless and hurrying, unfit, panting, ridiculous in its very femininity," she says. "It seemed like my father could just look out of his big front window and see me naked, chest heaving, breasts, thighs, and buttocks jiggling, dignity irretrievable" (114–15). That Ty, in his stubborn hopefulness, sees and encourages no other response for Ginny than that of the demeaned and silent sufferer reveals the degree to which he seeks comfort rather than truth and contributes to the failure of his own marriage. "Ty's attitude intruded itself, soothing me. . . . So I served up [my father's] food silently and told myself that he wasn't senile. . . . My job remained what it had always been—to give him what he asked of me" (115).

Ginny's self-denial takes the further form of her constant efforts to be sociable, accommodating, and philosophical—as passive before the world as she is before her father. "Of course it was silly to talk about 'my point of view,'" she says. "When my father asserted his point of view, mine vanished" (176). She has neither opinion nor perception, and is afraid of both. Even as Rose prods her, conversation by conversation, toward acknowledgment of her abuse, Ginny tells her "I'm afraid to see" (211). She hardly needs the urging of Henry Dodge, the minister, to take refuge in a world of appearances in order to "preserve a way of life that we believe in" (266). All the more reason, then, for her to be drawn to Jess—the attractive prodigal son whose face "seemed to promise a meaning" (144)—and the hope of recovering through one man the self that has been damaged by another. Smiley suggests broader implications in that Ginny's failure to see is a characteristic shared by many in the book. It is shared with Ty, either unwilling or unable to understand Ginny's sense of imminent disaster after Larry's driving accident. "You must be blind" (143), she tells her husband. It is shared with Caroline, shallowly involved and ill-informed by her occasional visits to farm and family. It is shared with violent and tyrannical Harold Clark, whose anhydrous ammonia accident (intended by Pete for Larry) makes him literally blind, housebound, and unable to farm any longer. And failure of vision is characteristic of

Larry himself, whose progressive loss of reason and self-possession are accompanied by paranoia and an inability to comprehend responsibly either the present or the past. The cumulative effect of all this blindness is collective anomie and resignation and an inclination to look toward the future with something like despair.

Ginny's lack of vision is matched by her lack of speech. This voicelessness is consistent with the nature and circumstances of her incest experience; in a life of the unsaid, "you don't have to remember things about yourself that are too bizarre to imagine. What was never given utterance eventually becomes too nebulous to recall" (305). Her voicelessness replicates that of her mother, whose illness and death are "almost muffled," whose laughter is reported rather than remembered, and whose fear for her daughters' well-being is only conveyed, obliquely and late, through Mary Livingstone (93). While Rose's reactions to the condition of her life are open rebellion as an adolescent and retaliation as an adult, Ginny's reaction is silence. She is reluctant to speak, to differ, to argue, and turns reticence and circumspection into an art, just as Ty makes quiet endurance a virtue. Ginny's repression of adolescent trauma is revealed in her inclination toward consciously keeping other secrets of various kinds—regarding the pregnancies and miscarriages that will devastate Ty, her affair with Jess, the poisoned sausage intended for Rose. The sausage in particular constitutes an elaborate exercise in secrecy and disclosure that combines the novel's key themes. Ginny's sausage can be read as a "domestic" gesture, consistent with her lifelong role and restrictive domain; a marker in her love-hate relationship with Rose, her sister, fellow victim, messenger of truth, and rival in love; a symbolic containment of male power and domination; an exorcism and objectification of the emotional poison of incest that impinges on the present and future; and an effort to manipulate a natural world (specifically, the water hemlock) that now seems more fatal than fertile. Perhaps the most telling aspect of Ginny's use of the sausage is her "hiding" it in the cellar, eventually to be "discovered" by another rather than overtly delivered by her. Even in such a definitive action of an outraged spirit, she behaves atavistically; even in expressing a lifetime of woe she works in terms of equivocation, indirection, and delay.

Ginny's chilling acknowledgment of her incest experience, made possible by a return to her old room and a solitude created by Rose's (more than likely) calculated absence, expresses buried pain and the shock of recognition. "I screamed in a way that I had never screamed before, full out, throat-wrenching, unafraid-of-making-a-fuss-and-drawing-attention-to-myself sorts of screams that I made myself concentrate on, becoming all mouth, all tongue, all vibration" (229). This is, for her, the beginning of speech, and with Rose's death she will have to speak for them both. She has survived to tell the tragic story of a thousand acres, to acknowledge "the loop of poison we drank from" (370) and stand on a drainage grate in order to "faintly hear the eternal drip and trickle of the sea beneath the soil" (365).

In Ginny's epilogue, the sound and fury of the Cook family's tragic drama fades into the hum of air conditioning and the whine of cars on Interstate 35. In self-imposed Minnesota retreat, Virginia Cook Smith waits tables and lives out an unromantic version of the escape fantasy Rose had once envisioned for them and their mother. In her Minnesota apartment Ginny hears the news of Larry's unremarkable (albeit ironic) death in a supermarket cereal aisle; she learns of Jess's predictable flight west after only four months with Rose and organic farming—still self-centered, shallowly committed, and intent on reaping the benefits of the "good boy." In the restaurant on the interstate Ginny listens to Ty confirm the disintegration of the farm and his stubborn refusal to understand how it was lost ("I was on the side of the farm, that was all"). And when Ty offers a last-word defense of his ambitions and an *apologia* for wanting to maintain the status quo—"My plan was to . . ." (342)—Ginny rejects firmly and finally Larry Cook's philosophy and rhetoric of possession. This repudiation constitutes Smiley's ending, but hardly a resolution of larger issues.

"Our thousand acres seems to have gone to The Heartland Corporation," Ginny reports in the epilogue. Having absorbed the Ericsons and others—a matter of discipline, opportunity, and economic reality, Larry might have said—the Cooks are in turn taken over by a larger, more powerful element of American agribusiness. Their lives are finally bracketed by the inducements of Marv Carson and the benedictions of the Boone Brothers Auction House, and Ginny's elegiac description provides a sad contrast to the rich prospect of home and family that opened the novel.

> The Chelsea, that once came on a train, was too big to move, so they bulldozed it. Rose's bungalow went to Henry Grove, as it had once come from Columbus, and my house, too, was taken down to make room for an expansion of

> the hog buildings to give them a five-thousand-sow capacity. When you stand at the intersection of County 686 and Cabot Street Road now, you see that the fields make no room for houses or barnyards or people. No lives are lived any more within the horizon of your gaze. (368)

It is as if the consciously shaped, consciously objectified English countryside of Larry Cook's eighteenth-century forebears has in fact reached a bleak perfection in America. The land Ginny once described as having been made "flat as a table" is not unlike the "made" landscape described by Raymond Williams, "a rural landscape emptied of rural labour and labourers . . . from which the facts of production had been banished."[12]

In an interview shortly after the publication of *A Thousand Acres,* Smiley suggested that, given prevailing economic and demographic trends,

> What will happen is the huge transfer of land to large-scale farming interests and a huge changeover to more factory farming. This will cause a revolution in our whole way of approaching who is responsible for the land. And since nobody really cares in the cities, these corporations will be able to do what they want. Most people in the business of critiquing agriculture right now are pretty convinced Iowa is the next Alabama—that Third World way of life of tenant farms and big absentee landlords, factories with low-paying jobs in little towns, migrant workers who come to the little towns for low-paying jobs and towns full of elderly people. The only business of the towns is social

services. That's what's coming, and it's directly attributable to government policies, to industrial propaganda about how to farm and to university research that has promoted industrialized farming over anything else.[13]

CHAPTER NINE

Moo

In an interview for National Public Radio upon the publication of *Moo* (1995) Smiley offered some insight into her long-standing anticipation of writing the novel. "I knew before *A Thousand Acres* that I wanted to write both a tragic and a comic novel," she said. "And I knew that they would both have the theme of American agriculture, and so I had conceived of what I wanted to do with *Moo,* I even had thought of the title, before I even began *A Thousand Acres,* and I was gathering material, mostly in the form of apocryphal stories about life on the various campuses around the country."[1] What Smiley apparently failed to anticipate was the way *Moo* was received.

After the conclusion of the twenty-four-day book tour set up to publicize the novel, Smiley reported that the writing was revitalizing for her, but dealing with the reception of the book was not: "Writing *Moo* was a yearlong revel in irreverence, a tone of voice that my aunts, uncles and cousins have cultivated for generations—a prolonged stylistic reunion with my roots. But then perfect strangers, like reviewers and interviewers, read *Moo* as a license to be confrontational and edgy, as well as ironic and irreverent, with me."[2] The tour itself resulted in scores of conversations and a host of interviews—during which Smiley apparently responded to anticipated questions with agreeable consistency and to most others with intelligence and wit. The literal subtext of the tour was the steady stream of reviews and feature articles that began upon the book's publication and multiplied in the wake of Smiley's progress across the country. This descriptive and evaluative commentary—from the laudatory to the disappointed, confrontational, and dismissive—offers insight into more than the world of reviewing. It also provides access to an understanding of what *Moo* is and isn't, what the book accomplishes and what it does not. The rhetoric of this reception is revealing and instructive.

The most predictable (and rhetorical) interview question concerned the apparent connection between Moo U. and Iowa State University, at which Smiley had been teaching since 1981 and at which she served on the Faculty Senate from 1987 to 1989. Her equally predictable answer on all occasions and in all public forums, from National Public Radio and the *Chronicle of Higher Education* to the Ames *Daily Tribune,* was always some version of "there isn't any"—to which she added (in the case of the *Des Moines Register*), "I not only didn't consciously base it on Iowa State, I didn't subconsciously base it on Iowa State."[3] In short: Moo U. is a fully imagined place, a mythical institution—and the book is, after all, a novel.

The most predictable opening for a *Moo* review could be summarized as "Who'd have imagined" this "surprising departure" from the tragic vision of *A Thousand Acres* by an author whose "agreeable change of pace" can be compared to taking "a holiday from more draining work"?[4] In subject matter and fictional strategy *Moo* took most reviewers far from the familiar modes and textures of Smiley's most successful and familiar work, specifically *The Age of Grief, Ordinary Love and Good Will,* and her Pulitzer Prize–winning novel, *A Thousand Acres.* In several cases the apparent shift away from domestic realism and family tragedy resulted in reviews that explained more about what wasn't happening in *Moo* than what was. These perplexed and off-balance responses were understandable but limiting; a departure in subject and tone does not necessarily signal a complete break with fundamental issues and convictions.

Not surprisingly, the great majority of reviewers focused on one or another aspect of genre and mode—that is, they discussed *Moo* as satire, as academic novel, as comic fiction—with a range of analytical precision and interpretive success. (It should be noted, though, that Smiley's minimalist title does little in its own right to encourage this particular line of thinking, and even Knopf's dust jacket refers to "comic" and "comedy," but not "academic novel" or "satire.") Reviewers' references to traditional literary types were usually made for the purpose of asserting that *Moo* might be too forgiving to be effectively satirical and too serious in its ideas to be engagingly comic. The prevailing critical assumption was that a novel set in the academy could only be compelling if it were a comic putdown—a putdown of the "take no prisoners" kind. The reviewers for the *Atlantic, Nation, Washington Post, Los Angeles Times,* and *Wall Street Journal* declared *Moo* to be weak satirical tea, the last of these (in one of the most thoroughly negative evaluations) calling Smiley "handicapped by her unwillingness to cause offense . . . [because] she lacks the requisite measure of rage or disgust to succeed as a satirist. She is too eager to think well of her characters, even the most repellent among them." Gary Krist, in *Hudson Review,* asserted that Smiley was too cautious and that her "villains and good guys" are almost all "depicted from the same safe ironic distance, relegating all to the same level of comic absurdity. Such a democracy of mild ridicule," Krist added, "may be laudable from the viewpoint of journalistic fairness, but it makes for a rather wan comedy."[5] Smiley herself has occasionally acknowledged—as in her *Moo* tour *Washington Post* interview a Midwesterner's reluctance to argue, embarrass, or cause offense. The problem, as Valerie Miner described it, is that "Since the power of satire is dependent as much on persuasive world view as on comedic skill, this genre may demand of readers more shared philosophical sympathies than some other frame."[6]

Even this would seem to be beside the point that the mode of satire assumed, if not preferred, by many critics was more visceral than cerebral, characterized by the ridicule and scorn favored by Juvenal and Swift rather than the sympathetic wit of Addison and Horace. In fact, the constantly changing point of view in *Moo* reflects the discontinuous conversation of the university as a community; this in turn suggests an understanding on Smiley's part of the academy's need for collegial tolerance and discourse. Similarly, the intertextuality of *Moo*—its absorption and interweaving of the idioms and written documents that sustain academic culture—testifies to the way the various discipline-based, administrative, and pedagogical rhetorics constantly overlap and impinge on each other. In short, the rhetorical diversity and structural discontinuity of *Moo* seem driven by the freewheeling antistructural impulses of a Laurence Sterne. All of this adds up to an intuitive (if not intentional) affinity in Smiley for the literary "anatomy" (as brought into critical conversation by Northrop Frye's *Anatomy of Criticism*), signaled most strikingly by her weaving into the novel samples of written text from offices all over the campus. Commenting on the novel's point of view, Trudy Bush (among those to feel that Smiley's satire is strong enough) observed that its omniscience is "rather like what we hope God's might be as he looks down on our muddled world—kind, amused, approving of some of us and not completely rejecting even the worst."[7]

A number of reviewers also invoked "the academic novel"—usually without defining it but suggesting that it is inherently comic and typically involves a satiric agenda—from May Sarton's *Faithful Are the Wounds* (1955) and Kingsley Amis's *Lucky Jim* (1958) through Randall Jarrell's *Pictures from an Institution* (1968), and David Lodge's *Changing Places* (1975) and *Small World* (1984).[8] Yet the range and variety of this list suggest that knowing where the story takes place is only minimally useful for explaining its meaning and significance. In one of the few reviews actually to attempt a definition of "academic novel," Cathleen Schine cited "the race for tenure and sex and grants and love and grades and enlightenment," adding that "in this insular world, the imperfect flourish like Darwin's mutant finches, making Moo U. rich, full, and strong." Beyond this, there is the popular assumption that the academy is (and is discussable as) a "closed society"—idiosyncratic (if not harmlessly quaint), isolated, out of touch with the "real world." As Lorrie Moore observed in her wry commentary on *Moo,* "Within a university there can be no true sense of proprietors versus outsiders . . . because all academics are outsiders of a sort. And so a culture of community complaint, artful vying, caustic comment, witty self-loathing, operatic head-shaking, kvetching, and general wringing and throwing up of hands pervades such a place, and no one, finally, is particularly threatened or surprised."[9] But this perspective oddly determines a reading of the novel by concentrating the reader's focus on Moo U. as an object to be skewered rather than a subject that might engage sensibilities and command sustained attention for larger issues. To be sure, there is human fallibility enough to be mocked in academia as an institution. Particularly in ambitious, research-conscious, "second-rate" schools such as Moo U.—striving, after all, to achieve fallibility on a first-rate level—there is plenty of evidence for considering the university one of the most curious enclaves of American cultural life. But Smiley's point is precisely that Moo U. is *of* rather than separate from the culture at large, and social foibles generally are the main business of comedy.

Nevertheless, as a comic novel *Moo* proved equally problematic for reviewers. For some it was "uproariously funny"; others were not amused. In an interview with the *Baltimore Sun,* Smiley acknowledged: "I finally decided that comedy is really a much more complex form—it's less predictable how people will react to it, because humor is much more a matter of personal taste than a 'serious' or tragic novel." In the *Civilization* article, her analysis of the reviewers' mixed assessment is succinct: "Here's what I forgot: There's a lot more to comedy than the good times. Comedy is (didn't I realize this before?) contentious."[10] In any case, the search by some readers for a comic protagonist to lead an unauthorized, irreverent tour through academia seems misguided, especially given Smiley's placement of Earl Butz, the inertia-embraced seven-hundred-pound Landrace hog, at the geographical center and institutional heart of Moo U. Earl is at once an immoveable symbolic presence and a reminder that no individual human being (despite the assumptions of some and the ambitions of others) is the heroic center of the institution.

Silliness to be satirized and comic fun are never absent from *Moo,* but Smiley constantly works to transform these into social commentary of a higher order. Campus satire is great sport, but not, finally, the game she wants to play. (No reader of Smiley's preceding fiction, with its egotists and idealists and their inescapable "real world" lives, should find this surprising.) As Schine explained, "As a metaphor for the intrinsic corruption of the modern university, not to mention society at large, a pig is about as crudely satirical as you can get. But, incredibly, *Moo* is not a satire. Smiley subverts satire, making it sweeter, and ultimately more pointed. She has written a generous and, therefore, daring book . . . has transformed the genre by embracing a different tradition altogether. Ostensibly an academic comedy, *Moo* is really a social comedy." The ethos of *Moo* is insistently sympathetic and communal, then, precisely because the antic egos of two dozen individuals have a way of complementing and neutralizing each other, and the larger university community survives the chaos and manages to function despite itself. The "inefficient" productivity of Moo U. might not be widely understood (research must actually be carried out *before* the conclusions are drawn, the reports submitted, and the patents applied for, for example), but the self-corrective tendencies of the place drive its ironies and help sustain its commitments and its antic *joie de vivre.* Smiley, Schine went on to say, "has created what modern novel readers have until now been able only to dream about, that elusive, seemingly impossible thing: a fresh, literary, modern, twentieth-century nineteenth-century novel."[11] Like Dickens's *Pickwick Papers,* Smiley's novel is a bulky ensemble piece in which all the actors have peripatetic roles in loosely connected vignettes, sustaining each other in what she has referred to on several occasions as an ecosystem-like structure. The smaller stories add, incrementally and in the manner of collage, to the patchwork whole. *Moo* is (again, after Dickens) a comedic *Bleak House,* in which the muted effects of larger social and political institutions and issues are, more than individual lives, the primary focus. The novel's ending is marked, as in Austen's *Emma,* by the comic resolution of marriage—the drawing of even endemically troublesome individuals into the social order—in radical contrast to the epic doom of *The Greenlanders* or the tragic revelation of *A Thousand Acres.* Had Smiley been inclined to identify her novel by genre, she might have cited Fielding's notion of a "comic epic in prose." Had Smiley wanted a descriptive subtitle for her novel, she could have borrowed from Thackeray and *Vanity Fair,* "A Novel Without a Hero."

The college community Pat Ricks described as a diversely populated "island" and Lorrie Moore referred to as an "academic Lilliput" is often characterized by other readers as a microcosm of the larger society, but in the context of Smiley's preceding work it might better be thought of as a specialized enclave of an ambitious, acquisitive culture—in its own way more like than unlike the Greenlanders' settlement, Bob Miller's "self-sufficient" farm in "Good Will," the (Iowa) farm of Virginia Cook Smith's family story in *A Thousand Acres.*[12] Moo U. is, after all, a land-grant institution, invoked by democracy and pragmatism via the Morrill Act and driven ever since by a belief in meliorism through science, a mission most recently interpreted as the transforming of research funding into applied technology. Moo U., like Earl Butz, may be set off from the larger culture, but it is never cut off, a lifeline of money being necessary for its well-being and growth. Where thematic revelations in *A Thousand Acres* lay in the flow of water, the thematic lifeline of *Moo* is revealed in the flow of money, the raw material out of which come new products, new patents, and more arguments for more grants. Reading *Moo* as a pejorative critique of the larger culture, Juliet Fleming (one of a few who noted the similarities rather than the differences between Smiley's eighth and ninth books) pointed out that *Moo* "is characterized by a strong distrust of men in families; and by a hatred of agribusiness, *laissez-faire* capitalism and the self-complacency of those in power."[13] Further, to Smiley's mind, at the end of the twentieth century any colony must be understood as not only extending the hegemony of a particular society, but also having an irreversible impact on the colonizers and the colonized world—in this case, the world outside the university and the world far beyond it (for example, Costa Rica). The indigenous skraelings finally witnessed the end of their Icelandic-Norwegian occupation, Smiley suggests in *The Greenlanders,* but by the 1990s native peoples and habitats have little chance against empire-builders. In her *Baltimore Sun* interview Smiley asserts that in *Moo*

> I was writing about a specific point about a specific type of university. . . . It's very similar in theme, I think, to *A Thousand Acres.* My overall subject is not academia. It's a

> larger point about technology and agriculture. *A Thousand Acres* has a lot of sub-themes and motifs about how the world these people have lived in has been destroyed by such things as pesticides in the water supply and this giant machinery. The other side of that thematic coin takes place at the university. This university is very closely tied to the farm. So I would never have written an ivory-tower comic novel. I call my novel a slippery-slope academic novel, in which academia is not cut off from the world, but is constantly contaminating the world, is constantly both re-creating the world in its own image and re-creating the world.[14]

A crucial biographical point of reference for this environmental theme in Smiley's work was her early exposure to John H. Storer's primer on ecology, *The Web of Life:* "I remember feeling at 13, 'This is a revelation, this is how it is, this is how life works.' I would say everything I've ever written grows out of that revelation."[15] This intellectual provocation was supplemented, beginning in 1971, by years of living in Iowa and studying the culture of agriculture—from its philosophy and economics to its vocabulary and discourse—first as a rural commuter student in the graduate program at the University of Iowa and later as a faculty member at Iowa State University. That Smiley might or might not have encountered a real-life Lionel Gift ("Homo Economicus") is beside the point of his economic philosophy, the fact that this philosophy is fundamental to his being a distinguished professor, and the reader's awareness that in and beyond Moo U. the wheel of production-consumption is, for many, the engine of life itself. "His first principle was that all men, not excluding himself, had an insatiable desire for consumer goods, and that it was no coincidence that what all men had an insatiable desire for was known as 'goods,' for goods were good, which was why all men had an insatiable desire for them."[16] This is the seamless logic of consumer capitalism, a tautology of which Earl Butz (the research project) is the blissfully oblivious embodiment. (The hog's human antecedent, once but no longer a household name, served as Agriculture Secretary under presidents Richard Nixon and Gerald Ford and was an advocate of the "get big or get out" philosophy of farming; he resigned from office in October 1976 after a racial slur he made became public knowledge.) The catastrophic fate of the "white as cream cheese or sugar" (4) Landrace hog—a disoriented, panic-stricken, overloaded death—is Smiley's representation of what awaits a thoughtlessly consumerist humanity in the abattoir of history.

The equally pale human representatives of Moo U. history, ethos, and aesthetic are, most prominently, Ivar and Nils Harstad, "the Albino Nordic Twins." As bland products of the institution's limited ambitions when it was still just a "cow college," the provost and extension dean are, more than (for example) the university president or right hand/left hand Jack Parker/Bob Brown, positioned to marvel at Moo now that it is a university. As the provost observes, their "benign army of [faculty] uncles" with crewcuts has been succeeded by "other uncles in Afros, ponytails, razor cuts as up-to-the-minute as any on Wall Street, as well as by aunts in bobs or curls or chignons, aunts in blue jeans whose locks flowed to their waists . . . ," teaching all over the university "in a universal diversity of accents" (385). Sold aggressively to "all sorts of constituencies" with promises of "everything to everyone," Moo U. "had become, more than anything, a vast network of interlocking wishes, some of them modest, some of them impossible, many of them conflicting, many of them complementary" (386). Thus the fugal structure of the book and the contrapuntal relationship among its voices, which Smiley has shaped so as to give virtually everyone—from Chairman X to Marly Hellmich and from Bob Carlson to the coeds in Dubuque House—his or her telling moments of action and revelation, demonstrating the university's capacity, at all levels, for thinking (or at least scheming), doing, and surprising. The apparent exceptions to Smiley's tolerance are the two outsider-insiders who are virtually oblivious to the notion of learning—as opposed to a comfortable bottom line—as a goal of higher education: Governor O. T. Early and Arlin Martin, the chicken king.

Thus also the overall charity with which Smiley handles Moo U. and the idea of the university. The academy, like Earl Butz, is both the object of rather broad humor and the sympathetic protagonist of Smiley's book. Beyond this, it is not difficult to consider Moo U. a large, sprawling, never-quite-blended family, antic and unruly, familiar after all to readers conversant with Smiley's domestic realism. And in the sense that the university as family suffers under paternal misrule, it is the determinedly nondomestic but highly successful Lionel Gift and Ivar Harsted whom Smiley holds most to blame. As psychology professor William Garcia might put it, these men are "competent in groups that mimicked the playground, incompetent in groups that mimicked the family" (34). By contrast, the classic comic-ending union of Chairman Jake and the Lady Beth constitutes evidence that the domestic impulse will never disappear from Moo U.

Smiley's imagination, then, like that of Mrs. Loraine Walker, is never at work on only a single level or isolated project, and it refuses to accept the notion that the various units of Moo U. are discrete fiefdoms, no matter what some faculty might wish or believe. Her ecological consciousness brings with it a recognition of species diversity, commensal relationships, and organic community—in short, a web of life. The warp and woof of the web would seem to be money and paper trails (from catalogue copy to news releases, but most tellingly entwined in the trickle-down paperwork of chapter 68). The imaginative and ludic energies of Moo U. lie in the urges of love and power, and sometimes (the infatuation with artificial insemination and genetic manipulation notwithstanding) even conventional sex and reproduction. However, as the diverse pairings and activities of chapter 20 demonstrate, "Who's In Bed with Whom" becomes a seriously problematic question once it leaves behind the romantic, erotic, experimental, and sexual-preference level of lovemaking. As an ecosystem of intersecting capabilities and potentials, Moo U. is messy-but-productive. As a research-and-development arm of the corporate establishment ("agriculture and mechanics" having given way to science *as* technology) Moo U. finds itself on Smiley's ethical "slippery slope."

The essence of Smiley's critique in *Moo* is the funny-sad reality that "Dr. Lionel Gift is in bed with Arlen Martin, billionaire, but only in the Washington, D.C., sense" (104); that "Get big or get out" economics is finally disastrous for Earl Butz; and that the extension of Moo U. expertise to distant forests in Costa Rica is destined to result in even greater catastrophe. The problem at Moo U. is that love in its various forms (including the expression of human sexuality, from youthful experimentation to the ardor of longstanding affections) is manifested privately for the most part, while power is the currency of public conversation, from the governor on down. For her own part, Smiley seems to have found the preoccupation of many with *Moo* as strictly academic satire both misdirected and frustrating, since that aspect of the book distracted attention from her environmental thesis:

> The joke was on me. . . . I thought I knew what I was doing when I wrote that novel. I thought its ecosystem-like structure would be not only obvious but appreciated. I thought the way in which the liberal characters used and transcended their self-centeredness to stop something they disapproved of would, could, should become a model for how well-meaning people can act together for a larger interest. I thought my own passions were finally on display, that this was clearly my most personal effort. All these things went unnoticed, unmentioned.[17]

Although it would be wrong to see Smiley in any particular character—even Loraine Walker, the secret mover of life (that is, money)—at Moo U., Smiley has asserted that she and Tim Monahan share certain (unspecified) characteristics. Any attentive reader of Smiley's fiction and essays might also detect the authorial presence in Helen Levy's culinary predilections, Chairman X's leftist sentiments, and Joy Pfisterer's intimate understanding of horses.

There are fundamental reasons for being melancholy about Moo U. on a daily basis, including administrators with ambitions rather than vision, faculty caught up in reputation-building and grant-writing rather than paper-grading, and students who are now considered "customers," of which the more the merrier. Smiley's placement of the provost's "What is a university?" reflection in chapter 66 is her way of asking this serious question as close to the end of the novel as her comic denouement will permit. "At the very very least," could students "expect to slip the parental traces, get drunk, get high, have sex, seek passion, taste freedom and irresponsibility surrounded by the best facilities that money could buy"? Could the university, "its limits expanding at the speed of light . . . teach a kid, male or female, to do anything from reading a poem to turning protein molecules into digital memory, from brewing beer to reinterpreting his or her entire past"? (386) Could the university do much of this at all, Smiley asks, while trying to balance the budget on a slippery slope? No stranger to the challenge and potential offered in class rosters containing the likes of Gary, Sherri, Keri, Mary, and Diane, an experienced teacher of creative writing might be inspired to do something more than wonder. And, since Smiley genuinely likes the university as a possibility too much to wish it irredeemable ill will, even in its current incarnation, the ambivalence the reviewers detected in her—described by Moore in terms of the book's "true and stubborn, amused and brokenhearted tenor"—is an ambivalence of vexation leavened by hope.[18]

But where there is an identifiable culture there are also cultural margins, and at the margins of Moo U. land-grant culture are several African-American figures—Mary Jackson, Margaret Bell, and John Vernon Cates (as well as his Ghanian wife)—whose highly-recruited presence at Moo serves, sadly enough, only to reveal how white the place continues to be. Cates has long since retreated into a world of technical distractions, Bell finds herself overwhelmed by committee work in which she is more a token presence than a voice, and Mary, finally,

> could not imagine herself here. She could watch herself walk across the campus, enter classrooms, study in the library, eat in the commons or in the Dubuque House dining room, dance with Hassan at a party, but still not grasp where she was going or why she was doing anything. When she thought of the campus or her classes or even her room, she was absent. There wasn't even a space where a black person should be . . . the longer she stayed here, and here was the whitest place she had ever been, as white as any world she would have to succeed in in order to satisfy [her sister] Carol, the less she seemed to exist. (381)

From the perspective of these insiders who are also outsiders, Moo U. is still in the process of becoming the place it ought to be; it is unlikely to get there anytime soon, Smiley suggests (comic coincidence and inventor's luck notwithstanding), if business continues as usual.

Also at the margins of the now-sprawling cow college is the eccentric and paranoid farmer-inventor, Loren Stroop, whose labor of love and inspiration arrives serendipitously from off-campus "nowhere" to save the budget and university jobs and enable the Moo U. enterprise to continue. Unknowingly, he has relinquished his remarkable invention to the very enemy he has always feared, the same one, Smiley suggests, that bulldozed the Cook farm in *A Thousand Acres.* Stroop's new invention is elegant in its practical simplicity, but will it finally be enough to make farming better? His distant, helpless moo-ing is at once a lament and a pathetic benediction. Even as *Moo* appeared on the best-seller lists, several of the major agricultural states including Iowa were engaged in heated arguments regarding the impact of "factory farming"—in particular, large-scale hog confinement facilities—on family farming as an institution, on the well-being of rural communities, and on the quality of small-town life generally.

At the level of genre, then, Smiley has written *Moo* in the prose tradition of the anatomy; the book is erudite, intellectually playful, textually diverse, and discontinuous in its narration. (But it is worth remembering that the ongoing readership of such similar books as Laurence Sterne's *Tristram Shandy,* Jonathan Swift's *Gulliver's Travels,* John Barth's *Giles Goat–Boy,* and Thomas Pynchon's *Gravity's Rainbow* is as small as it is serious.) At the ideological level, *Moo* requires that readers leap intellectually from the doomed innocence of Earl Butz to the mega-corporation paranoia of Loren Stroop to the fate of the last virgin cloud forest in Costa Rica. But in his anthropomorphic sadness Earl is so proximate and substantial and Central America so distant and ethereal (this is finally one of Smiley's points) that the former becomes embedded in the consciousness as insistently as the latter does not. At the intimate level of characters and relationships, *Moo* is written, essentially, in the tradition of modern (and, indeed, domestic) realism, with its dependence on circumstantial detail, social nuance, and psychological verisimilitude—a tradition to which the bulk of Smiley's writing contributes.

In the end, it may be that nuance and detail (so useful for humanizing Smiley's people and demystifying the academy, and so fundamental to her practice of the art of fiction), comedy (so fundamental to the conception of *Moo*), and an environmental critique are mutually distracting, even disorienting. Lorrie Moore seemed to suggest as much, in her critically affectionate review: "As portraiture, perhaps *Moo* is more Van Eyck than, say, Goya. Instead of the quicker, satirical strokes of the Spaniard, we have, with *Moo,* the fantastically overstudied picture: Giovanni Arnolfini (with his tricky mirror), his bride, his tenure, his chairman, the chairman's family, students, staff, lovers, the departmental votes, administrative memorandums, text from student catalogs. . . . It is a little like the author as clipping service. The book bulges and spins. It throbs and fizzes. It is a plethora."[19] At the intersection of detail, action, and ideology the resolution of issues in the novel is neatly (because coincidentally) accomplished through the timely actions of key individuals—from Mrs. Walker to the Warren County Pork Queen—who act according to their best impulses when the occasion presents itself. For many readers, though, the several levels and directions of real-world and intellectual action, distributed across a score of antic characters, may be too numerous for passionate attention.

Moo is a kinder, gentler *Animal Farm,* with the pigs replaced by people, it is *Gulliver's Travels* with Laputa amplified, and scarcely a true Yahoo in sight. *Moo* is Smiley's "novel without a hero." As such, Smiley's eighth book of fiction, like *The Greenlanders,* captures a small but devoted audience—and a somewhat different one at that. With *Moo,* Smiley also completes the third part of a four-part project she assigned herself when conceiving *The Greenlanders:* to write novels in each of four traditional Western literary modes—epic, tragedy, comedy, and romance.

CHAPTER TEN

The All-True Travels and Adventures of Lidie Newton

In *The All-True Travels and Adventures of Lidie Newton* (1998) Smiley addresses several issues fundamental to mid-nineteenth-century culture in the United States. She examines the romantic preoccupations of the time and the sentimental inclinations of its literature, as well as its social and political realities. She scrutinizes what was then a largely unexamined dogma of marriage and domestic life. She re-imagines a time when travel across the continent meant for many a new beginning in a "New World," and sometimes an abrupt end. In *Lidie Newton* Smiley evokes the moment when the trans-Mississippi region was a geographic magnet for ambition, money, and missionary zeal—when Kansas Territory was the battlefield of choice for the slavery debate. It is the moment when American politics, economics, and religion—cynicism, idealism, opportunism, and hypocritical compromise—joined to transform the Midwestern frontier and give rise to "Bleeding Kansas." Smiley's ninth book of fiction is almost as ambitious and demanding in what it knows and tries to do as was *The Greenlanders.*

Lidie Newton is also, in oblique fashion, the romantic novel that Smiley wanted to write, after turning out novels in the epic, tragic, and comic modes. To the extent that Lydia Harkness's brief courtship and impulsive marriage to a Massachusetts abolitionist thrust her into both domestic life and the moral, social, and political conflict over slavery that anticipated the Civil War, her story is one of deeply felt, often transcendent passions. To the extent that Lidie Newton's 1855–56 emigration from Quincy, Illinois, to Kansas Territory enables her to experience the unusual, witness historic events, test her survival skills, question received ideas, acquire new knowledge, and develop a radically expanded sense of self—all of which would otherwise have been, socially and pragmatically speaking, beyond the experience of a twenty-one-year-old woman of her time and place—her story is a version of "romance." Because Lidie Newton's travels and adventures in Kansas Territory evoke fear and wonder, prod the imagination and nourish ambition, inspire hope and (for a while, at least) allow for the denial of some fundamental realities of western life, her story is not inconsistent with the larger "romantic" narrative of American destiny. At mid-century her country is fascinated with its presumed attributes, national ambitions, and abstract possibilities: its ability to cobble a viable political system out of the raw materials of Enlightenment thought, its supposedly exceptional status among nations and cultures, its awe at the sheer scale of an intimidating geography (particularly in the West), its vast inventories of natural resources, its barely addressed potential for food production, and its promise, given all this, for rewarding aggressive individualism. The rhetoric that shapes Lidie's life includes the handbill puffery of territorial expansionists and western land speculators, a plethora of books (fiction as well as nonfiction) having to do with female conduct and domestic instruction, the vast literature of nineteenth century reform, notably that of abolition, and the widely popular travel articles and books of both amateur and professional writers—many of them "literary women." In the end, however, Smiley is a realist, and *Lidie Newton* is a realist's reading of a "romantic" time.

Smiley's thinking on the crucial issues that inform *Lidie Newton* was apparently brought to a focus by a rereading—and subsequent reevaluation—of *Adventures of Huckleberry Finn* during an extended period of recuperation after falling from her horse and breaking a leg in 1995.[1] In "Say It Ain't So, Huck," published in *Harper's Magazine* in 1996, Smiley takes issue with both the fact and the manner of the canonization of Mark Twain's novel, concluding that the book is badly compromised in several ways, but most notably by Twain's own "moral failure" in not taking Jim's desire for freedom seriously and in losing focus on "the true subject of the work: Huck's affection for and responsibility for Jim." Smiley accuses Twain of "lip service to real attachment between white boy and black man," of finally thinking "that Huck's affection is a good enough reward for Jim" and that good feelings are a reasonable substitute for positive action. And, finally, Smiley suggests, Twain and his less critical readers ultimately "opted for the ultimate distraction, lighting out for the territory."[2] In the same article Smiley praises *Uncle Tom's Cabin,* "which for its portrayal of an array of thoughtful, autonomous, and passionate black characters leaves *Huck Finn* far behind," because in her 1852 novel Harriet Beecher Stowe "never forgets the logical end of any relationship in which one person is the subject and the other is the object. No matter how the two people feel, or what their intentions are, the logic of the relationship is inherently tragic and traps both parties until the false subject/object relationship is ended."[3]

Lidie Newton is a slightly older and more socially interesting alternative to Huck Finn, and Smiley does Twain one better in transporting her to the "territory" to which Huck refers at the end of his own narrative—a place of further adventures to which Twain took Huck in manuscript but from which he was unable to deliver him in a finished book.[4] Smiley's heroine is older "sister" to nephew Frank Brereton's Huck and (given her ability to swim, shoot, and ride a horse) clearly surpasses him in both survival skills and serious interest for the reader. In manner and voice Frank is fundamentally a creature of "boy book" conventions and limitations —"Huck Finn" decentered (and, finally, criticized) in the narrative precisely because of his thoughtless treatment of life as a barter system, a mercantile game. In *Lidie Newton* Smiley speaks to the little-anticipated possibility—but not uncommon reality—that life in the territory might be something other than a game and more than an adventure, and not be the easiest stuff to write home about. She rearticulates through the experience of a capable, free-willed young nineteenth-century woman the fundamental social issues that Stowe confronted in *Uncle Tom's Cabin* but that Twain's nostalgia for his Hannibal boyhood seduced him into holding at a distance.[5] Lidie Newton's travels to Kansas Territory offer Smiley not only an opportunity to address the fundamental conundrum of slavery as an American institution, but also to reexamine American domestic life and its ideology through the eye of realism.

If Twain's "lighting out for the territory" was essentially a version of romantic escapism (finally, Smiley would argue, a male fantasy), then learning and addressing what it takes for a woman to struggle and survive in the violent cultural borderland of 1850s Kansas is Smiley's way of confronting the messy business of nation building as a social enterprise. As such, *Lidie Newton* is akin to *The Greenlanders,* Smiley's ponderous commentary on ambition, adventuring, and empire building in the fourteenth century, and to *A Thousand Acres,* her study of possessiveness and abuse as forces that shape and sustain a patriarchal kingdom in the twentieth. As the legacy left by nineteenth-century women writers such as Caroline Kirkland reveals, literary realism was inscribed in the disillusioned domestic record of emigration and settlement at least as early as it emerged in the local-color literary humor that anticipated Twain. Smiley's clear-eyed rendering of the realities that belied the naive fantasies of westward expansion makes it possible to appreciate the myth-resisting function of Kirkland's recently recovered *A New Home—Who'll Follow?* (1839) as well as the more familiar naturalistic prose of Edgar Watson Howe and Hamlin Garland later in the century.

In fact *Lidie Newton* contains numerous irony-freighted reminders of Twain's famous adventure book, enough to reveal Smiley in the process of tweaking *Huckleberry Finn* as a cultural artifact and icon of literary realism. There are numerous references to Lidie's own intimate relationship with the Mississippi, including her almost boylike response to its seductive power—"You couldn't stay away from the river; at least I couldn't" (36)—and her impulsive, self-absorbed immersion at the age of nineteen that ends with the sensation of an awakening (37). There is the Newtons' emigration voyage up first the Mississippi and then the Missouri, marked by references to locations and navigational phenomena familiar to Huck Finn or (alternately) his creator. And even after the Newtons have arrived in "K.T.," Lidie's figurative evocation of Twain's idyllic river (and thus Smiley's evocation of Twain) is apparently irresistible: "The fact is that in those days, our little cabin floated like a raft in a populous sea. We were certainly observed. . . . But . . . I couldn't rid myself of the impression that we were far away from everything and everyone, safe in a wilderness of space and nuptial contentment" (115).

Here and elsewhere, Smiley's allusions to Twain are ironic and skeptical because Lidie's nuptial "raft," more arbitrarily and tragically than Huck's fraternal one, is vulnerable to the "civilized" world of chicanery, harassment, beatings, thievery, and servitude. Promotional literature had convinced Lidie that the civilization east of the Mississippi had already been replicated west of it, and she had already begun to make her choices: "Salley Fork, Nebraska, where the grid of streets ran down a gentle southern slope to the sandy, oak-shaded banks of the cool, meandering Salley River and where the ladies' aid society had already received numerous subscriptions for the town library . . . Morrison's Landing, Iowa, on the Missouri, where the soil was of such legendary fertility and so easy to plow that the farmers were already reaping untold wealth from their very first plantings . . . Walnut Grove, Kansas, where the sawmill, the gristmill, and the largest drygoods emporium west of Independence, Missouri were already in full operation" (7). Smiley's ironic nod in this context toward Laura Ingalls Wilder's "Walnut Grove" confirms Lidie's early ignorance of territorial realities and the naivete of her vision of a picture-book little house on the prairie.

In the early 1850s the ungoverned social space of K.T.—a far cry from the moderately climed, picturesque fiction of the promoters' advertisements—is a domain of chaotic liminality. K.T. is filling up at a disorienting pace with a border-crossing hodgepodge of scarcely compatible individuals and interest groups, variously driven by simple curiosity, moral fervor, personal history, political ambition, and the need to make money: expansionists, social reformers, merchants, slave catchers, land speculators, "Border Ruffians," ministers turned horse dealers, would-be "farmers" with little understanding of agriculture. Perhaps most strikingly, there are numerous live-by-your-wits individuals whose common denominator is self-interest—enterprising and inventive loners who can also be unscrupulous, unpredictable, and indifferent to expectations of social compact. In Smiley's book the illusion of the noble isolato who finds a unique calling on the borderland is a troubled and troublesome romantic indulgence. Frank/Huck, whose talent for scavenging was considered entertaining back home in Quincy, is seen in less generous perspective in lawless K.T., where he narrowly escapes permanently becoming a scavenger of a less endearing sort. The civilized institutions that Lidie presumes to be in place will not be established for some time, and in their absence individual idiosyncracy has free play and troubling implications.

For Lidie Newton domestic life (like K.T. itself) is a cultural mystery, a vaguely imagined goal, and a personal threat. Having lost both parents, she receives sympathy and suffers alienation at the hands of siblings and experiences the disorientation of the displaced; she is kin to other nineteenth-century literary orphans, from Dickens's Pip to Melville's Ishmael, and including the abused and abandoned Huck Finn himself. Given plentiful evidence of a high rate of maternal mortality and the prevalence in popular literature of the self-sacrificing wife and mother figure, Lidie is in danger of becoming a sacrifice and a statistic, and she knows it. In the face of Lidie's sisters' nagging domesticity, only Catherine Beecher's demeanor while teaching at the short-lived Quincy Female Seminary offers an alternative role model for female identity and conduct. In her writing Beecher offers abundant anecdotal testimony regarding the physically debilitating potential of marriage, childbearing, and domestic life—a metaphor inscribed over and over in both the domestic fiction and didactic writing of the time. Lidie's recollection of her own invalid mother is that of a plain woman with scant prospects for marriage who was "invited" by a widower, silent and vain, to "come over to him, to care for his six daughters and bear him a son." Lidie speculates, not without bitter regret, that "perhaps she was gratified at being chosen at last for the very usefulness she had cultivated so long" (6). That Cora Mary Harkness died of exhaustion and cholera at age forty-seven, having given birth to seven more children and survived by only the last, is hardly inspiration for that sole survivor to cultivate "useful" domestic skills.

Lidie's sense of an alternative, nondomestic female self is also set in implicit contrast to a more physically sound but not unrelated cultural marker, Dickens's Florence Dombey, an icon of self-sacrifice who personifies the guiding tenets of a culture of sentiment. When Florence—"beautifully transfigured by the desire to give her filial love entirely to her father"—is dramatized in Quincy, she evokes from the audience a tearful, acquiescent, culturally appropriate response. But Lidie's more complex, conflicted awareness of her own and others' reaction to the performance derives from an unvoiced fear of what acceptance of such a shared vision of female identity might finally mean for her. "I entertained myriad poignant regrets at my own useless selfishness and felt much chastened and revivified by the whole experience when the interval came. Annie was in tears. Horace was in tears. I wasn't in tears, but beneath many layers of what I knew to be passing sentiment induced by the art of Mrs. Duff, I did feel a hard nub of fear. No one I knew knew what was to become of me, and I didn't know, either" (23). In the end Lidie's ambivalence and confusion mark an early stage of radical alienation from the sentimental model of womanhood.

Among the readings that contribute to Lidie's domestic education, only Beecher's *Treatise on Domestic Economy* offers intimations of an alternative ethos for making a home.[7] In reading the *Treatise,* Lidie finds Beecher's insistence on intelligent observation, common sense, self-reliance, and unvarnished descriptions of the hazards of married life a refreshing change from the conventional wisdom passed on by her sisters. In Beecher, Lidie sees a woman who "did what she pleased and wasted no time" (31), a mentor of vigorous sensibility who is committed to "loose clothing and undergarments" rather than the usual restrictive layers, and daily calisthenics in a large room with open windows in all seasons. Lidie also understands Beecher's *Treatise* to be a manual of enabling practical advice, finds stimulating Beecher's contention that women are beings of intelligence and sensation, and is intrigued by Beecher's observations on human physiology: "Now, in addition to looking forward to a strange future in a strange place with a strange man (and all men were strange enough to me), I, with my *cerebellum* and my *left ventricle* and my *lacteals* and my *follicles,* was strange as well" (32).

Smiley the realist makes clear that social and cultural biases combine with scant (and unreliable) "information" to make an adventure of her heroine's passage into Kansas and across the landscape of marriage. Prior to marriage, Lidie considers matrimony a curious necessity and Thomas Newton primarily an engaging intelligence and large presence. She is effectively seduced into marriage by Newton's observation that her otherwise anomalous (and, in Quincy, all but androgynous) skills—from swimming to riding and shooting—"prepared me wonderfully well for Kansas" (33). In fact her impulse to marry precedes both love for her husband and any useful grasp of domestic life as a lived experience. Her need to achieve that love and understanding engages her attention as long as making a home in Kansas remains an expectation—and despite her husband's brooding morality, metaphysical tendencies, and emotional distance. "My husband's intentions continued to be a mystery to me that I dared not plumb," Lidie recalls. "I would have said then that I loved him as a wife should do, that he was kind to me, and that I felt no desire to be secretive myself. . . . But he afforded me no answering self-revelation. In Illinois, this had seemed to be simply his nature—not secretive but laconic. In K.T., it seemed to be his design—not merely laconic but conspiratorial" (99). Marital intimacy is deflected by Newton's New England rectitude and reformist mission, and since Lidie is impulsive and prefers to immerse herself in experience, forging a shared life becomes a personal challenge. She would like to understand her husband: "This sense that a life was being lived in my presence that was partly, or largely, unrevealed to me seemed eerie—the very hallmark of marriage. My sisters seemed to have learned to live with this other life by either ignoring it or dismissing it, which I attributed to their common lack of imagination. My aim was . . . some sort of apprehension of him, out of which the other things would grow. That was what I called love. The mysteries of Thomas . . . seemed like a treasure that it was my God-given task to explore" (104). Lidie, like the protagonist at the end of Smiley's early story "The Pleasure of Her Company," effectively concludes that one of "the secrets of marriage" is that "it's worth finding out for yourself."[8]

Lidie's struggle to establish a domestic life with Thomas Newton is a crucial measure of territorial life. Because the unaccompanied emigration of an unmarried woman would have been unusual in her time, marriage is the necessary precondition for her travels and adventures. The irony of Lidie's coming to desire domesticity and "nuptial contentment" at a far remove from the culture in which their conventions are established and sustained is the essence of her new condition. For Thomas civilization is morality, rooted in the "higher-law" ideology of antislavery; for Lidie civilization is a domestic paradigm recognized with reluctance and anxiety in her half sisters' marriages: "My sisters were as fixed in their various homes as stones, and as difficult to lift" (8). The prospect of a life like those of Alice, Harriet, and Beatrice—regimented, submissive, predictable, and oppressively "useful"—appalls her. She views with a mixture of horror and sarcasm Alice's daughter Annie, describing her niece to Thomas as "a remarkably useful girl . . . it's only a matter of months before some widower with a dozen or more small children offers to make her the happiest girl in the world" (27). Lidie's fear of the "strange languor" (6) of an unmarried life spent with one of their families is accompanied by an instinctive alienation from household duties: "That hole of kitchen work was one I didn't care to fall into, because it was easy to see how those women would pull up the ladder and there you'd be, hauling wood and water, making fires and tea, for the rest of your life" (4).[9] That the circumscribed satisfactions of marriage can hardly sustain even Beatrice, Harriet, and Alice is revealed in their need to repudiate the alternative choices of their late, never-married sister Miriam, who made what they consider a wasted life of teaching the children of escaped slaves in Yellow Springs, Ohio.

In rendering the Newtons' husband-wife relationship, Smiley plays Lydia's effort to achieve a viable domestic self against Thomas's fixed convictions regarding slavery and his own role in trying to keep it out of Kansas Territory. It is moral certainty as well as self-irony that leads him to remark that "Many would say that any practice performed by New Englanders soon amounts to a religion" (28). The obvious sign of (and ironic commentary on) his idealistic abolitionism is the box of Sharps rifles, the "harness" with which Thomas surprises Lidie and that becomes part of the baggage with which the Newtons start their married life. That Thomas offers Lidie only belated revelation of the fact of the rifles says a lot about gender prerogatives and marital relationships in their time. That Thomas has agreed to accompany the rifles across the country, while possessed of minimal skill at shooting and little apparent understanding of how such weaponry is changing the nature of the social and political conversation, suggests something about both his own naïveté and the pace of change in K.T. Lidie herself recognizes that, curiously enough, she owes her marriage to the rifles, but she cannot know until their potential violence is realized what their presence in her life really means. "Suffice it to say that all things were fresh to me, and the moments, which passed slowly, were full of shock, interest, and some fear. I sense that Mr. Newton, too, felt more strange than he expected to . . . I knew he was full of wonder at how little we had foreseen, he had foreseen, the consequences of our impulses" (45). In fact, in a place and time where both sides in the slavery debate have been demonized by a rhetoric of ignorance and pride, firearms supersede even horses and "rectified whiskey" as empowering commodities. The lived experience of Kansas puts rifles—as well as restlessness, courage, moral conviction, and hope—in a new light.

Once events overtake Lidie's insecure dependence on Beecher's *Treatise* as a guide to her new life—"I have to say that there was nothing in Miss Beecher about hunting game over the prairie" (102)—she has to marshal her own intuition and resources in adapting to circumstances and, when this proves impossible, is forced to remake herself. Typically, throughout their relationship, Lidie's intuitive perception illuminates and reveals the limitations of Thomas's intelligence. Simultaneously the chapter-opening quotations from Beecher function as ironic running commentary (the irony as much Smiley's as Lidie's own) on the irrelevance of conventional notions of domestic economy in a socially unstable, aggressively undomestic space. In 1855 K.T. is an opportunity to extend borders and ambitions, but at a time when two incompatible social and economic systems seek to establish hegemony. K.T. is thus a place where vandalism, beatings, claim-jumping, arson, and murder become a way of life. "'Here it seems like anything is a reason to kill you,'" Thomas observes shortly after they have entered the territory; "'disagreement on the slavery question is one thing, but just how you talk or how you look is another, or, maybe, just how the killer feels at that moment. Killing you might just be boasting by other means'" (66). The place the Newtons have chosen to start their married life is in fact the domain of numerous individuals in the process of reinventing themselves and redefining their relationship to society, including those for whom domestic life is irrelevant and in whom entrepreneurship and opportunism are indistinguishable and virtually unthreatened by unselfish motives. There are, of course, enough fanatical John Browns and "romantic adventurer" Jim Lanes to go around, but the antidote to romantic illusion is no farther away than men such as David B. Graves—nominally an antecedent of Jane Graves Smiley—the garrulous and uncouth itinerant Missourian who, bad-penny-like, seems as unavoidable in Lidie Newton's Kansas experience as he is essential to her story.[10] Thomas Newton's ethical arguments regarding slavery are all but lost to Graves and others who refer to slavery (in an amorally comic euphemism) as "the goose question" and are content to bide their time while waiting "to see what happens" (58). What happens, of course, is that anarchy overtakes order at every turn.

When the Newtons arrive, the territory is in a state of social and political incoherence, so their hopeful domestic ambitions fall victim to Kansas's violent ideologues, social chameleons, and soldiers of fortune. "K.T." is a conception held together by opinions and understood in terms of gossip, a culture finally driven by eccentric impulses, and in K.T. the meaning of any reported event is hardly ever clear. In fact, Smiley's effort to convey constantly changing circumstances is occasionally stymied by the disparate and recalcitrant facts of K.T. Even for an age of oratory and oral information, some characters' dialogue can take on an expository heft—as with the Bush-Jenkins conversation in chapter 7 and some of Louisa Biskit's profeminist expostulations—notwithstanding the reader's need, over a century and a half later, for historical data and the articulation of issues.

The education of Lidie Newton is a function of her disillusionment—that is, the lived experience that initiates her into the real world of the midcentury American West and the real meaning of slavery as a disfiguring fact of American life. It is an education that socially incoherent K.T. both enables and requires her to pursue. The territory's instability makes possible an expanded version of the incidental freedom for which Lidie discovers a taste at sister Alice's, "the freedom of not being attended to" (117)—in fact the kind of freedom that resulted in Lidie's swimming across the river at age 19. Lidie feels this expansive new condition when she instinctively resists Miss Anabelle Tonkin's assertion (and Smiley's jab at Twain) to the effect that "the adventure is for the men, my dear; that's the way of it here in the West" (42); when she notes that the Kansas heat makes the emigrants' once-obligatory beards, corsets, and layers of clothing impractical and irrelevant; and when she describes K.T. as a place "where women went almost everywhere" (187). Lidie's first overt exercise of her K.T. freedom is her purchase of Jeremiah, an impulsive and consciously perverse act given that her domestic obligation is to buy a stove for her new home. That the horse costs more than the stove she eventually buys and that the money for both is left over from the sale of her father's house (that is, a vestige of her patrimony) attests to the shifting nature of priorities and values in K.T. Lidie's ambivalence regarding the appropriateness of her purchase of Jeremiah in Thomas's absence is assured by Mrs. Bush's criticism, and Lidie's regret, if only temporary, is real. But her flurry of domestic activity the next morning is more than a guilt-inspired transaction that creates an opening for her to ride him for the first time, more than an exchange of labor for pleasure; it is an early example of her negotiation of gender roles as they relate to independence and autonomy, a key concern of book 1 of the novel: "I was certainly the only woman I saw who was riding like a man," Lidie recalls. "Most were walking, some were seated in wagons, all glanced at me . . . but here in K.T., where petticoats and buttons and manners were all loose and loosening further, I decided that I would ride my horse as I pleased, the Missourians and their brawls notwithstanding. That would be the compensation for everything else" (89).

When in chapter 14 Lidie accedes to Frank's suggestion that they race Jeremiah, her misgivings on behalf of propriety are consistent with her status as Thomas's wife, and her contrary decision is consistent with having earlier bought the horse before the stove. After her fears of her husband's displeasure are confirmed—and, given her own temperament of free will, perhaps because of this—she affirms her selfish impulse and finally feels less culpable than exhilarated. But here, too, ambivalence leads to internal negotiation:

> But then a new argument began, this one not so much between what I had done and what I ought to have done as between the two halves of what I was. As it happened . . . I had devoted almost every thought and every action since August to Thomas Newton. Everything about my situation in K.T. was bound up with our marriage and his desires. . . . This day, though, all unbeknownst at the time, I had set a little space between us when I watched the race and thrilled to it and came home half-pleased with myself and wholly pleased with Jeremiah. I resented my husband for not allowing me to communicate what I saw—that was the root of my resentment—but then I knew also that I could not have communicated what I saw to him . . . because he hadn't the interest or capacity or phrenological bump to be thrilled by such a thing. (191–92)

This tendency on Lidie's part to ponder her condition is reminiscent of similar inclinations in such earlier Smiley narrators as Rachel Kinsella in "Ordinary Love" and Ginny Smith in *A Thousand Acres.* The questioning of gender expectations and behavioral norms informs Lidie's spontaneous experiment with cross-dressing when she and Frank join the confrontation with the Missourians, is reinforced by Louisa Biskit's contention that

"Woman should not be subject to male whim, as we are, but should live in full exercise of her capacities" (170), and ultimately sustains her role-playing as Lyman Arquette. Such a contrarian ability in Lidie Newton to be a constantly thinking, identity-shifting self also makes Thomas expendable to Smiley, since, given nineteenth-century mores, Lidie's chafing at the restrictions imposed by her subordination through marriage can only end if her marriage ends. In fact Thomas's growing bewilderment over the gap between the moral wrongness of slavery and the reductive violence of territorial politics suggests that he, a stubbornly consistent abstract thinker and writer, is being overtaken even faster than Lidie is by the vertiginous reality of Kansas.

The almost simultaneous killings of Thomas and Jeremiah bring to an abrupt end one phase of Lidie's life and complicate her internal debate concerning domestic issues by linking it with more fundamental questions. Having to live the truth of her earlier observation that "K.T. made you see the world as it was" (250), Lidie also finds herself having to accept that "Sentiment was a deadly thing in K.T. Folks back in the U.S. didn't know that about K.T., did they?" (257) Emotionally Lidie has been moving toward a new life since she noted that Kansas was hardly a petticoat culture, and the metamorphosis in appearance and gender that carries her into book 2 begins when she rips off the bottom of her skirt in order to run for help after the shootings. It is hardly necessary for her to tell the reader that "Now I was a new person, one I had never desired nor expected to be" (262).

Lidie is, in the domestic sense, free, and the freedom that enables (but also requires) her to become a man, from hat to gait to voice, also enables her to continue to examine both gender and race as conditions of living in that time and place. In fact Lidie is made to realize almost immediately that her status as a woman will restrict her in pursuing revenge against her husband's killers and keep her from confronting, even through casual public conversation, the issue that led to his death. In Missouri in general and male-populated, business-and-politics Kansas City in particular (as opposed to abolitionist Lawrence), it would be impossible for Lidie, as a woman, to ride, bear firearms, and travel freely without inviting attention and repression. As earlier, the catalyst for change is David B. Graves, this time cajoling and maneuvering her toward safe passage to Saint Louis on the *Missouri Rose* but reminding her of the terms under which safety might be had. Since Lidie is apparently "unsound on the goose question," she "would be wise to maintain a womanly silence and gentleness of demeanor at all times, because though all Missourians and southerners honor the fair sex, by habit and from their earliest childhoods, no one can answer for the general irritability that I see all around me here. I am feeling that you should take your cabin on the *Rose* and stick to it and not say too much about your troubles in K.T." (284). Lidie's status as an unaccompanied widow would dictate that once again she resign herself to claustral quarters, the indoors of designated "female" space, a prospect that once made even the comforts of Quincy worth leaving. Her impulse, as before, is flight, on the grounds that safety is relative and that, "When all was said and done, freedom was all, wasn't it?" (290)—a phrase that resonates throughout her shared adventures with Lorna. Even so, while Lidie is quite aware of the ironic implications for her of even a temporary reversion to acquiescent womanly behavior, she is surprised by the emotional weight of her husband's clothing and apparently unaware that briefly wearing it (and thus symbolically becoming Thomas) is a necessary prelude to pursuing her goals and experiencing yet other selves: "I saw at once that as long as I was a man, I would be able to do whatever I wanted, and that I would have a taste of freedom that no woman I had known, even Louisa, had ever had" (294). For Lidie, cutting off a lifetime of hair (and thus conventional female beauty) is not only a symbolic offering to Thomas, but a matter of "lightness and relief" (292).

Adopting the male ethos of "big strides and nothing in your way" (295), Lidie, cross-dressed as "Lyman Arquette" of Palmyra, Missouri, experiences the prerogatives of the dominant, masculine "subject" in a territorial culture where women and slaves are, in their respective ways, objects. For Lyman Arquette "the institution of Negro servitude was a righteous and inevitable disposition of natural, and scripturally justifiable, inequality" (337). As a young male reporter Lidie can gaze at the world "as if it were my prerogative to watch without being watched" (340) and offer a proslavery version of it in his columns. Ironically enough with regard to the "goose question," the moral position to which she begins to feel closest is the one shared by her abolitionist sister and Thomas Newton—as implied through her periodic recollections of Miriam and her talismanic attachment to her husband's watch. While Lyman is able to adopt a white male Missourian discourse of possession, Lidie cannot ignore the faces and voices of slaves, entreating salvation of anyone who will listen. The further irony of Lidie's gender switching is that being a man requires of her a coarsened sensibility and the keeping of low company. Lidie's feelings and opinions are in constant ironic conflict with Lyman's social situations. Nevertheless, as long as the masquerade lasts, she can leave behind female restrictions and pursue her personal agenda.

In book 2, then, Lidie Newton lives through the implications of the moral and ethical issues raised by the chapter 5 steamboat incident in which a slaveowning woman challenges a northern woman to trade her dress and hat for a slave girl's freedom. In that early incident Lidie's peevish disappointment at the outcome of the altercation and her own smugly imagined solution to the dilemma—"You see, you could always take off your shoes right then and there, and that would be a seizing of the advantage" (54)—confirm that she married an abolitionist and set out for contested territory with a few untested sentiments concerning slavery, but no viable and sustaining convictions. Traveling up the Mississippi toward Kansas, she fails to understand the objectification-commodification underpinnings of slavery and her own subject/object relationship to the slave girl she wishes were free. Wanting to see a solution in a specific instance draws Lidie into responding to slavery as barter (that is, a financial transaction) rather than a moral issue. As Thomas explains, the northern woman is simply unable even to "put a girl and a dress in the same category" (54). In chapter 20, however, the issue is joined for Lyman/Lidie when Lidie's abolitionist sensibility is violated by Lyman's need to write proslavery articles for Morton's *Missouri Freeman*—to do the job that will supposedly enable her to pursue her intention to revenge Thomas's death. Lidie's confusion of conscience over being proud of her writing and ashamed of its sentiments echoes ironically the passage in *Huckleberry Finn* in which Huck decides he will go to hell rather than submit Jim to the authorities. "I thought my disguised self could go ahead and write up those boys' story in the style of Mr. Morton's paper and that it would remain outside of me," Lidie recalls. "But what I found out was that my piece had a way of talking back to me. Every lie I put down on the paper made a claim, and every claim those lies made, made me mad. But I couldn't seem to stop them. . . . The truth seemed to protest, but it couldn't really get in there. There wasn't a place for it, for one thing, and my project couldn't afford it, for another" (320–21). Given Smiley's sense of the harsh terms of survival in slave-holding Missouri—and her contention that Twain sometimes disregarded them—Lidie and the reader can hardly be allowed a conscience-clearing agenda uncontaminated by immediate and ongoing real-world considerations.

In chapter 21, with Lyman/Lydia on an unsure course (literal and symbolic) to Independence, the incident involving "Master Phillip" and the slave child provides another test of Lidie's abolitionist convictions. That she fails to respond to the child's explicit pleas to her *as* an "Ablishinist" she immediately attributes to her feminine weakness in a world that men control; but after this she must acknowledge that aside from becoming "a hater"—"the sort who wanted to hang, shoot, dismember, clear out, and otherwise dispose of those who wanted to hang, shoot, dismember, clear out, and otherwise dispose of me"—she is indeed an abolitionist who "hadn't many instinctive feelings about slavery" (343). This failed test of Lidie's antislavery convictions results in yet another crisis of conscience, but again one with no visible repercussions for Lidie in the real world. "Only afterwards did that child's voice come back to me as the voice of my conscience, you might say. I only knew what I should have done by surmising what Thomas would have done, and by then, of course, it was too late. It wasn't just having to hide among my enemies that made it hard to be an abolitionist in Missouri; it was also having no friends" (343). The impact is internal. The more her own condition begins to resemble that of a fugitive slave, the more difficult it is for her actually to do anything productive in the interests of freedom.

Lidie's feeling, thinking, and identity shifting reach a crisis point when miscarriage and physical collapse overtake her at Day's End Plantation, and she is again reborn into yet another new life and an entirely new set of possibilities and challenges. Having lost everything from her prior life, "including, at the moment, my very name and history" (352), Lidie is forced to reclaim her female identity as "Louisa"—instinctively becoming namesake and kindred spirit to her outspoken feminist and antislavery companion from Lawrence—and she has to invent yet another personal history. Yet, as an invalid female without connections or resources, she must also accede to local mores while she is cooked for and nursed back to health by slaves. It should not be overlooked that as a domestic servant, Lorna must be useful at precisely those tasks for which Lidie has declared herself useless. The ease with which Lidie's invalidism merges comfortably into a supposedly healthy feminine passivity—one that is not unattractive to Papa Day—suggests the ease with which social convention can reassert its control. Ultimately Louisa/Lidie must confront once more the seductive and conflict-ridden domestic status quo: listening to Helen gossip about clothing, courtship, and marriage; being waited on and cared for by Delia and Lorna; appreciating the comforts and aesthetics provided by the house and grounds; making polite conversation with Papa about English writers and books (but not politically questionable Americans such as the Emerson, Lowell, Stowe, and Beecher who share her travels); and betraying the memory and moral principles of Miriam Harkness and Thomas Newton. As a reading farmer Papa Day is both amiably odd and frighteningly reminiscent of the desperate widowers Lidie escaped by marrying Thomas Newton. As a neo-Jeffersonian agrarian Papa Day believes in the nearly edenic quality of plantation life, on which money is a fundamental blight while slavery is not. To him slaves are childlike, loving, loyal, dependent, and dependable adjuncts to family life. In the Day's End episode—Smiley's alternative treatment of issues raised in Twain's much-analyzed Phelps farm episode—"Louisa" is faced with two choices: a domestic life of enforced leisure predicated on the forced labor of others or a fugitive existence through which she might leave slave territory and return to Illinois.

Lidie's confusion regarding how this fugitive status might be achieved and the form her flight might take disappears with Lorna's recognition of Lidie's true identity and insistence on their running away together. In Lorna's reading of their relationship "You cain' gi' me four dollar one time and walk away from me de nex," and with regard to Lidie vis-à-vis Thomas, "dis is somethin' you gone do fo' him" (403). The difference between the two women is that while Lidie is fleeing an unwanted domestic life in a society that fosters slavery, Lorna is fleeing slavery itself, the institution that has destroyed her domestic life by enabling Papa Day to sell her husband, Jake. Because race is the definitive marker for classifying people in Missouri, race divides

Lidie and Lorna even in their shared search for freedom; it dictates the terms under which they can travel together at all. Lorna's sense of how differently the two women are culturally situated is a matter of internalized understanding; by contrast, Lidie's recognition that slave-holding society expects her to demonstrate that she is superior to and in control of her slave comes reluctantly, at best. Her awkward, apologetic efforts to learn from Lorna something about servitude as a condition of life amount to intelligence trying to catch up with vague notions and good intentions. Through her association with Lorna Taler, Lidie Newton learns that it is easier for a woman to pass as a man and for an abolitionist to pass as a slaveholder than it is for a black woman to travel alone and unfettered—let alone ever to be free. A related irony in all this for Lidie the strong-minded woman is that she herself could only leave Illinois and enter K.T. when accompanying a man. The irony for Lidie the abolitionist is that her best hope of escaping Missouri and helping Lorna run away is to demonstrate her ownership by mistreating the black woman in public. The sad irony for Lidie the widow is that "Of course, Lorna was right. Aiding in her escape was the thing I had to do for Thomas that would somehow restore him to me" (403–44).

Whether Lidie's aiding Lorna without success is sufficient might be best determined by Lorna herself, who "invested me with the power to move" (443), who is responsible for the actual escape plan, whose confidence and stamina on the road sustains them both, and who apparently suffers an even harsher fate than does her husband. The truth is, Lidie confesses, that she had counted on Lorna to save *her.* The reality is that while aiding a slave to escape is nominally a crime punishable by hanging,

Lidie's risk as a white woman is finally less than Lorna's as a black one, particularly after Lawrence is no longer a secure abolitionist refuge. The further reality of their story together is that they are caught because Lidie is recognized, not Lorna. Lidie is forced to sell to an outfitter the last relics of her earlier life, including Thomas's watch and their books, and she is caught and locked up for a while; but finally Lidie escapes hanging because she is white, female, and a widow—and because Papa Day's sentimental convictions prevail. Backtracking for both herself and Thomas, she ends up in Massachusetts, able to tell her tale. Lorna, sold south, disappears.

Lidie is deprived, in the end, of a sense of closure. Her married life ends suddenly, after only a ten-month acquaintance with Thomas, and their lost child is a permanently unrevealed mystery. Her adventures end not because she finds a home and embraces domestic life (however defined), but because her travels are brought to an end through the actions of David B. Graves, the unaffiliated commercial opportunist with an occasional, unpredictable impulse to do something kind—perhaps the prevailing spirit of K.T. itself. Already a failed Kansas adventurer, she fails to see Lorna to freedom and hardly returns to Quincy on anything like her own terms. Lidie's plotted murders of Samson and Chaney, who represent for her everything despicable and unworthy in K.T., are made impossible by her inability to identify definitively the face of evil in the suspects she encounters. Her questions regarding the ultimate fate of Lorna yield only the information that she has been sold south. Lidie's guilt and resignation regarding what has been permanently lost are real, as is her sense of pathos: "It was hard to see Lorna simply, as another desperate woman powerless against the institution of servitude, against Missouri and Kansas and guns and horses and catchers and dogs and distance and lack of funds and chance, but that's what she was in the end, wasn't she? And the ways she would have to pay for her mistake in trusting me I would never get to know and always be tempted and terrified to imagine" (443). But short of the end of the territorial war in which Thomas Newton's shooting was an obscure skirmish, and the Civil War to follow, there is no closure for the quandary of Kansas and Missouri. What Lidie has achieved in the course of her adventures is yet another new self, this one alienated from the mannerly silence of Saint Louis, the willed ignorance of sisters such as Harriet and other women generally, and the misinformation and distorted rhetoric of an increasingly polarized political world. Her friend Louisa was right, after all, in claiming that Lidie would not be able to live back there after experiencing K.T.; after Kansas, Lidie is, emotionally speaking, a permanently dis-placed person.

The view of Kansas from New England vexes Lidie Newton, and at best it provides her with a sardonic perspective for contemplating her adventures. The K.T. of the Boston imagination is a congeries of opinions and convictions that have found in Kansas a stage to be acted on, so Lidie's hard-earned but confusing testimony is as much of the truth of her experience as she is capable of giving and as coherent a reality as her audience is interested in knowing. By helping Thomas's family and abolitionist friends raise money for their cause, she is merely contributing to the purchase of more rifles—and the perpetuation of chaos, squalor, and despair. What was true in Kansas and Missouri cannot be described, she says, but "A sojourn in K.T. ought to prepare the soul for any other journey whatsoever" (262).

NOTES

Chapter 1—Understanding Jane Smiley

1. Interview with the author, 7 Aug. and 4–5 Nov. 1996. Unless otherwise indicated, comments in this chapter attributed to Smiley but not directly quoted are taken from this interview.

2. Interview with the author, 7 Aug. 1996.

3. See Jane Smiley, "Afterword: Gen-Narration," in *Family: American Writers Remember Their Own,* ed. Sharon Sloan Fiffer and Steve Fiffer (New York: Pantheon, 1996) 241.

4. Jane Smiley, "Shakespeare in Iceland" (Unpublished paper read before the Sixth World Shakespeare Congress, Los Angeles, 8 Apr. 1996) 3. Smiley's typescript is quoted here by permission.

5. Smiley, "Shakespeare in Iceland" 3.

6. Smiley, "Shakespeare in Iceland" 3.

7. Smiley, "Shakespeare in Iceland" 4.

8. Interview with the author, 7 Aug. 1996.

9. Smiley, "Shakespeare in Iceland" 4.

10. Interview with the author, 7 Aug. 1996.

11. Interview with the author, 4–5 Nov. 1996.

12. Interview with the author, 4–5 Nov. 1996.

13. Interview with the author, 4–5 Nov. 1996.

14. Smiley, "Shakespeare in Iceland" 7.

15. Negative criticism of *A Thousand Acres* could be summarized in the words of a British reviewer, Jonathan Mirsky, who saw the novel as overwhelmed by issues and catastrophes. Smiley, he wrote, "hasn't found the solution. She has constructed a pastiche of *King Lear* . . . [and] has to resort to ominous 'Little did I know that morning what would happen by evening' tags designed to keep us turning the pages; and to coincidences and revelations which come from nowhere. What we have here, in fact, is a not-bad thriller masquerading as a bucolic

tragedy" ("Bitter Harvest," *The Observer* [London], 15 Nov. 1992, 64). See also James Wood, "The Glamour of Glamour," *London Review of Books* 14 (19 Nov. 1992): 17.

16. Alexander Neubauer, "An Interview with Jane Smiley," *AWP Chronicle* 26 (Mar./Apr. 1994): 4.

17. Neubauer 5.

18. Jane Smiley, "Reflections on a Lettuce Wedge," *Hungry Mind Review,* no. 27 (Fall 1993): 13. Once asked what her favorite word is, Smiley responded, "garlicky"; see *The Logophile's Orgy: Favorite Words of Famous People,* ed. Lewis Burke Frumkes (New York: Delacort, 1995) 180–81.

19. Kenneth Pins, "This Story's Still Being Written, but the Plot Is Thickening," *Des Moines Register,* 25 Jan. 1987, 1B.

20. Jane Smiley, "So Shall We Reap," *Sierra* 79 (Mar.–Apr. 1994): 74–82, 140–41.

21. Smiley's earliest in-print expression of her sense of middle-class stability and security appeared in a short interview in which Smiley noted that "she didn't have 'a past full of suffering . . . my family had its share of death, disease and craziness, but I'm essentially a product of the middle class'" (James Kaufmann, "*Barn Blind:* Smiley Experiments with a Family," *The Daily Iowan,* 2 July 1980, 3E). Characteristically, Smiley added that in fiction writing, the most important thing "is not what you've done, ultimately, but how you have thought about it." The one non-middle-class, nonestablishment figure among Smiley's antecedents, her maternal great-grandmother Nicolena Olson Doolittle, was the only ancestor within living memory who was undeniably "an immigrant."

22. Jane Smiley, untitled commentary on "Lily," in *American Voices: Best Short Fiction by Contemporary Authors,* ed. Sally Arteseros (New York: Hyperion, 1992) 214.

23. As several of her readers have noted, Smiley's characters (whether in the fourteenth or twentieth century) are not unconscious consumers of food. See, for example, Alison Lurie, "Hog Heaven,"

New York Times Book Review, 2 Apr. 1995, 26; and Lorrie Moore, who writes that "it is one of the oddities of Smiley's work that she so frequently falls into rather intoxicated anthropological listings of food," in "Fiction in Review," *Yale Review* 83 (Oct. 1995): 138. (All of the stories in *The Age of Grief,* for example, eventually have something to do with recipes, menus, kitchens, and meals, and might serve as a convenient starting place for a study of Smiley's phenomenology of food.)

24. John Gardner, *On Moral Fiction* (New York: Basic Books, 1978) 126.

25. Kelly A. Marsh, "The Neo-Sensation Novel: A Contemporary Genre in the Victorian Tradition," *Philological Quarterly* 74 (Winter 1995): 99–123.

Chapter 2— *Barn Blind*

1. Jane Smiley, "Horse Love," *Victoria* 6 (May 1992): 40. Smiley's affection for equestrian sports is also expressed in "My Gelding, Myself," *Outside* 20 (Nov. 1995): 112–18, 159; "*Puissance,*" *Flyway* 1 (Spring 1995): 23–32; "North Carolina's Equestrian Heaven," *New York Times Magazine* (17 Sept. 1995): 55–61; and, with a somewhat different emphasis, "The Call of the Hunt," *Outside* 19 (Nov. 1994): 114–22.

2. Jane Smiley, *Barn Blind* (New York: Harper & Row, 1980) 38. Subsequent references will be incorporated parenthetically into the text.

3. Mary Loudon, "Jane's Addiction," *Guardian Weekend,* 27 May 1995, 36.

4. Jane Smiley, "Can Mothers Think?" *The True Subject: Writers on Life and Craft,* ed. Kurt Brown (Saint Paul: Graywolf, 1993) 8.

5. Loudon 36.

6. Jane Smiley, "Idle Hands," *Hungry Mind Review,* no. 33 (Spring 1995): 13.

7. Smiley, "Can Mothers Think?" 3, 6–7, 13.

8. Smiley, "Can Mothers Think?" 13, 14–15.

Chapter 3—*At Paradise Gate*

1. Jane Smiley, *At Paradise Gate* (New York: Simon and Schuster, 1981) 118–19, 164. Subsequent references will be incorporated parenthetically into the text.

2. Interview with the author, 4–5 Nov. 1996.

3. Valerie Miner, "Domestic Novels," *New York Times Book Review,* 22 Nov. 1981, 15.

4. Miner, 15.

5. Susan Wood, "Family Circles," *Washington Post,* 27 Oct. 1981, C6. Perhaps a more valid complaint would be that, beyond references to place names, Des Moines and Iowa—as opposed to Anna's house itself—remain a textureless larger setting for *At Paradise Gate.* Smiley's primary interest and commitment here are clearly to the rendering of interior reality.

6. Jane Smiley, "Afterword: Gen-Narration," in *Family: American Writers Remember Their Own,* ed. Sharon Sloan Fiffer and Steve Fiffer (New York: Pantheon, 1996) 241.

Chapter 4—*Duplicate Keys*

1. Lois Gould, "When the Sharing Had to Stop," *New York Times Book Review,* 29 Apr. 1984, 14. See also Sarah Montague, "Metaphysical Murder Mystery," *Newsday,* 25 Mar. 1984, Ideas section, 18; and Arthur Krystal, "Two Tales of a City," *Village Voice,* 14 Aug. 1984, 45.

2. Jane Smiley, *Duplicate Keys* (New York: Knopf, 1984) 100–101. Subsequent references will be incorporated parenthetically into the text.

3. Gould 14. Or, in more urbane terms, "*Duplicate Keys* makes some intelligent links between detective work and more general forms of perspicacity" (Laura Marcus, "Families and friends," *Times Literary Supplement,* no. 4247 [24 Aug. 1984]: 953).

4. Marcus 953; Jennifer Crichton, "In Short," *Ms.* 12 (Apr. 1984): 32; Mary Ann Riley, "Friends and Their Mysteries," *Des Moines Register,* 8 Apr. 1984, 6C; Jane S. Bakerman, "Renovating the House of Fiction: Structural Diversity in Jane Smiley's *Duplicate Keys,*" *Midamerica XV* (1988): 111–20.

5. Others who have noted the culinary—and gastronomical—texturing throughout Smiley's story include Riley 6C, and Geraldine R. Foty, "Young People Coping in 'Big Apple,'" *Worchester (Mass.) Telegram,* 10 June 1984, 12D.

6. Smiley offers a different kind of post-1960s requiem in "*Fahrvergnügen,*" *Playboy* 38 (Dec. 1991): 102–4, 112, 196–99.

7. Krystal 45.

8. John Preston, untitled rev., *Time Out* (London), 14 June 1984, 37; Alice Cromie, "Tales Calculated to Keep You Shivering This Summer," *Chicago Tribune Book World,* 8 July 1984, 32.

9. "Water on Stone: Long-Term Friendships in Jane Smiley's *Duplicate Keys* and Charlaine Harris' *A Secret Rage,*" *Clues: A Journal of Detection,* 10 (Fall/Winter 1989): 50. Bakerman reads *Duplicate Keys* as a female "maturation novel" or "delayed *Bildungsroman,*" in which violent disruption and victimization trigger the protagonist's transformation.

10. Kenneth Pins, "This Story's Still Being Written, but the Plot is Thickening," *Des Moines Register* (25 Jan. 1987): 5B. Alice is thirty-one years old in the novel, which takes place in 1980; Smiley was born in 1949.

Chapter 5—*The Age of Grief*

1. Jane Smiley, "Shakespeare in Iceland" (Unpublished paper read before the Sixth World Shakespeare Congress, Los Angeles, 8 Apr. 1996) 7; interview with the author, 4–5 Nov. 1996.

2. Jane Smiley, *The Age of Grief* (New York: Knopf, 1987) 9. Subsequent references will be incorporated parenthetically into the text.

3. Seen in the larger context of Smiley's work, the fully represented, onstage demonstration of Kevin's anger in the form of a calculated and vicious violation of Nancy's selfhood can be seen as notification that from this point on, such abuse will not only be reported, as in *At Paradise Gate,* but taken on and called to account, as in *A Thousand Acres.*

4. "Books of the Times," *New York Times,* 26 Aug. 1987, C21.

5. Mary Loudon, "Jane's Addiction," *The Guardian Weekend,* 27 May 1995, 36.

6. Loudon 36.

7. Jane Smiley, "Can Mothers Think?" *The True Subject: Writers on Life and Craft,* ed. Kurt Brown (Saint Paul: Graywolf Press, 1993) 13. And, Smiley says, "Need I add that there's always a mess to be cleaned up afterward that is not the concern of the dead tragic hero? A mother's vison would encompass survival . . . would encompass the cleaning up of messes."

8. Smiley, "Can Mothers Think?" 15.

9. Smiley, "Can Mothers Think?" 13.

10. Raymond Carver, "Gazebo," *What We Talk About When We Talk About Love* (New York: Random) 27.

11. Representative of these are Kakutani; Anne Bernays, "Toward More Perfect Unions," *New York Times Book Review,* 6 Sept. 1987, 12; James Atlas, "Poignant Prose," *Vanity Fair* 50 (Sept. 1987): 186; Rob-

ert Wilson, "*The Age of Grief:* Fiction Worth Celebrating," *USA Today,* 4 Sept. 1987, 6D; Karen Rile, "In Jane Smiley's Stories, Reflections on Inner Lives," *Philadelphia Inquirer,* 22 Nov. 1987, 5; Alice H. G. Phillips, "The Periodicals: *The Quarterly,*" *Times Literary Supplement,* no. 4424 (15–21 Jan. 1988): 60.

Chapter 6—*The Greenlanders*

1. Jane Smiley,"Shakespeare in Iceland" (Unpublished paper read before the Sixth World Shakespeare Congress, Los Angeles, 8 Apr. 1996) 5.

2. Steve Paul, "A Daunting Saga of Life in Twilight," *Kansas City Star,* 3 Apr. 1988, 10G.

3. Howard Norman, "They Should Have Listened to the Skraelings," *New York Times Book Review,* 15 May 1988, 11.

4. Marcelle Thiébaux, "Jane Smiley," *Publishers Weekly* 233 (1 Apr. 1988): 65–66. A more personal motive for getting to the heart of the Greenlanders' ethos and voice is suggested in Smiley's comment in "Shakespeare in Iceland" that "I grew up in a family of story-tellers, gossipers, natural narrators. We did not mimic voices or take parts or perform. We specialized in irony of tone. When I discovered the Icelandic sagas, I discovered us" (3).

5. Thiébaux 66. A somewhat differently slanted comment appears in "Shakespeare in Iceland": "In studying Old Icelandic and in writing and researching *The Greenlanders,* I engaged for ten years or so with a distinctly pre-modern mind, as expressed in the stories and the style of the Icelandic sagas and the poetic Edda, and yet, because the sagas were written prose narratives about the social consequences of unrestrainable conflict in the polity, they were also strangely modern,

strangely American. I always thought of *Njáls saga* as the great proto-American novel, halfway here in place and time" (7).

6. David Streitfeld, "Smiley's People," *Washington Post Book World,* 28 Jan. 1990, 15.

7. Jane Smiley, "*Puissance,*" *Flyway* 1 (Spring 1995): 25–28. A follow-up piece to "*Puissance*" is "My Gelding, Myself," *Outside* 20 (Nov. 1995): 112–18, 159.

8. Thiébaux 65.

9. Paul 10G.

10. Paul 10G; Thiébaux 65; interview with the author, 4–5 Nov. 1996.

11. Interview with the author, 4–5 Nov. 1996; Thiébaux 66.

12. Kenneth Pins, "This Story's Still Being Written, but the Plot is Thickening," *Des Moines Register,* 25 Jan. 1987, 5B.

13. "Shakespeare in Iceland" 7.

14. Interview with the author, 4–5 Nov. 1996.

15. Jane Smiley, *The Greenlanders* (New York: Knopf, 1988) 120. Subsequent references will be incorporated parenthetically into the text.

16. Smiley's attention to issues surrounding land stewardship is ongoing; see, for example, her essay "So Shall We Reap," *Sierra* 79 (Mar./Apr. 1994): 74–80, 82, 140–41; and "Losing the Farm," *New Yorker* 72 (3 June 1996): 88–92, a review of Victor Davis Hanson's *Fields Without Dreams.*

17. Thiébaux 66.

18. Smiley is quoted in her *Publishers Weekly* interview to the effect that Steinunn is one of the characters in her novel who appear in the Icelandic Annals: "'Steinunn was seduced through witchcraft by a Greenlandic man and he was burned at the stake and Steinunn went crazy from the grief'"; Thiébaux 66.

19. Erik Eckholm, "Her Saga of a Giant Island," *New York Times Book Review,* 15 May 1988, 11.

Chapter 7—*Ordinary Love and Good Will*

1. Jane Smiley, *The Age of Grief* (New York: Knopf, 1991) 154.

2. Michiko Kakutani, "Pleasures and Hazards of Love in the Family," *New York Times* (31 Oct. 1989): 14. Valerie Miner was among the less positive reviewers, arguing that much remains undeveloped in "Good Will" and that Smiley is an "authentically circumscribed" writer of "fair-enough, writing-from-your-own-experience fiction"; "Middle-class Moods," *Women's Review of Books* 7 (Apr. 1990): 18.

3. Vince Passaro, "Smiley's People," *7 Days,* 29 Nov. 1989, 67. Others who praise Smiley's achievement in the art of the novella include David Leavitt, "Of Harm's Way and Farm Ways," *Mother Jones* 14 (Dec. 1989): 44; and Josephine Humphreys, "Perfect Family Self-Destructs," *New York Times Book Review,* 5 Nov. 1989, 1. In his review of *Ordinary Love and Good Will,* Richard Panek refers to novellas as "those literary works of uncommon length, no commercial prospects and indeterminate identity"; "Two Novellas With the Warmth of Home," *USA Today,* 3 Nov. 1989, 7D.

4. Jane Smiley,"Shakespeare in Iceland" (Unpublished paper read before the Sixth World Shakespeare Congress, Los Angeles, 8 Apr. 1996) 3; Jane Smiley, "Can Mothers Think?" *The True Subject: Writers on Life and Craft,* ed. Kurt Brown (Saint Paul: Graywolf Press, 1993) 7; Hillel Italie, "Iowa Author Jane Smiley Dips Into Heartbreak In Heartland," *Omaha World-Herald Sunday Magazine,* 4 Feb. 1990, 15.

5. Smiley, "Can Mothers Think?" 10.

6. Smiley, "Can Mothers Think?" 10–11.

7. Jane Smiley, *Ordinary Love and Good Will* (New York: Knopf, 1989) 104. Subsequent references will be incorporated parenthetically into the text.

8. Mary Loudon, "Jane's Addiction," *The Guardian Weekend,* 27 May 1995, 36.

9. Suzanne Berne, "*Belles Lettres* Interview," *Belles Lettres* 7 (Summer 1992): 38.

10. See Loudon 36.

11. Kakutani 14.

12. See Smiley, "Can Mothers Think?" 13; Richard Grant, "Jane Smiley: Homebody Makes Good," *Telegraph Magazine* (20 May 1995): 38; and Berne, "*Belles Lettres* Interview" 38.

13. Suzanne MacLachlan notes that "Smiley writes as if she were sitting at the kitchen table telling a story to a friend" ("Kitchen-Table Tales of Desire and Will," *Christian Science Monitor,* 30 Oct. 1989, 13). Dean Flower remarks that "Smiley's narrators just seem to tell us what they think, or just plain what happens" (*Hudson Review* 43 [Summer 1990]: 315).

14. Jane Smiley, "Can Writers Have Friends?" in *Between Friends: Writing Women Celebrate Friendship,* ed. Mickey Pearlman (Boston and New York: Houghton Mifflin, 1994) 46–47.

15. Smiley adds: "I'm always asked why I write about 'ordinary' people. But why would I write about princesses or executives in big oil companies? Their lives are probably less interesting in a lot of ways. They're protected from a lot of things that others aren't" (Italie 15).

16. Ursula K. Le Guin, "The Carrier Bag Theory of Fiction," *Dancing at the Edge of the World: Thoughts on Words, Women, Places* (New York: Harper & Row, 1989) 169.

Chapter 8—*A Thousand Acres*

1. Jane Smiley, "Shakespeare in Iceland" (Unpublished paper read before the Sixth World Shakespeare Congress, Los Angeles, 8 Apr. 1996) 3, 8.

2. "Shakespeare in Iceland" 7–8.

3. See Wendell Berry, *The Unsettling of America: Culture and Agriculture* (San Francisco: Sierra Club Books, 1977); Deborah Fink,

Agrarian Women: Wives and Mothers in Rural Nebraska, 1880–1940 (Chapel Hill: University of North Carolina Press, 1992); Osha Gray Davidson, *Broken Heartland: The Rise of America's Rural Ghetto* (New York: Doubleday, 1990); and Jane Smiley, "So Shall We Reap," *Sierra* 79 (Mar./Apr. 1994): 74–80, 82, 140–41.

4. Jane Smiley, *A Thousand Acres* (New York: Knopf, 1991) 4–5. Subsequent references will be incorporated parenthetically into the text.

5. Suzanne Berne, "*Belles Lettres* Interview," *Belles Lettres* 7 (Summer 1992): 36.

6. Rupert Christiansen, "Sharper Than the Serpent's Tooth," *The Observer* (London), 25 Oct. 1992, 1.

7. Peter Conrad, "Expatriating Lear," in *To Be Continued: Four Stories and Their Survival* (Oxford: Clarendon, 1995) 133–34. In Raymond Williams's analysis, the ownership-production-management pattern of agrarian capitalism was well established in England by the time Sam Davis and John Cook would have emigrated in the late nineteenth century. That is, economic and cultural developments in Zebulon County can be seen as "logical" extensions of an attitude toward the land that had been evolving for over two hundred years. See *The Country and the City* (New York: Oxford University Press, 1973), especially chapters 5–8.

8. See, for example, Glenda Riley, *The Female Frontier: A Comparative View of Women on the Prairie and the Plains* (Lawrence: University Press of Kansas, 1988), which covers the years 1815–1915, and especially chapter 9; Fink, *Agrarian Women* (cited above), especially chapter 8, "Agrarian Contradiction"; and Deborah Fink, *Open Country, Iowa: Rural Women, Tradition, and Change* (Albany: State University of New York Press, 1986), which corroborates a continuing pattern of dependency and exploitation for farm women after World War II.

9. Katie Roiphe, "Making the Incest Scene," *Harper's* 291 (Nov. 1995): 65, 68. By contrast, see Jack Fuller, "King Lear in the Middle West," *Chicago Tribune Books,* 3 Nov. 1991, 1, 4.

10. Interview with the author, 4–5 Nov. 1996. Donna Rifkind notes that "this is a novel whose characters overshadow the plot: Their shifting points of view are often more breathtaking than the action itself" ("A Man Had Three Daughters . . . ," *Washington Post Book World,* 27 Oct. 1991, 13); Joan Bunke suggests that "some of Ginny's psychologizing sounds more like the theorizing of an author than a character" ("Revenge, Rage on *Lear* Farm," *Des Moines Sunday Register,* 3 Nov. 1991, 4C).

11. Berne 37. Ginny's post-traumatic behavior is consistent with that observed in formal studies; see, for example, Judith Lewis Herman, *Trauma and Recovery* (New York: Basic Books, 1992), especially chapters 2–4: "Terror," "Disconnection," "Captivity." Smiley has also cited Akira Kurosawa's film *Ran* as having prompted her to change the perspective—and the gender of the perspective—in retelling the *King Lear* story. See Christiansen, "Sharper."

12. Williams 125.

13. Karin Winegar, "In Her Book, Earth, Women are Victims of Mistreatment," *Star Tribune* (Minneapolis), 9 Apr. 1992, 3E.

Chapter 9—*Moo*

1. Noah Adams, "Author Talks About New Novel Centered at Moo University," *All Things Considered,* National Public Radio, 4 Apr. 1995.

2. Jane Smiley, "And Moo to You Too." *Civilization* 2 (Nov./Dec. 1995): 75. Elsewhere, Smiley observed that *Moo* elicited "the worst reviews I've ever gotten for a book" (Janice Harayda, "Sharp 'Moo' to Faith in Technology," *The Plain Dealer* [Cleveland], 21 May 1995, 7K). For Smiley's post-*Moo* response to the phenomenon of reviewing—a satirical meditation that can be read as a companion piece to "And Moo to You Too"—see "Making Enemies: Your Bad Review," *Hungry Mind Review,* no. 40 (Winter 1996–1997): 21.

3. The opening sentence of the *Chronicle* interview-cum-profile reads, "Jane Smiley wants everyone to know that her latest novel, *Moo,* is not based on Iowa State University," and at the end of an interview for her local paper Smiley contends that "there's nothing in it that ever happened at Iowa State that I know of." Liz McMillen, "Moo U. Follies," *Chronicle of Higher Education,* 12 May 1995, A19–A20; Jeffrey Bruner, "Smiley's Pulitzer Follow-up *Moo* Set for April Release," *Daily Tribune* (Ames, Iowa), 24 Feb. 1995, A1, A3; Noah Adams, "Author Talks"; Joan Bunke, "Smiley's People," *Des Moines Register,* 11 Apr. 1995, 1T–2T.

4. Joanne Kaufman, "Picks and Pans: *Moo,*" *People Weekly* 43 (24 Apr. 1995): 29; Joanne Wilkinson, untitled rev., *Booklist* 91 (1 Feb. 1995): 971; untitled rev., *Kirkus Reviews* 63 (1 Feb. 1995): 101; Pico Iyer, "How High the Moo?" *Time* 145 (17 Apr. 1995): 69.

5. Phoebe-Lou Adams, "Brief Reviews," *Atlantic* 275 (May 1995): 126; Valerie Miner, "The Cow Pies of Academe," *Nation* 260 (8 May 1995): 639; Richard Eder, "Moo U: The Superheated Life of a University Community," *Los Angeles Times Book Review,* 2 Apr. 1995, 8; Jonathan Yardley, "Wallowing in Hog Heaven," *Washington Post Book World,* 26 Mar. 1995, 3; Brooke Allen, "On Campus Among the Sacred Cows," *Wall Street Journal,* 29 Mar. 1995, A12; Gary Krist, "Comedy," *Hudson Review* 48 (Winter 1996): 680.

6. Miner 639. This would seem to explain the equal number of positive reviews: for example, Iyer 68–69; Michiko Kakutani, "All Too Human Comedy On a Midwest Campus," *New York Times,* 21 Mar. 1995, C19; Trudy Bush, "War Wounds, and a Midwest Microcosm," *Christian Century* 112 (24–31 May 1995): 569–70.

7. Bush 569.

8. The diverse roster also includes, among others, George R. Stewart, *Doctor's Oral* (1939); Malcolm Bradbury, *Eating People is Wrong* (1960); Bernard Malamud, *A New Life* (1961); Hazard Adams, *The Horses of Instruction* (1968); Michael Frayn, *The Trick of It* (1989);

Michael Malone, *Foolscap* (1991); Cathleen Schine, *Rameau's Niece* (1993); and, in another vein, Vladimir Nabokov, *Pale Fire* (1962).

9. Cathleen Schine, "The Way We Live Now," *New York Review of Books,* 10 Aug. 1995, 38; Lorrie Moore, "Fiction in Review," *Yale Review* 83 (Oct. 1995): 139.

10. Smiley, "And Moo To You Too" 75; Tim Warren, "Author Smiley Takes Criticism of *Moo* with a Grain of Salt," *Baltimore Sun,* 3 May 1995, 1D. Among those amused were David Galef, "An Academic Romp," *New Leader* 78 (13–27 Mar. 1995): 18–19; Bill Holm, "Confused State," *San Jose Mercury News,* 2 Apr. 1995, 1B, 7B; Lorrie Moore; and Kakutani.

11. Schine 38.

12. Pat Ricks, untitled rev., *Austin (Tex.) American-Statesman,* 9 Apr. 1995, G7; Moore 138.

13. Juliet Fleming, "Death of a Porker," *Times Literary Supplement,* no. 4807 (19 May 1995): 20.

14. Warren 1D. Smiley adds: "I thought that was pretty explicit in this book, but others persist in seeing it as a novel about academia rather than a novel about technology or whatever." The strength of Smiley's convictions on this subject is measured by her making the same statement to the alumni magazine of Iowa State University, which finessed by reporting her as having "a lot of serious fun with the land-grant philosophy in her seventh work of fiction" (Steve Sullivan, "Smiley's Latest a Light Look at Land-grants," *The Iowa Stater,* Feb. 1995, 2).

15. Lorraine Adams, "The Moo the Merrier," *Washington Post,* 4 May 1995, D2.

16. Jane Smiley, *Moo* (New York: Alfred A. Knopf, 1995) 31. Subsequent references will be incorporated parenthetically into the text.

17. Smiley, "And Moo to You Too" 75. At least one reader who responded to *Moo* as Smiley intended referred to it as "not a comedy of manners but of morals. What we do matters. We see how infinite changes can be wrought by apparently inconsequential events, and how a single

good intention can, against great odds, achieve a reversal of misfortune" (Liz Heron, "Fiction," *Times Educational Supplement,* 7 July 1995, Centre Pages section, 13).

18. Moore 139.

19. Moore 135–36.

Chapter 10—*The All-True Travels and Adventures of Lidie Newton*

1. See Jane Smiley, "Two Plates, Fifteen Screws," in *The Healing Circle: Authors Writing of Recovery,* ed. Patricia Foster and Mary Swander (New York: Plume, 1998).

2. Jane Smiley, "Say It Ain't So, Huck." *Harper's* 292 (Jan. 1996): 62–63. This article evoked an energetic response from Twain scholars; see Justin Kaplan, "Selling *Huck Finn* Down the River," *New York Times Book Review* (10 Mar. 1996): 27; and "Letters," *Harper's* 292 (April 1996): 6–7, 83–85.

3. Smiley, "Say It Ain't So, Huck" 64, 65.

4. Twain's effort to take Huck to the territory exists only as a long fragment of a novel— "Tom and Huck among the Indians"—that was never completed.

5. The subject matter of Lidie Newton is essentially that of Jane Austen's novels as described by Smiley—"the moral lives of woman who, though dependent and circumscribed in many ways, are autonomous, thinking beings of intelligence and sparkling personality." Jane Smiley, "Jane Austen's Heroines," *Victoria* 9 (May 1995): 28.

6. Jane Smiley, *The All-True Travels and Adventures of Lidie Newton* (New York: Knopf, 1998) 120. Subsequent references will be incorporated parenthetically into the text.

7. Catherine Beecher was the daughter of Henry Ward Beecher and sister of Harriet Beecher Stowe; *A Treatise on Domestic Economy*

for the Use of Young Ladies at Home and at School was first published in Boston in 1841.

8. Jane Smiley, "The Pleasure of Her Company." *The Age of Grief* (New York: Knopf, 1987) 26.

9. Lidie shares with Smiley herself a disaffection for chores and for making them a condition of family life; see Jane Smiley, "Idle Hands," *Hungry Mind Review* 33 (Spring 1995): 13.

10. Interview with the author, 7 August 1996.

BIBLIOGRAPHY

Works by Jane Smiley

Items are listed chronologically by date of publication.

Novels

Barn Blind. New York: Harper and Row, 1980. London: Flamingo, 1994.

At Paradise Gate. New York: Simon and Schuster, 1981. London: Flamingo, 1995.

Duplicate Keys. New York: Alfred A. Knopf, 1984. London: Jonathan Cape, 1984.

The Age of Grief. New York: Alfred A. Knopf, 1987; London: Collins, 1988.

The Greenlanders. New York: Alfred A. Knopf, 1988. London: Collins, 1988.

Ordinary Love and Good Will. New York: Alfred A. Knopf, 1989. London: Collins, 1990.

The Life of the Body: A Story. Minneapolis: Coffee House Press, 1990. With six hand-colored linoleum cuts by Susan Nees. A limited edition ("Espresso Editions"); 170 numbered copies signed by the author and artist.

A Thousand Acres. New York: Alfred A. Knopf, 1991; London: Collins, 1991.

Moo. New York: Alfred A. Knopf, 1995. London: Flamingo, 1995.

The All-True Travels and Adventures of Lidie Newton. New York: Alfred A. Knopf, 1998; London: HarperCollins, 1998.

Short Stories and Excerpts from Novels

"And Baby Makes Three." *Redbook* 149 (May 1977): 231–34.

"Jeffrey, Believe Me." *Triquarterly,* no. 40 (Fall 1977): 81–87.

"I In My Kerchief and Mama In Her Cap." *Redbook* 150 (Jan. 1978): 157–61.

"New Poems." *Fiction* 5 (Spring 1978): 136–53.

"Good Intentions." *Playgirl* 6 (May 1979): 36–39.

"Sex." *Mademoiselle* 86 (July 1980): 154, 156–59.

"The Pleasure of Her Company." *Mademoiselle* 87 (Mar. 1981): 102 ff.

"The Blinding Light of the Mind." *Atlantic* 252 (Dec. 1983): 48 ff.

"Lily." *Atlantic* 254 (July 1984): 76–80, 83–86.

"Firing Jennifer." *TWA Ambassador,* Oct. 1984.

"A Spy Story." *Poet and Critic* 16 (Winter 1985): 32–52.

"Long Distance." *Atlantic* 259 (Jan. 1987): 68–75.

"The Age of Grief." *The Quarterly* 1 (Spring 1987): 104–89.

"Good Will." *Wigwag,* Nov. 1989, 52–81. Slightly abridged.

"Ordinary Love." *Fiction Network,* no. 13 (Fall/Winter 1989/90): 3–33. Slightly abridged.

"What the Women Said." *Wigwag,* July–Aug. 1990, 48–52.

"The Nickel Plan." *McCall's* 118 (Oct. 1990): 112–14, 144–46, 150–51.

"Turnpike." In *Voices Louder Than Words: A Second Collection,* ed. William Shore, 97–113. New York: Vintage Books, 1991.

"*Fahrvergnügen.*" *Playboy* 38 (Dec. 1991): 102 ff.

"Gregor: My Life as a Bug." *Harper's* 285 (Aug. 1992): 36–37.

"A Quarrelsome Peace." *New York Times Magazine,* 20 Dec. 1992, 26–28, 46.

"The Life of the Body." *Antaeus,* no. 75/76 (Autumn 1994): 190–206. Repr. in *Prize Stories 1996: The O. Henry Awards,* ed. William Abrahams, 251–69. New York: Doubleday, 1996.

"Creative Writing 101." *Esquire* 123 (Mar. 1995): 129–30. Chapter 6 of *Moo.*

"Moo." *Elle* 10 (Mar. 1995): 176–90. Chapters 2, 9, and 47 of *Moo.*

Nonfiction

Book

Catskill Crafts: Artisans of the Catskill Mountains. New York: Crown, 1988.

Uncollected Essays and Articles

"As Time Goes By." *Savvy* 9 (Jan. 1988): 96, 95.

"A Thousand Acres: How Much is Enough?" Iowa City: The Iowa Humanities Board, 1991 (broadside format). The 1991 Iowa Humanites Lecture, delivered 20 Oct. 1991, Iowa State University, Ames.

"Mirror Images." *Life* N. S. 15 (Mar. 1992): 87.

"Horse Love." *Victoria* 6 (May 1992): 38–40.

"All-American Garden." *House and Garden* 164 (June 1992): 122–29, 156.

"Imposing Values." *New York Times Magazine,* 20 Sept. 1992, 28–29.

"The Undresser." *Allure* 2 (Oct. 1992): 96–98.

Untitled commentary on "Lily." In *American Voices: Best Short Fiction by Contemporary Authors,* ed. Sally Arteseros, 213–14. New York: Hyperion, 1992.

"Wisconsin: Three Visions Attained." *New York Times Magazine,* 7 Mar. 1993, pt. 2 ("Sophisticated Traveler"), 28 ff.

"The Worth of a Bookstore." *Victoria* 7 (Aug. 1993): 71.

"Reflections on a Lettuce Wedge." *Hungry Mind Review,* no. 27 (Fall 1993): 13.

"Can Mothers Think?" *The True Subject: Writers on Life and Craft,* ed. Kurt Brown, 3–15. Saint Paul: Graywolf Press, 1993.

"Something Extra." *New York Times Magazine,* 10 Oct. 1993, pt. 2, p. 8.

"Can Writers Have Friends?" In *Between Friends: Writing Women Celebrate Friendship,* ed. Mickey Pearlman, 44–55. Boston and New York: Houghton Mifflin, 1994.

"Introduction." In *First Fiction: An Anthology of the First Published Stories by Famous Writers,* ed. Kathy Kiernan and Michael M. Moore, 13–21. Boston: Little, Brown, 1994.

Untitled introduction to "The Interview," by Ruth Prawer Jhabvala. In *You've Got to Read This: Contemporary American Writers Introduce Stories That Held Them in Awe,* ed. Ron Hansen and Jim Shepard, 272. New York: HarperCollins, 1994.

"So Shall We Reap." *Sierra* 79 (Mar./Apr. 1994): 74 ff.

"Borges, JCO, You, and Me." *Antaeus,* no. 73/74 (Spring 1994): 56–57. Includes a pen-and-ink self-portrait.

"The Call of the Hunt." *Outside* 19 (Nov. 1994): 114–22.

"Introduction." In *The Best American Short Stories 1995,* ed. Jane Smiley with Katrina Kennison, 10–18. Boston and New York: Houghton Mifflin, 1995.

Untitled entry in *The Logophile's Orgy: Favorite Words of Famous People,* ed. Lewis Burke Frumkes, 180–81. New York: Delacorte Press, 1995.

"Full Cry." In *Women on Hunting,* ed. Pam Houston, 186–98. Hopewell, N.J.: Ecco Press, 1995.

"A Novel Encounter." *Harper's Bazaar,* no. 3400 (Mar. 1995): 168–69.

"Tornadoes." *Outside* 20 (Mar. 1995): 72.

"Idle Hands." *Hungry Mind Review,* no. 33 (Spring 1995): 13.

"*Puissance.*" *Flyway: A Literary Review* 1 (Spring 1995): 23–32.

"Jane Austen's Heroines." *Victoria* 9 (May 1995): 28–29.

"North Carolina's Equestrian Heaven." *New York Times Magazine,* 17 Sept. 1995, pt. 2 ("Sophisticated Traveler"), 55 ff.

"Yes, Please, and One of Those . . . ," *Mirabella* 7 (Sept/Oct. 1995): 66, 68.

"The Big Soak." *Vogue* 185 (Oct. 1995): 256 ff. Also as "The Bathroom," in *Home: American Writers Remember Rooms of Their Own,* ed. Sharon Sloan Fiffer and Steve Fiffer, 106–15. New York: Pantheon, 1995.

"Confess, Early and Often." *New York Times Magazine,* 8 Oct. 1995, 62–63.

"Getting into Character . . . Psyche." *New York Times Magazine,* 29 Oct. 1995, 50.

"My Gelding Myself." *Outside* 20 (Nov. 1995): 112–18, 159.

"And Moo to You Too." *Civilization* 2 (Nov./Dec. 1995): 75.

"Nancy Drew." Introduction to Carolyn Keene, *Nancy's Mysterious Letter,* 3 pp., unnumbered. Facsimile Edition. Bedford, Mass.: Applewood Books, 1996.

"Say It Ain't So, Huck: Second Thoughts on Mark Twain's 'Masterpiece,'" *Harper's* 292 (Jan. 1996): 61–67.

"There Is Nothing Like a Dane." *Town & Country* 150 (Feb. 1996): 62–63.

"The Affair: Why It's Not Worth It." *Mirabella* 7 (Mar./Apr. 1996): 78–79.

"Okay, Go Ahead." *Hungry Mind Review,* no. 37 (Spring 1996): 13.

"Greenland." *Islands* 16 (July/Aug. 1996): 118–19, 143.

"Making Enemies: Your Bad Review." *Hungry Mind Review,* no. 40 (Winter 1996–1997): 21.

"Shakespeare In Action." *New York Times,* Dec. 1996, A13.

"Afterword: Gen-Narration." In *Family: American Writers Remember Their Own,* ed. Sharon Sloan Fiffer and Steve Fiffer, 241–47. New York: Pantheon Books, 1996.

"Two Plates, Fifteen Screws." In *The Healing Circle: Authors Writing of Recovery,* ed. Patricia Foster and Mary Swander, 99–106. New York: Plume, 1998.

"Mothers Should." *New York Times Magazine,* 5 Apr. 1998: 37–39.

"Taking It All Back." *Washington Post Book World,* 21 June 1998: 1, 8.

Reviews

"Getting Away from Daddy." *New York Times Book Review,* 13 Mar. 1988, 29. Rev. of Josephine Gattuso Hendin, *The Right Thing to Do.*

"Social Change 101." *New York Times Book Review,* 2 Oct. 1988, 13. Rev. of Paul Hoover, *Saigon, Illinois.*

"What Is This Thing Called Bronze?" *New York Times Book Review,* 16 July 1989, 12. Rev. of Jim Crace, *The Gift of Stones.*

"Searching for Secrets on This Side of the 'Moon.'" *USA Today,* 17 Mar. 1989, D4. Rev. of Paul Auster, *Moon Palace.*

"'The Hardest Thing I've Ever Done.'" *New York Times Book Review,* 7 Jan. 1990, 10. Rev. of Le Anne Schreiber, *Midstream.*

"Books." *Vogue* Apr. 1990: 278, 280–81. Rev. of Dori Sanders, *Clover;* Elinor Lipman, *Then She Found Me;* Sharlene Baker, *Finding Signs;* Sandra Dallas, *Buster Midnight's Café.*

"Someone's in the Kitchen With Freud." *New York Times Book Review,* 22 Apr. 1990, 1, 45. Rev. of Sue Miller, *Family Pictures.*

"Recipe for Riding Out a Storm." *New York Times Book Review,* 20 May 1990, 38. Rev. of Patricia Polacco, *Thunder Cake.*

"In One Small Town, the Weight of the World." *New York Times Book Review,* 2 Sept. 1990, 2. Rev. of Barbara Kingsolver, *Animal Dreams.*

"The Wild West Show." *Chicago Tribune Books,* 21 Oct. 1990, 6–7. Rev. of Larry McMurtry, *Buffalo Girls.*

"Matters of Appearance." *Chicago Tribune Books,* 17 Feb. 1991, 3. Review of Mary Gaitskill, *Two Girls, Fat and Thin.*

"In the Shadow of a Big Bad Boy." *New York Times Book Review,* 10 Mar. 1991, 6. Rev. of Susan Cheever, *Treetops: A Family Memoir.*

"You'd Never Suspect Kathleen." *New York Times Book Review,* 5 May 1991, 9. Rev. of Joyce Carol Oates, *The Rise of Life on Earth.*

"An Old World Seen in a New Way." *Boston Sunday Globe,* 26 May 1991, A13. Rev. of John Vernon, *Peter Doyle.*

"Caribbean Voices." *Chicago Tribune Books,* 6 Oct. 1991, 3. Review of Paule Marshall, *Daughters.*

"Wide-Eyed in the Big City." *New York Times Book Review,* 10 Nov. 1991, 14. Rev. of Terry Teachout, *City Limits: Memories of a Small-Town Boy.*

"Families and Other Works in Progress." *New York Times Book Review,* 19 Apr. 1992, 9. Rev. of Sandra Tyler, *Blue Glass.*

"Vogue Arts: Books." *Vogue* (May 1992): 158, 160. Rev. of Toni Morrison, *Playing in the Dark* and *Jazz.*

"New Wine from the Grapes of Wrath." *Los Angeles Times Book Review,* 11 Oct. 1992, 2, 7. Rev. of Toby F. Sonneman and Rick Steigmeyer, *Fruit Fields in My Blood: Okie Migrants of the West* and Dan Morgan, *Rising in the West: The True Story of an "Okie" Family From the Great Depression Through the Reagan Years.*

"Fiction in Review." *Yale Review* 81 (Jan. 1993): 148–62. Rev. of Garrison Keillor, *WLT;* David Lodge, *Paradise News;* Rupert Everett, *Hello Darling, Are You Working?;* Michael Malone, *Foolscap;* Stephen McCauley, *The Easy Way Out;* Walter Kirn, *She Needed Me.*

"Fine-Tuning One's Enemies." *New York Times Book Review,* 3 Jan. 1993, 6. Rev. of John Mortimer, *Dunster.*

"Snap, Crackle, Pop In Battle Creek." *New York Times Book Review,* 25 Apr. 1993, 1, 28. Rev. of T. Coraghessan Boyle, *The Road to Wellville.*

"From the New World." *Boston Sunday Globe,* 16 May 1993, B39, B42. Rev. of Isabel Allende, *The Infinite Plan.*

"In Distant Lands of Ice and Sun." *Washington Post Book World,* 24 Oct. 1993, 1, 11. Rev. of Peter Hoeg, *Smilla's Sense of Snow.*

"Something Is Wrong With This Life." *New York Times Book Review,* 13 Feb. 1994, 12. Rev. of Robert Olen Butler, *They Whisper.*

"Children's Books." *New York Times Book Review,* 5 June 1994, 30. Rev. of Patricia MacLachlan, *All The Places to Love.*

"Country Matters." *Washington Post Book World,* 5 Mar. 1995, 9. Rev. of Tim Pears, *In the Place of Fallen Leaves.*

"Losing the Farm." *New Yorker* 72 (3 June 1996): 88–92. Rev. of Victor Davis Hanson, *Fields Without Dreams.*

"Back to School." *Chicago Tribune Books,* 8 Sept. 1996, 1, 11. Rev. of David Denby, *Great Books.*

"In Custody." *New York Times Book Review,* 18 Aug. 1996, 13–14. Rev. of Paula Sharp, *Crows Over a Wheatfield.*

Smiley as Coeditor or Panelist

Pickerill, Martha and Bryan Sheeley. "Across the Table: S & H Profs Discuss the Changing Role of Education in the Modern World." *Ethos* (College of Sciences and Humanities, Iowa State University), Fall 1985: 12–17. Smiley is one of ten faculty members contributing to the discussion.

Iowa State University. "Women and Words." With Fern Kupfer and Mary Swander. Iowa State University: University Lecture Series, 1991. Sound recording, one cassette.

Hodnefield, Qory. "Teaching the Craft." *Ethos* (College of Sciences and Humanities, Iowa State University) 39 (Winter 1993): 9–11. Smiley is one of five faculty members discussing the Iowa State University creative writing program.

Iowa Public Television. "The Dames from Ames." Des Moines, Iowa, 1 May 1994, 30 min. A four-part "Living in Iowa" profile-interview of Iowa writers Smiley, Fern Kupfer, Mary Swander, and Saron Oard Warner.

The Best American Short Stories 1995. Selected from U.S. and Canadian Magazines by Jane Smiley with Katrina Kennison. With an introduction by Jane Smiley, x–xviii. Boston and New York: Houghton Mifflin, 1995.

Unpublished Work

"Notes of an Androphiliac." M.F.A. thesis, University of Iowa, 1976: v, 193 typescript pp.

"Harmes and Feares: Nine Stories." Ph.D. diss., University of Iowa, 1978: iv, 258 typescript pp.

"Shakespeare in Iceland." Paper read before the Sixth World Shakespeare Congress, Los Angeles, 8 Apr. 1996: 13 typescript pp.

Interviews and Statements

Formal Interviews

Thiébaux, Marcelle. "PW Interviews: Jane Smiley." Publishers Weekly 233 (1 Apr. 1988): 65–66.

Ross, Jean W. "[Smiley, Jane (Graves) 1949–] *CA* Interview." *Contemporary Authors* New Revision Series 30, ed. James G. Lesniak, 411–13. Detroit: Gale Research, 1990.

Berne, Suzanne. "*Belles Lettres* Interview." *Belles Lettres* 7 (Summer 1992): 36–38.

Pearlman, Mickey. "Jane Smiley." In *Listen to Their Voices: Twenty Interviews with Women Who Write,* 99–111. New York and London: W. W. Norton, 1993.

Neubauer, Alexander. "An Interview with Jane Smiley." *AWP Chronicle* 26 (Mar./Apr. 1994): 1–7. Repr. as "Jane Smiley," in *Conversations on Writing Fiction: Interviews with Thirteen Distinguished Teachers of Fiction Writing in America,* ed. Alexander Neubauer, 209–27. New York: HarperCollins, 1994.

Unpublished interview with the author, 7 Aug. and 4–5 Nov. 1996.

Interview Articles and Public Statements

Includes feature articles that contain quoted interview material.

Pins, Kenneth. "This Story's Still Being Written, but the Plot is Thickening." *Des Moines Register,* 25 Jan. 1987, 1B, 5B.

Horn, Miriam. "Raising the Curtain on a New Breed of Talent . . . Betwixt Iowa and Iceland." *U.S. News & World Report* 103 (28 Dec. 1987/4 Jan. 1988): 96, 98.

Hauser, Sylvia. "In Smiley's *Greenlanders,* History Explains Itself." *Ethos* (College of Sciences and Humanities, Iowa State University), Mar./Apr. 1988: 21.

Paul, Steve. "A Daunting Saga of Life in Twilight." *Kansas City Star,* 3 Apr. 1988, 1G, 10G. Includes some review commentary.

Eckholm, Erik. "Her Saga of a Giant Island." *New York Times Book Review,* 15 May 1988, 11.

Graeber, Laurel. "The Problem Is Power." *New York Times Book Review,* 5 Nov. 1989, 45.

Krapfl, Mike. "Ames' Jane Smiley Gains Literary Renown." *Daily Tribune* (Ames, Iowa), 2 Dec. 1989, Al, A4.

Gaffey, Abbie. "A Mid-Iowa Christmas." *Daily Tribune* (Ames, Iowa), 23 Dec. 1989, A3.

Pollock, Jim. "Iowa Author: Writing 'comes when I call.'" *Des Moines Register,* 28 Jan. 1990, 1F, 6F.

Streitfeld, David. "Smiley's People." *Washington Post Book World,* 28 Jan. 1990, 15.

"Writer Prefers Imagination." *Las Cruces (New Mex.) Sun-News,* 2 Feb. 1990, 6B. A syndicated article (AP).

Italie, Hillel. "Iowa Author Jane Smiley Dips Into Heartbreak In Heartland." *Omaha Sunday World-Herald Magazine,* 4 Feb. 1990, 15.

Winter, Michael. "Eavesdropping on the World." *Tampa Tribune,* 10 Mar. 1990, 1F, 7F.

Gibson, Debra. "Critics' Choice." *Visions* (Alumni Magazine, Iowa State University) Spring 1990: 30–35.

Anderson, Jon. "Author Finds Ample Fodder in Rural Midwest." *Chicago Tribune,* 24 Nov. 1991, sec. 5, pp. 1, 3.

Green, Michelle, and Barbara Kleban Mills. “Of Serpents’ Teeth in Iowa.” *People Weekly* 37 (13 Jan. 1992): 59–60.

Krapfl, Mike. “Ames Author Writes Another Winner.” *Daily Tribune* (Ames, Iowa), 31 Jan. 1992, A1, A3.

Fowler, Veronica. “Smiley Finds Iowa Fertile Ground for Fiction.” *Des Moines Sunday Register,* 23 Feb. 1992, 1A, 6A.

Baker, John F., and Calvin Reid. “17th NBCC Awards: Idealism Meets Commercialism.” *Publishers Weekly* 239 (23 Mar. 1992): 10.

Krapfl, Mike. “Ames Author Wins Pulitzer Prize.” *Daily Tribune* (Ames, Iowa), 7 Apr. 1992, A1–A2.

Winegar, Karin. “In Her Book, Earth, Women Are Victims of Mistreatment.” *Star Tribune* (Minneapolis), 9 Apr. 1992, 1E, 3E.

Christiansen, Rupert. “Sharper Than the Serpent’s Tooth.” *The Observer* (London), 25 Oct. 1992, 63.

Bruner, Jeffrey. “Jane Smiley: A Year Later.” *Daily Tribune* (Ames, Iowa), 3 Apr. 1993, A1, A7.

Shulins, Nancy. “Winning the Pulitzer Has Its Perks and Its Problems.” *Daily Tribune* (Ames, Iowa), 16 July 1994, A1, A7. A syndicated article (AP).

Daria, Irene. “Jane Smiley on Writing for the Love of It.” *Writer’s Digest* 75 (Feb. 1995): 7.

Sullivan, Steve. “Smiley’s Latest a Light Look at Land-grants.” *The Iowa Stater* (Iowa State University Alumni Association and ISU Foundation), Feb. 1995, 1–2.

Bruner, Jeffrey. “Smiley’s Pulitzer Follow-up *Moo* Set for April Release.” *Daily Tribune* (Ames, Iowa), 24 Feb. 1995, A1, A3.

Schneider, Bethany. “A Few Words with Jane Smiley.” *Elle* 10 (Mar. 1995): 190.

Adams, Noah. “Author Talks about New Novel Centered at Moo University.” *All Things Considered* (National Public Radio), 4 Apr. 1995. Transcript no. 1807–6.

O’Donnell, Thomas R. “Smiley’s People.” *Des Moines Register,* 11 Apr. 1995, 1T–2T.

Donahue, Deirdre. "Smiley Lets Out a Comic *Moo.*" *USA Today,* 13 Apr. 1995, 6D.

Peres, Daniel. "Smiley's People." *Women's Wear Daily,* 27 Apr. 1995, 20.

Warren, Tim. "Author Smiley Takes Criticism of *Moo* with a Grain of Salt Bordering on the Comic." *Baltimore Sun,* 3 May 1995, 1D.

Adams, Lorraine. "The Moo the Merrier." *Washington Post,* 4 May 1995, D1–D2.

McMillen, Liz. "Moo U. Follies." *Chronicle of Higher Education,* 12 May 1995, A19–A20.

Madigan, Tim. "*Moo* Could be a Bigger Cash Cow Than Pulitzer-winning Predecessor." *Daily Tribune* (Ames, Iowa), 17 May 1995, B8. Repr. from *Fort Worth Star-Telegram.*

Grant, Richard. "Jane Smiley: Homebody Makes Good." *Telegraph Magazine,* 20 May or June 1995: 36–39.

Harayda, Janice. "Sharp 'Moo' to Faith in Technology." *The Plain Dealer* (Cleveland, Ohio), 21 May 1995, 1K, 7K.

Loudon, Mary. "Jane's Addiction." *The Guardian Weekend,* 27 May 1995, 34–36, 39.

Mehren, Elizabeth. "Writing That Springs Fully Formed." *Los Angeles Times,* 4 June 1995, Orange County edition, E2.

Wagner, Jay P. "Days of Swine and Roses: Pigs Permeate Pop Culture." *Des Moines Register,* 26 June 1995, 1A–2A.

"From the Heartland." *CBS Sunday Morning with Charles Osgood,* 11 Feb. 1996.

Diliberto, Gioia. "King Lear's World, Reborn on a Farm In the Heartland." *New York Times,* 8 Dec. 1996, sec. 2, pp. 22, 24.

Brady, Thomas J. "The Further Adventures of Jane Smiley." *Des Moines Register,* 6 Apr. 1997, 5C.

Callahan, Sedona. "The Winner's Circle." *Gallery Magazine* (*Monterey County [Calif.] Herald*), 13 Apr. 1997, 6–8.

O'Donnell, Thomas R. "Pulitzer Novelist Smiley Undecided on Future at ISU." *Des Moines Register,* 5 Aug. 1997, 5M.
Heldt, Diane. "Jane Smiley Resigns from ISU Faculty Post." Ames, Ia. *Daily Tribune,* 13 Septl 1997, A7.

Works About Jane Smiley

Biographical Sources

"Jane Smiley." *Des Moines Register,* 23 Feb. 1992, 6A. A biographical profile.

Criticism: Articles and Sections of Books

Bakerman, Jane S. "'The Gleaming Obsidian Shard': Jane Smiley's *A Thousand Acres.*" *Midamerica XIX* (1992): 127–37. Discusses the book as a complex pattern of perceptions and events that reflect the appearance and reality of American culture.
———. "Renovating the House of Fiction: Structural Diversity in Jane Smiley's *Duplicate Keys.*" *Midamerica XV* (1988): 111–20.
———. "Water on Stone: Long-term Friendships in Jane Smiley's *Duplicate Keys* and Charlaine Harris' *A Secret Rage.*" *Clues: A Journal of Detection* 10 (Fall/Winter 1989): 49–63.
Conrad, Peter. "Expatriating Lear." In *To Be Continued: Four Stories and Their Survival,* 131–34, 141, 143, 151. Oxford: Clarendon, 1995. Includes discussion of *A Thousand Acres* as a reworking of *King Lear.*
Heller, Dana. "Father Trouble: Jane Smiley's "The Age of Grief." In *Family Plots: The De-Oedipalization of Popular Culture,* 94–112. Philadelphia: University of Pennsylvania Press, 1995.
"Jane (Graves) Smiley 1949– ." *Contemporary Literary Criticism* 53, ed. Daniel G. Marowski and Roger Matuz, 344–51. Detroit: Gale

Research, 1989. Selected earlier reviews of *Barn Blind, At Paradise Gate, Duplicate Keys, The Age of Grief,* and *The Greenlanders,* some excerpted.

Kaplan, Justin. "Selling *Huck Finn* Down the River." *New York Times Book Review,* 10 Mar. 1996, 27. In response to Smiley's "'Say It Ain't So, Huck'" article in *Harper's,* Jan. 1996.

Kellman, Steven G. "Food Fights in Iowa: The Vegetarian Stranger in Recent Midwest Fiction." *Virginia Quarterly Review* 71 (Summer 1995): 435–47. Includes discussion of food as "the language of communication" in *A Thousand Acres.*

Kirby, Jack Temple. "Rural Culture in the American Middle West: Jefferson to Jane Smiley." *Agricultural History* 70 (Fall 1996): 581–97. Surveys the impact of empire-building and capitalism on the Jeffersonian vision of agrarian life, with *A Thousand Acres* and *Moo* among contemporary points of reference.

Marsh, Kelly A. "The Neo-Sensation Novel: A Contemporary Genre in the Victorian Tradition." *Philological Quarterly* 74 (Winter 1995): 99–123. Discusses *A Thousand Acres* as one of several contemporary versions of a "recrudescent genre" that offers a critique of certain postmodern notions.

N[elms], B[en] F. "Transformations: Classics and Their Cousins." *English Journal* 83 (Mar. 1994): 94. Briefly discusses *A Thousand Acres* as a recasting of *King Lear.*

Roiphe, Katie. "Making the Incest Scene." *Harper's* 291 (Nov. 1995): 65–71. A largely negative review of recent fiction, including *A Thousand Acres,* for the "political predictability" of its use of incest.

Rozga, Margaret. "Sisters in a Quest—*Sister Carrie* and *A Thousand Acres:* The Search for Identity in Gendered Territory." *Midwestern Miscellany* 22 (1994): 18–29.

Seelye, John, et al. "Letters: Twain Sold Down the River?" *Harper's* 292 (Apr. 1996): 6–7, 83–85. In response to Smiley's "'Say It Ain't So, Huck'" article in *Harper's,* Jan. 1996.

Shapiro, Laura. "They're Daddy's Little Girls." *Newsweek* 123 (24 Jan. 1994): 66. Discusses the use of incest as a theme in contemporary fiction, including *A Thousand Acres.*

Selected Reviews

Barn Blind

B[rosnahan], J[ohn]. Untitled rev. *Booklist* 76 (1 July 1980): 1594.

"Fiction: *Barn Blind.*" *Publishers Weekly* 217 (25 Apr. 1980): 74.

Forster, Margaret. "Truly Interesting Horses." *Spectator* (London) 272 (30 Apr. 1994): 39.

Graeber, Laurel. "New and Noteworthy." *New York Times Book Review,* 16 May 1993, 40.

Grumbach, Doris. "A Fanfare for Five First Novels." *Washington Post Book World,* 15 June 1980, 4.

H., B. H. "*Barn Blind* Lacks Clue." *Anniston (Ala.) Star,* 3 Aug. 1980, 11C.

Hildebrand, Holly. "A Fine First Novel by a Former St. Louisan." *St. Louis Globe-Democrat,* 19–20 July 1980, 4E.

Kaufmann, James. "*Barn Blind:* Smiley Experiments with a Family." *Daily Iowan* (University of Iowa), 2 July 1980, 3E.

Leber, Michele M. Untitled rev. *Library Journal* 105 (15 June 1980): 1410–11.

Malone, Michael. "Four Novels." *New York Times Book Review,* 17 Aug. 1980, 10, 14.

McCall, J. G. "Illusion of Happiness." *Wichita Falls (Tex.) Times Sunday Magazine,* 24 Aug. 1980, 23.

Quinn, Anthony. Untitled rev. *Times Literary Supplement,* no. 4754 (13 May 1994): 21

Selway, Jennifer. "Dad's the Word." *The Observer Review* (London), 1 May 1994, 23.

Smith, Dee. "Iowa Bookshelf: *Barn Blind.*" *Cherokee (Iowa) Daily Times,* 14 July 1980, 9. A syndicated review (Iowa Daily Press Association).

At Paradise Gate

Christiansen, Rupert. Untitled rev. *Times Literary Supplement,* no. 4846 (16 Feb. 1996): 22.

D[onavin], D[enise] P. Untitled rev. *Booklist* 78 (15 Oct. 1981): 288.

"Fiction: *At Paradise Gate.*" *Publishers Weekly* 220 (4 Sept 1981): 45–46.

"Fiction Reprints." *Publishers Weekly* 224 (9 Dec. 1983): 49.

Graeber, Laurel. "New and Noteworthy Paperbacks." *New York Times Book Review,* 29 Aug. 1993, 20.

Howard, Jane. "Books." *Mademoiselle* 87 (Nov. 1981): 52.

Leber, Michele M. Untitled rev. *Library Journal* 106 (1 Nov. 1981): 2155.

Miner, Valerie. "Domestic Novels." *New York Times Book Review,* 22 Nov. 1981, 15, 42. Reviewed with Marian Seldes, *Time Together.*

"New and Noteworthy." *New York Times Book Review,* 5 Feb. 1984, 34.

Richardson, Kathleen. "Incisive Insight." *Des Moines Register,* 15 Nov. 1989, 4C.

S., M. Untitled rev. *Chattanooga Times,* 24 Oct. 1981, B5.

Solomon, Charles. "Paperbacks." *Los Angeles Times Book Review,* 22 Aug. 1993, 8.

Untitled rev. *Kirkus Reviews* 49 (1 Aug. 1981): 963.

Wood, Susan. "Family Circles." *Washington Post,* 27 Oct. 1981, C6.

Duplicate Keys

Boyd, Malcolm. "The Song Ends, Murder Lingers." *Los Angeles Times Book Review,* 18 Mar. 1984, 7.

Crichton, Jennifer. "In Short." *Ms.* 12 (Apr. 1984): 32.

Cromie, Alice. "Tales Calculated to Keep You Shivering This Summer." *Chicago Tribune Book World,* 8 July 1984, 32.

D[onavin], D[enise] P. Untitled rev. *Booklist* 80 (1 Mar. 1984): 945.

"Fiction: *Duplicate Keys.*" *Publishers Weekly* 224 (23 Dec. 1983): 53–54.

"Fiction Reprints." *Publishers Weekly* 228 (11 Oct. 1985): 64.

Foty, Geraldine R. "Young People Coping in 'Big Apple.'" *Worcester (Mass.) Sunday Telegram,* 10 June 1984, 12D.

Gould, Lois. "When the Sharing Had to Stop." *New York Times Book Review,* 29 Apr. 1984, 14.

Krystal, Arthur. "Two Tales of a City." *Village Voice,* 14 Aug. 1984, 43, 45.

Marcus, Laura. "Families and Friends." *Times Literary Supplement,* no. 4247 (24 Aug. 1984): 953. Reviewed with Vickery Turner, *Focusing.*

Montague, Sarah. "Metaphysical Murder Mystery." *Newsday,* 25 Mar. 1984, Ideas section, 18.

Nerboso, Donna L. Untitled rev. *Library Journal* 109 (15 Feb. 1984): 389.

Ott, Bill. "What They Wrote Before Their Ships Came In." *American Libraries* 24 (Dec. 1993): 1056.

Preston, John. "Books and Poetry . . . Fiction." *Time Out* (London), 14 June 1984, 37.

Riley, Mary Ann. "Friends and Their Mysteries." *Des Moines Sunday Register,* 8 Apr. 1984, 6C.

Wordsworth, Christopher. "Crime Ration." *The Observer* (London), 15 July 1984, 20.

The Age of Grief

Atlas, James. "Poignant Prose." *Vanity Fair* 50 (Sept. 1987): 186.

Bernays, Anne. "Toward More Perfect Unions." *New York Times Book Review,* 6 Sept. 1987, 12.

Bonnell, Paula. "Character Revelation and Zingy One Liners." *Belles Lettres* 3 (July/Aug. 1988): 14.

Brandmark, Wendy. "Love Knots." *The Listener* (London) 3 Mar. 1988: 30. One of three books reviewed.

Blades, John. "In Search of the Secret of Psychic Pain." *Chicago Tribune,* 6 Nov. 1987, sec. 5, p. 3.

Caldwell, Gail. "Playing Well the Hand That You're Dealt." *Boston Globe,* 15 Nov. 1987, 99–100.

Carper, Leslie. "Smiley's *Grief:* Subtle and Gritty." *Des Moines Sunday Register,* 4 Oct. 1987, 4C.

Corcoran, Marlena. "Smiley's *Age of Grief* Morally Engaging." *Daily Iowan* (University of Iowa), 7 Dec. 1989, 5B.

Dalley, Jan. "Utterly Scrutable Chinese." *The Observer* (London), 31 Jan. 1988, 27. Brief review.

"Fiction: *The Age of Grief.*" *Publishers Weekly* 231 (10 July 1987): 56–57.

"Fiction Reprints." *Publishers Weekly* 234 (15 July 1988): 62.

Furman, Laura. "The Barriers of Circumstance." *Los Angeles Times Book Review,* 18 Oct. 1987, 6.

H[ooper], B[rad]. Untitled rev. *Booklist* 84 (15 Sept. 1987): 110.

Hegi, Ursula. "Lonely Characters Eluding Closeness." *Newsday,* 8 Nov. 1987, Ideas section, 18.

Howard, Philip. "Winning and Unwinding." *The Times* (London), 4 Feb. 1988, 17.

Ingoldby, Grace. "A Potent Atmosphere Spiked with Risk." *Sunday Times* (London), 6 Mar. 1988, G6. Rev. with Howard Norman, *The Northern Lights.*

Johnson, George. "New and Noteworthy." *New York Times Book Review,* 12 Nov. 1989, 62.

Kakutani, Michiko. "Books of The Times." *New York Times,* 26 Aug. 1987, C21.

Kaufman, Joanne. "Picks & Pans: Pages . . . *The Age of Grief.*" *People Weekly* 29 (18 Jan. 1988): 14.

Kaveney, Roz. "Acceptable Behaviour." *Times Literary Supplement,* no. 4433 (18–24 Mar. 1988): 302.

Lacy, Robert. "Smiley's *The Age of Grief* is Moving, Poignant." *Minneapolis Star Tribune,* 18 Oct. 1987.

O'Leary, Theodore M. "*The Age of Grief* for a Young Family: Trials of Living Complicate Pain." *Kansas City Star,* 29 Nov. 1987, 9I.

Phillips, Alice H. G. "The Periodicals: *The Quarterly.*" *Times Literary Supplement,* no. 4424 (15–21 Jan. 1988): 60. Rev. of *The Quarterly,* citing "The Age of Grief."

Rile, Karen. "In Jane Smiley's Stories, Reflections on Inner Lives." *Philadelphia Inquirer,* 22 Nov. 1987, 5.

Rinzler, Carol E. "For Whom the Blurbs Toll." *Vogue* 177 (Sept. 1987): 475–76.

"Short Takes: Fiction." *Ms.* 16 (Sept. 1987): 34. Brief mention.

"Shorts." *Time Out* (London), 7–14 Dec. 1988, 38. Brief mention.

Smith, Starr E. Untitled rev. *Library Journal* 112 (Aug 1987): 145.

Sokolov, Raymond. "Them Too: A Family Affair." *Wall Street Journal,* 8 Sept. 1987, 30.

Solomon, Charles. "Current Paperbacks." *Los Angeles Times Book Review,* 19 Nov. 1989, 14.

Wilson, Robert. "*The Age of Grief:* Fiction Worth Celebrating." *USA Today,* 4 Sept. 1987, 6D.

The Greenlanders

Adams, Phoebe-Lou. "Brief Reviews." *Atlantic* 261 (May 1988): 94.

Askham, Suzanne. "Connections: Books." *New Woman* (London), Dec. 1988, 25. Brief review.

Blake, Fanny. "Books." *Options* (London), Jan. 1989, 127. Brief review.

Bonnell, Paula. "A Hypnotic Saga." *Belles Lettres* 4 (Fall 1988): 9.

"Books: Briefly Noted." *New Yorker* 64 (15 Aug. 1988): 82.

Dally, Emma. "Books." *Cosmopolitan* (London), Dec. 1988, 13. Brief review.

"Fiction Reprints." *Publishers Weekly* 235 (3 Mar. 1989): 100.

Foty, Geraldine R. "Norse Folklore Helps Shape Ambitious Novel." *Worcester (Mass.) Sunday Telegram,* 29 May 1988, 12D.

Freely, Maureen. "Gunnar Lore." *The Observer* (London), 11 Dec. 1988, 47.

Gilbert, Matthew. "A Compelling Novel of 14th-Century Greenland." *Boston Globe,* 8 Apr. 1988, 40.

"*The Greenlanders.*" *Publishers Weekly* 233 (25 Mar. 1988): 50.

H[ooper], B[rad]. Untitled rev. *Booklist* 84 (1 Mar. 1988): 1049.

Howard, Jane. "Critics' Choices for Christmas." *Commonweal* 115 (2 Dec. 1988): 658.

Johnson, George. "New and Noteworthy." *New York Times Book Review,* 7 May 1989, 42.

Klinkenborg, Verlyn. "News from the Norse." *New Republic* 198 (16 May 1988): 36, 38–39.

Mouland, Bill. "A Tale of Vanishing Vikings." *Today* (Kent, England), 8 Dec. 1988, 36. One of five books reviewed.

Norman, Howard. "They Should Have Listened to the Skraelings." *New York Times Book Review,* 15 May 1988, 11.

Øverland, Orm. "Mektig gronlendinge saga." *Bergens Tidende* (Bergen, Norway), 7 Dec. 1988, 59.

Panek, Richard. "The Mean Life." *Chicago Tribune Books,* 3 Apr. 1988, 5.

Pate, Nancy. "*Greenlanders* Brings Lost Colony Back to Life." *Orlando Sentinel,* 27 May 1988, E5.

Paul, Steve. "Book's Unconventional Demands Create Glorious Effect." *Minneapolis Star Tribune,* 5 June 1988, 8Fx. A syndicated review (Scripps Howard).

Pressley, M. Melissa. "A Stark Saga of an Icy Island Settlement in the Dark Ages." *Christian Science Monitor,* 7 Sept. 1988, 18.

Smith, Starr E. Untitled rev. *Library Journal* 113 (15 Apr. 1988): 96–97.

Spafford, Roz. "When Life Was Short, Brutal, Cold." *San Francisco Chronicle Review,* 1 May 1988, 3–4.

Spanier, Muriel. "The Grief-Stricken World of Greenland's Settlers." *Newsday,* 17 Apr. 1988, 20, 17.

Theodore, Lynn. "Saga Of Hot Passions, Cold Beauty." *St. Louis Post-Dispatch Book Review,* 3 July 1988, 1.

Untitled rev. *Kirkus Reviews* 56 (15 Feb. 1988): 240.

W., T. "*The Greenlanders.*" *West Coast Review of Books* 13, no. 6 (1988): 27–28.

Walton, David. "A Saga of Greenland." *St. Petersburg Times,* 17 Apr. 1988, 6D.

Yolen, Jane. "Passion & Strife in a Bleak Land." *Washington Post,* 13 May 1988, D4.

Ordinary Love and Good Will

"Books." *Me* (London) 12 Feb. 1990: 87.

Brandmark, Wendy. "Abnormal Conformists." *Times Literary Supplement,* no. 4543 (27 Apr.–3 May 1990): 456. One of four books reviewed.

Christiansen, Anne. "Two Novellas: One Insightful Author." *Ethos* (College of Sciences and Humanities, Iowa State University) Jan. 1990: 16–17.

Dunlap, Lauren Glen. "Here's How Paradise Gets Lost." *Seattle Times/ Post-Intelligencer,* 19 Nov. 1989, L7.

Eder, Richard. "Twisted Lives of Isolated People." *Los Angeles Times,* 16 Nov. 1989, E7.

Fiction: *Ordinary Love and Good Will.*" *Publishers Weekly* 236 (1 Sept. 1989): 76.

"Fiction Reprints." *Publishers Weekly* 237 (14 Dec. 1990): 64.

Fisher, Ann H. Untitled rev. *Library Journal* 114 (15 Sept. 1989): 137.

Flower, Dean. "Story Problems." *Hudson Review* 43 (Summer 1990): 315–16.

Gilbert, Ruth. "Hot Line . . . Books." *New York* 22 (27 Nov. 1989): 32.

Grambs, Marya. "Two Novellas Detail Frayed Family Ties." *San Francisco Chronicle Review,* 24 Dec. 1989, 3.

Humphreys, Josephine. "Perfect Family Self-Destructs." *New York Times Book Review,* 5 Nov. 1989, 1, 45.

Hunter, Timothy. "Good Stories of Grim Subjects." *The Plain Dealer* (Cleveland), 26 Nov. 1989, 10H.

Johnson, George. "New and Noteworthy." *New York Times Book Review,* 3 Feb. 1991, 32.

"Just Released in Paper." *Los Angeles Times Book Review,* 10 Feb. 1991, 14.

Kakutani, Michiko. "Pleasures and Hazards Of Love in the Family." *New York Times,* 31 Oct. 1989, 14.

Kaufmann, Joanne. "Picks & Pans: Pages . . . *Ordinary Love & Good Will.*" *People Weekly,* 4 Dec. 1989, 42–43, 45.

Leavitt, David. "Of Harm's Way and Farm Ways." *Mother Jones* 14 (Dec. 1989): 44–45.

MacLachlan, Suzanne. "Kitchen-Table Tales of Desire and Will." *Christian Science Monitor,* 30 Oct. 1989, 13.

Mathews, Laura. "Matched Pearls." *Glamour* 87 (Nov. 1989): 180.

McPhillips, Robert. "Jane Smiley's People." *Washington Post Book World,* 19 Nov. 1989, 8.

Mesic, Penelope. Untitled rev. *Booklist* 86 (1 Oct. 1989): 263.

Miner, Valerie. "Middle-class Moods." *Women's Review of Books* 7 (Apr. 1990): 17–18. Rev. with Ellen Gilchrist, *Light Can Be Both Wave and Particle.*

"Notes on Current Books." *Virginia Quarterly Review* 66 (Summer 1990): 94.

Panek, Richard. "Two Novellas with the Warmth of Home." *USA Today,* 3 Nov. 1989, 7D.

Passaro, Vince. "Smiley's People." *7 Days,* 29 Nov. 1989, 67.

Riley, Mary Ann. "Smiley Novellas: Studies in Nuance." *Des Moines Sunday Register,* 26 Nov. 1989, 4C.

Rubin, Merle. "Storytelling, the Second Oldest Profession." *Wall Street Journal,* 29 Nov. 1989, Eastern edition, A12.

Solomon, Andy. "The Sins of the Parents." *Philadelphia Inquirer,* 12 Nov. 1989, 1F, 4F.
Solomon, Charles. "Paperbacks." *Los Angeles Times Book Review,* 17 Feb. 1991, 10.
Stone, Laurie. "Books." *Vogue,* Oct. 1989, 284.
Thomas, Jane Resh. "2 Smiley Novellas Probe Darkness of Our Souls, Areas We Need to Explore." *Minneapolis Star Tribune,* 24 Dec. 1989, 8F.
Untitled rev. *Antioch Review* 48 (Winter 1990): 122.
Walton, David. "The Quiet Power of Jane Smiley's Novellas." *Chicago Tribune Books,* 12 Nov. 1989, 6.

A Thousand Acres

Armstrong, Karen. Untitled rev. *Times Educational Supplement,* 24 Dec. 1993, 8.
Bunke, Joan. "Revenge, Rage on *Lear* Farm." *Des Moines Register,* 3 Nov. 1991, 4C.
Carlson, Ron. "King Lear in Zebulon County." *New York Times Book Review,* 3 Nov. 1991, 12.
Christian, Rupert. "Speaking Less Than She Knowest." *Spectator* (London) 269 (10 Oct. 1992): 38–39.
Conrad, Peter. Untitled rev. *The Observer* (London), 29 Nov. 1992, Christmas Books section, 1.
Duffy, Martha. "The Case for Goneril and Regan." *Time* 138 (11 Nov. 1991): 92–94.
Eder, Richard. "Sharper Than a Serpent's Tooth." *Los Angeles Times Book Review,* 10 Nov. 1991, 3, 13.
Fisher, Ann H. Untitled rev. *Library Journal* 116 (1 Oct. 1991): 142.
Henderson, Pam. "King Lear on an Iowa Farm." *Farm Journal* 116 (Feb. 1992): I2.
"Fiction Reprints." *Publishers Weekly* 239 (31 Aug. 1992): 72.
Fuller, Edmund. "Kind and Unkind Daughters." *Sewanee Review* 101 (Spring 1993): 50–52.

Fuller, Jack. "King Lear in the Middle West." *Chicago Tribune Books,* 3 Nov. 1991, 1, 4.

Graeber, Laurel. "New and Noteworthy." *New York Times Book Review,* 4 Oct. 1992, 32.

Just, Julia. "Lear in Iowa: Family Farm, Family Trouble." *Wall Street Journal,* 13 Nov. 1991, A14.

Lehmann-Haupt, Christopher. "On an Iowa Farm, a Tragedy With Echoes of Lear." *New York Times,* 31 Oct. 1991, C20.

Marks, M. Lewellyn. "Finalists for the 1991–1992 *Los Angeles Times* Book Prizes." *Los Angeles Times Book Review,* 13 Sept. 1992, 14.

McAnany, Lisa. "*A Thousand Acres.*" *Daily Tribune* (Ames, Iowa), 7 Mar. 1992, B6. A syndicated review (AP).

Mirsky, Jonathan. "Bitter Harvest." *The Observer* (London), 15 Nov. 1992, 64.

"Notable Books, 1993." *Booklist* 89 (15 Mar. 1993): 1324.

Olson, Ray. Untitled rev. *Booklist* 88 (1 Sept. 1991): 5.

Purkiss, Diane. "Uncovering Iowa." *Times Literary Supplement,* no. 4674 (30 Oct. 1992): 20.

Rifkind, Donna. "A Man Had Three Daughters . . . ," *Washington Post Book World,* 27 Oct. 1991, 1, 13.

Shapiro, Laura. "*A Thousand Acres.*" *Newsweek* 118 (18 Nov. 1991): 84.

Steinberg, Sybil. "Best Books of 1991." *Publishers Weekly* 238 (1 Nov. 1991): 20.

"*A Thousand Acres.*" *Publishers Weekly* 238 (23 Aug. 1991): 44.

Untitled rev. *Kirkus Reviews* 59 (15 Aug. 1991): 1041.

Walter, John. "Environment." *Successful Farming* 90 (Apr. 1992): 63.

Williams, Linda. "Critics' Voices." *Time* 138 (2 Dec. 1991): 14.

Wood, James. "The Glamour of Glamour." *London Review of Books* 14 (19 Dec. 1992): 17–18.

Moo

Adams, Phoebe-Lou. "Brief Reviews." *Atlantic* 275 (May 1995): 125–26.

BIBLIOGRAPHY

Allen, Brooke. "On Campus Among the Sacred Cows." *Wall Street Journal,* 29 Mar. 1995, A12.

Barrett, Andrea. "Review: Books." *Outside* 20 (May 1995): 154.

Battersby, Eileen. "Keeping Them Down on the Farm." *The Irish Times,* 7 June 1995, News Features section, 12.

"Books for Vacation Reading." *New York Times Book Review,* 11 June 1995, 26.

Bunke, Joan. "Smiley's *Moo:* A Degree in Mockery." *Des Moines Sunday Register,* 9 Apr. 1995, 4C.

Bush, Trudy. "War Wounds, and a Midwest Microcosm: A Fiction Roundup." *Christian Century* 112 (24–31 May 1995): 567–70. Reviewed with five other books.

Caldwell, Gail. "Smiley, Down on the Farm." *Boston Globe,* 2 Apr. 1995, B36.

Campbell, Jane. "Hot Fudge." *London Review of Books* 17 (19 Oct. 1995): 38.

Carlson, Michael. "Very Flat, Iowa." *Spectator* (London) 274 (27 May 1995): 44.

Chappell, Helen. "Moo-ing Through the Intrigues of Academia." *Baltimore Sun,* 26 Mar. 1995, 5F.

Diehl, Digby. "Books." *Playboy* 42 (June 1995): 34.

Edelman, Dave. "Satire Without the Bite." *Baltimore Sun,* 5 June 1995, 11A.

Eder, Richard. "Moo U.: The Superheated Life of a University Community." *Los Angeles Times Book Review,* 2 Apr. 1995, 3, 8.

Fisher, Ann H. Untitled rev. *Library Journal* 120 (15 Mar. 1995): 99.

Flansburg, James. "The Real World of Jane Smiley." *Des Moines Register,* 30 Mar. 1995, 11A.

Fleming, Juliet. "Death of a Porker." *Times Literary Supplement,* no. 4807 (19 May 1995): 20.

Foster, Aisling. "Stuffed on Animal Farm." *The Independent,* 11 June 1995, "Sunday Review," 35.

Freely, Maureen. "Be Not Cowed." *The Observer Review* (London), 11 June 1995, 14.

Fry, Donn. "*Moo* Turns into Wake-up Call Amid Paramilitary, Hate Groups." *Seattle Times,* 18 May 1995, E5.

Galef, David. "An Academic Romp." *New Leader* 78 (13–27 Mar. 1995): 18–19.

Gerber, Eric. "Satirical *Moo* Amuses All Too Infrequently." *Houston Post,* 2 Apr. 1995, G13.

Govier, Katherine. "*Moo* Wallows in Its Satirical Effort." *The Financial Post,* 1 July 1995, sec. 2, p. 22.

Hale, Babette Fraser. "*Moo.*" *Houston Chronicle,* 16 Apr. 1995, Zest section, 25, 29.

Harrison, Claire. "*Moo* Sounds the Call that Smiley is a True Master." *Ottawa Citizen,* 25 June 1995, B3.

Heron, Liz. "Fiction." *Times Educational Supplement,* 7 July 1995, *TES 2* (Centre Pages section), 13.

Holm. Bill. "Confused State: Jane Smiley Makes Fun of Aggies, and All of Us." *San Jose (Cal.) Mercury News—Books,* 2 Apr. 1995, 1B, 7B.

Iyer, Pico. "How High the Moo?" *Time* 145 (17 Apr. 1995): 68–69.

Kakutani, Michiko. "All Too Human Comedy On a Midwest Campus." *New York Times,* 21 Mar. 1995, Late N.Y. edition, C19.

Kaufman, Joanne. "Picks and Pans: *Moo.*" *People Weekly* 43 (24 Apr. 1995): 29.

Krist, Gary. "Comedy." *Hudson Review* 48 (Winter 1996): 679–80.

Linfield, Susan. Untitled rev. *Entertainment Weekly,* no. 275 (19 May 1995): 56–57.

Lowenstein, Andrea Freud. "Good vs. Evil." *Ms.* 5 (May 1995): 74.

Lurie, Alison. "Hog Heaven." *New York Times Book Review,* 2 Apr. 1995, 1, 26.

Mesic, Penelope. "Midwestern School Daze." *Chicago Tribune Books,* 9 Apr. 1995, 1, 8.

Messud, Claire. "Piggy in the Middle." *Guardian Weekly,* 4 June 1995, 29.

Miner, Valerie. "The Cow Pies of Academe." *The Nation* 260 (8 May 1995): 638–39;

"*Moo.*" *Publishers Weekly* 242 (6 Feb. 1995): 75–76.

Moore, Lorrie. "Fiction in Review." *Yale Review* 83 (Oct. 1995): 135–43. Reviewed with Anne Tyler, *Ladder of Years.*

Moynahan, Molly. "Trivial Pursuits." *Dallas Morning News,* 2 Apr. 1995, 8J–9J.

Pearl, Nancy. "Life at Moo U.—Jane Smiley's Wise, Knowing Dig at Academia." *Seattle Times,* 9 Apr. 1995, M2.

"Piggy in the Middle." *The Economist* 335 (10 June 1995): 78.

Press, Joy. "Read Me." *Details* 13 (Apr. 1995): 128.

"Recommended Reading." *New Yorker* 71 (8 May 1995): 91.

Ricks, Pat. "Reviews: *Moo.*" *Austin (Texas) American-Statesman,* 9 Apr. 1995, G7.

Rubin, Merle. "A Lively Satire of Derring-do at Moo U." *Christian Science Monitor,* 4 Apr. 1995, 14.

Schine, Cathleen. "The Way We Live Now." *New York Review of Books,* 10 Aug. 1995, 38–39.

Scott, R. C. "Fattening the Metaphor." *Washington Times,* 30 Apr. 1995, B7.

Skenazy, Paul. "School for Scandal." *San Francisco Chronicle,* 26 Mar. 1995, Sunday Review section, 1.

Taylor, Laurie. "Pork-Barrel Politics." *New Statesman and Society* 8 (9 June 1995): 37.

Untitled rev. *Kirkus Reviews* 63 (1 Feb. 1995): 101.

Wilkinson, Joanne. Untitled rev. *Booklist* 91 (1 Feb. 1995): 971.

Willeford, Betsy. "Smiley's *Moo* Lows with Academic Satire." *Palm Beach Post,* 21 May 1995, 6J.

Yardley Jonathan. "Wallowing in Hog Heaven." *Washington Post Book World,* 26 Mar. 1995, 3.

INDEX

INDEX